REMINISCENCES
OF GENERAL HERMAN HAUPT

THE RAILROADS

REMINISCENCES
OF GENERAL HERMAN HAUPT

[Herman Haupt]

ARNO PRESS

A New York Times Company
New York • 1981

Editorial Supervision: Steve Bedney

Reprint Edition 1981 by Arno Press Inc.
Reprinted from a copy in the University of Michigan Library

THE RAILROADS
ISBN for complete set: 0-405-13750-8
See last pages of this volume for titles

Manufactured in the United States of America

Library of Congress Cataloging in Publication Data

Haupt, Herman, 1817-1905.
    Reminiscences of General Herman Haupt.

    (The Railroads)
    Reprint of the 1901 limited autograph ed.
printed by Wright & Joys Co., Milwaukee, Wis.
    1. United States--History--Civil War, 1861-1865--
Campaigns and battles.   2.   Haupt, Herman, 1817-1905.
3.   United States--History--Civil War, 1861-1865--
Transportation.   4.   United States. Bureau of
Military Railroads.   5.   United States--History--
Civil War, 1861-1865--Personal narratives.
6. Generals--United States--Biography.
7. United States. Army--Biography. I. Title.
II. Series: Railroads.

E470.2.H37   1981   973.7'15'625 [B]   80-1314
ISBN 0-405-13786-9

REMINISCENCES

OF

GENERAL HERMAN HAUPT

GENERAL HERMAN HAUPT AT 84.

REMINISCENCES

OF

GENERAL HERMAN HAUPT

Director, Chief Engineer and General Superintendent of the
Pennsylvania Railroad
Contractor and Chief Engineer for the Hoosac Tunnel
Chief of the Bureau of United States Military Railroads in the
Civil War
Chief Engineer of the Tidewater Pipeline
General Manager of the Richmond & Danville and
Northern Pacific Railroads
President American Air Power Company
Etc   Etc

GIVING

HITHERTO UNPUBLISHED OFFICIAL ORDERS,

PERSONAL NARRATIVES OF IMPORTANT MILITARY
OPERATIONS,

AND

INTERVIEWS WITH PRESIDENT LINCOLN, SECRETARY STANTON, GENERAL-
IN-CHIEF HALLECK, AND WITH GENERALS MCDOWELL, MC-
CLELLAN, MEADE, HANCOCK, BURNSIDE, AND OTHERS
IN COMMAND OF THE ARMIES IN THE FIELD,
AND HIS IMPRESSIONS OF THESE MEN

[WRITTEN BY HIMSELF]

WITH NOTES AND A PERSONAL SKETCH BY
FRANK ABIAL FLOWER

Illustrated from Photographs of Actual Operations in the Field

1901

WRIGHT & JOYS CO.,
ENGRAVERS,
PRINTERS,
MILWAUKEE, WIS.

PREFATORY NOTE.

THERE is too much truth in the Irish observation that "No one thinks of strewing flowers on a friend's grave till after he is dead."

The writer entertained a decided feeling that a man like General Haupt, full of years, of goodness, of unselfish patriotism, and of widely fruitful deeds, certainly should have his "grave" bestrewn with the very choicest flowers while yet there was life to enjoy their fragrance.

This feeling led to the publication of the present volume.

The main portion of it, which is General Haupt's, was committed to writing by him in 1889. He had no intention of publishing the collection—merely desired to get into record form, for the gratification of his grandchildren and other immediate descendants, many important facts concerning our civil war which had entirely escaped the attention of historians—especially those in which he was either the foremost or a conspicuous actor. They embrace personal interviews with the President, Secretary of War, General Halleck, and the Generals in command of the armies in the field, of which there are no official records.

While going over his manuscript in search of material to verify certain portions of a *Life of Edwin M. Stanton,* the writer discovered not only the general historical value of the matter, but that the almost abnormal modesty of the narrator had resulted in so much self-submergence as to entirely deprive him of many important honors to which he was incontestably entitled.

General Haupt was, therefore, besought to consent to the publication, during his lifetime, of a limited edition of his formal military story, prefixed by such a condensed but general sketch of his life as would afford an indication of at least the mountain-peaks of his remarkably long and honorable career.

This seemed the more necessary because the meagre records of the Government disclose not even the shadow of a reason for his sudden retirement from the army at the very zenith of his splendid achievements as Director of the Military Railroads of the United States, thus leaving the impression, perhaps, that there had been something discreditable in his conduct.

He yielded to this importunity, with the result that 900 numbered autograph copies of his story are available for such personal friends, army officers and libraries as care to subscribe for them. **F. A. F.**

ILLUSTRATIONS.

ILLUSTRATIONS.

CONTENTS.

HERMAN HAUPT AT 34.

GENERAL HERMAN HAUPT.

G ENERAL HAUPT, now in his 85th year and the active head
of an important manufacturing enterprise in the United
States, is one of the most interesting, as he certainly is one of the
most remarkable, figures in our history.

Few men have participated in so much that has contributed
to the growth and grandeur of our country, yet how little the
world knows of his career, how reluctant the trumpeters have been
to herald his achievements!

A designer and builder of roads and bridges; a constructor
of railroads and tunnels; a professor and author; an inventor and
master mechanic; a military strategist and civil counsellor; a
railway manager and canal engineer; a manufacturer and organizer of great enterprises; a military and civil engineer, still up-
to-date and a leader of progress, he links the old with the new, the
slow and sleepy past with the swift and dashing present in a way
that is entirely exceptional.

He was born in Philadelphia on March 26, 1817. His father,
Jacob Haupt, died in 1828, leaving a widow and six children.

WEST POINT COMMISSION DATED AHEAD.

In 1830, through the help of John B. Steriger, Member of
Congress from Pennsylvania, he received an appointment to West
Point from President Andrew Jackson; but as he was only 13, the
commission was dated a year ahead. He entered in June, 1831,
at the age of 14, and graduated in 1835, at the age of 18, in a
class with General George G. Meade and others who became distinguished in the civil war.

Of that early class of fifty-six members, there are no sur-
vivors except General Haupt, and in the entire list of graduates
of the United States Military Academy the only senior is General
Thomas A. Morris (1834) of Indianapolis, Ind.

In the fall of 1835 he resigned his commission in the army to become assistant engineer, under H. R. Campbell, in surveying a railroad from Norristown to Allentown, in Pennsylvania, and subsequently in locating the Norristown & Valley Railroad.

For many years the State of Pennsylvania built, owned and managed railways and canals, and in 1836, although only 19, Haupt was appointed principal assistant in the service of the State, and, as such, located a railroad from Gettysburg across South Mountain to the Potomac—now a part of the Western Maryland system.

In 1838, on becoming 21, he was married to Miss Ann Cecilia, daughter of his pastor, Rev. Benjamin Keller, of Gettysburg. A lively, cheerful and accomplished woman, she shared his fortunes for fifty-three years and became the mother of eleven children, of whom Professor Lewis M. Haupt, formerly of the University of Pennsylvania, and now a member of the Isthmian Canal Commission, is the third son.

A DECISIVE EVENT.

In 1840 he was engaged to aid in the construction of the York & Wrightsville Railroad—an event which ultimately was the means of developing the magnificent possibilities of railway and bridge construction which have since astonished the world.

On this road were a number of lattice bridges for which the plans had been prepared previously, and the timbers already ordered.

Young Haupt deemed them too weak for the duty they were designed to perform and at once sought advice from all the prominent engineers of the country as to the proper mode of calculating the strength of a trussed bridge.

He was astonished to find that, with one exception,* not an engineer in the United States, or in the world, so far as he could discover, ever attempted to calculate the strength of a truss—except in a triangular system. The members were generally all of the same dimensions; the counter-brace was either unknown or its

---

* NOTE.—Benj. H. Latrobe, of the Baltimore & Ohio Railroad, appeared to calculate the strains upon his bridges, but his structures were simple triangular systems in which pressure at the apex was transmitted in the direction of the two sides to the base—the abutments or other points of resistance, as in the Fink and Bollman trusses—in which the problem was solved by the parallelogram of forces.

office not understood, and the fact that there were vastly different strains at different points of the same system was generally unrecognized.

STUDYING BRIDGE CONSTRUCTION.

Unwilling to admit that the problem could not be solved, he continued to search for the laws governing the transmission of strains and to attempt to originate formulæ by which strain sheets could be calculated and the strength of any truss, however complicated, might be accurately determined.

Being in a country town, without books of reference or access to scientific apparatus, he was compelled to evolve his own formulæ and invent his own modes of experimentation.

Commencing with experiments on the resistance of timbers, he discovered that the strains could be represented by the ordinates of conic sections, which led to a new but simple mode of obtaining formulæ and determining strains on beams in all possible positions. He then experimented with models of his own design and construction, and took observations on bridges during the passage of trains until certain conclusions which he had reached were so well established that he published, anonymously, in 1841, a pamphlet entitled, "Hints on Bridge Construction," which attracted much attention and led to some controversy.

On completing the York & Wrightsville Road, General Haupt was appointed Professor of Mathematics and Engineering in Pennsylvania College at Gettysburg. In 1844 he began the preparation of a general text-book on civil engineering, but, on reaching the subject of bridges, abandoned everything for the purpose of renewing his previous attempt to solve the very important problem of calculating the strains in this class of structures.

SOLVES THE GREAT PROBLEM.

Having acquired a greater profundity in general mathematics, and being strengthened by added years and experience, he was able to solve riddles which before had baffled him. In due time he had ready the manuscript of the noted work which finally reached all civilized countries—"General Theory of Bridge Construction."

For five years, however, he was unable to get his book before the public, because he could find no engineer capable of reviewing it and no publisher who dared to put it forth—the manuscript being generally returned without any comment for or against it. In 1851 D. Appleton & Co. undertook its publication, and were rewarded with its prompt success. The volume met a very general want, and its sales were large.

This pioneer work became a text-book in schools and colleges, and Professor Gillespie, of Union College, wrote to Haupt from London reporting the strong terms of commendation with which it was received by Robert Stephenson and his associates.

From that time engineers began to calculate strain sheets and distribute material properly to meet the varying requirements of self-supporting pendant structures, without which the marvelous achievements of engineering science, as exemplified throughout the world to-day, would have been impossible.

As, beyond question, transportation is the chief of the basic elements of civilization, Mr. Haupt belongs in the front rank of the most distinguished benefactors of mankind.

CONSTRUCTING THE PENNSYLVANIA RAILROAD.

In 1846 the Pennsylvania Railroad was chartered. Haupt applied to President Samuel V. Merrick for a position with the company, but was told that engineers were as plentiful as blackberries and that there were scores of applicants for every open position, so he returned to Gettysburg.

John Edgar Thomson had been appointed Chief Engineer, with Edward Miller associate on the Western, and William B. Foster on the Eastern Division. Foster had been a canal engineer, and filled his division with his old assistants, who knew little or nothing about railroads. The consequence was that after the location of sixty miles of the Juniata Division, the chief engineer walked over the line and decided that an entire revision must be made before construction could begin, although the contractors had built shanties and were ready to commence work.

In this dilemma he sent for Mr. Haupt, who accepted the position offered, and not only relocated the entire division without delaying the work, but effected great improvement in the line and a large reduction in cost.

His leisure hours were still devoted to the study of bridge

problems. One day he was surprised by a visit from Chief Engineer Thomson. It was the first appearance of that officer, and on a very cold day in the winter of 1848. After he had become sufficiently thawed out to turn his head, he discovered the model of a bridge truss resting on two chairs and loaded with weights.

With a smile he remarked: "Some fellow has been trying to make a bridge and don't know anything about it. He has got his braces in the wrong way."

Haupt replied: "Excuse me, Mr. Thomson, if I presume to differ from you. I think they have been put in the *right* way. They are not braces, but counter-braces. It is a model of a counter-braced arch."

Proceeding to explain the model and the results of his investigations, for about an hour he gave, in fact, a lecture on bridge construction, during which Mr. Thomson was a very attentive listener, occasionally nodding, or giving an expression of acquiescence as some new point was made which met his approval.

After the bridge explanation was finished the railroad maps were examined and much gratification expressed over the improvements made, and Haupt was immediately promoted to principal assistant.

On Mr. Thomson's return to Harrisburg he sent to Haupt a large roll of the bridge plans that had been prepared for the road, with a line in pencil: "I would like to have your opinion about these."

The opinions were given, merits and defects being pointed out in writing, and the roll returned. As a result another assistant was sent at once to relieve Haupt, who was ordered to report at Harrisburg to assume the important duties of examining and criticising the plans of location and construction from all parts of the line and suggesting necessary changes.

ORGANIZES AND OPERATES THE PENNSYLVANIA RAILROAD.

When the first division approached completion, Haupt was selected as General Superintendent and directed to visit the principal roads of New England for the purpose of examining their systems of accounts, plans of organization, snowplows, machinery, and everything connected with the operation of a road.

On his return he submitted a plan of organization and management, with forms and blanks for every branch of the business, which was adopted without change, and which, modified to meet subsequent new conditions and features in transportation, is in use to this day on what is generally regarded as the best-managed railway property in the world.

Haupt at once urged upon the Board of Directors the policy of developing the local business of the line, especially in coal, lumber, iron and agricultural products, by reduced rates during the season when, from the close of navigation on the Ohio, the equipment was not fully employed.

Up to this time the impression prevailed that nothing could be carried on a railroad without loss that did not pay over 2 cents per ton per mile.

To settle this question Haupt made a careful analysis of the business of the preceding year, classifying the fixed and variable items and the extent to which cost would be affected by volume of transportation. He demonstrated that, if the volume were increased to a million tons per year, as it could be by proper encouragement of local traffic, the cost per ton-mile would be reduced to six mills from points east and seven mills from points west of the Alleghanies.*

This was the first careful and scientific analysis published, or perhaps made, of the cost of railway transportation, which was subsequently elaborated by Albert Fink, A. M. Wellington and others.

It caused much astonishment and the declaration that by proper encouragement the freight business of the Pennsylvania Railroad could be increased to a million tons was regarded as the utterance of a visionary enthusiast.

Ultimately, however, Haupt saw his plan of encouraging local industries fully adopted and never abandoned, and the extra million tons of freight which he advocated as a certainty in the near future was very soon added, and then multiplied over and over again more than fifty times.

---

* NOTE.—See 4th and 5th Annual Reports of the Pennsylvania Railroad, 1851-1852; also his final report on retiring from the office of General Superintendent, pages 81-85.

On January 15, 1852, he submitted a series of papers opposing the policy of a State tax on railroad traffic to sustain the public canals, and also an analysis of the increased cost of conducting transportation due to enforced connections with State improvements (canals and railways) and the conflicting schedules of the two interests.

In the Sixth Annual Report, H. J. Lombaert, his successor, said: "During the greater portion of the year (1852) the operations of the road were conducted under the direction of H. Haupt, late General Superintendent, to whose ability and success the results of the present and preceding years' operations abundantly testify, and to whom no one will more readily, than your present Superintendent, award all the credit."

On page 32, *et seq.,* of the Seventh Annual Report of the Pennsylvania Railroad, Mr. Haupt says: "To secure a traffic of 1,000,000 tons and make the road an instrument of incalculable good to the citizens of the State, *low rates, with moderate dividends,* must indicate the settled policy upon which the operations are to be conducted."

The entire report is to-day as remarkable for wisdom and foresight as it was when made, almost a half-century ago, when railway management was crude, unscientific and haphazard. In fact, if the policy advocated by Haupt had been adopted and adhered to, the Pennsylvania Railroad would have been out of debt years ago and kept out, and would be now altogether the most economical artificial freight-carrier of great proportions in the world.

Soon after he became General Superintendent his efforts to unify and classify rates resulted in a meeting of trunk-line presidents and other officials at the St. Nicholas Hotel, in New York. In this, the first meeting of the kind ever held in America, Mr. Haupt took the initiative in effecting an organization, bringing on discussion and coming to conclusions. Similar meetings were held afterwards and resulted in mutually valuable understandings.

In 1853 he notified the Board of Directors, who had twice declined to receive his resignation, that he had accepted the position of Chief Engineer of the Southern Railroad of Mississippi, and that his connection with the company would terminate at a given date. He recommended that Herman J. Lombaert, his assistant, be made his successor, and Thomas A. Scott, then agent at Hollidaysburg, be appointed Assistant Superintendent, which selections were ratified.

This promotion enabled Colonel Scott, some years after, to succeed to the presidency of the Railroad Company, and to live in history as one of the great railway managers of the country.

The location of the Southern Railroad occupied about six months, when Mr. Haupt was recalled to take the position of Chief Engineer of the Pennsylvania Railroad, which he retained until the completion and opening of the whole line to Pittsburg, including the Allegheny Mountain tunnel.

He was also elected by the councils of Philadelphia as a director of the company to represent the stock held by the city—a very distinguished mark of confidence and respect.

THE FAMOUS HOOSAC TUNNEL CONTEST.

We now come to a very important and interesting portion of Mr. Haupt's career, which involves his fortune and reputation, the honor and integrity of the State of Massachusetts, and an account of the vicissitudes of constructing the great railway tunnel through the Hoosac Mountain.

In 1855, while Chief Engineer of the Pennsylvania Railroad and director of that company for the City of Philadelphia, he was requested to make an examination of the proposed Hoosac tunnel, on the line of the Troy & Greenfield Railroad, in Massachusetts, and give his opinion as to its practicability. He reported favorably and, after much solicitation, was prevailed upon to take an interest in the contract for its construction and assist in raising $100,000 as additional capital—a portion of which came from his associates in the Pennsylvania Railroad.

The contract was for $4,000,000. The State of Massachusetts had agreed to loan its credit to the extent of $2,000,000; the company had made an issue of $900,000 in bonds and was to provide, from town and individual subscriptions, a liberal amount of additional cash.

The contract was signed in 1856, when he resigned from the Pennsylvania Railroad and began a vigorous prosecution of the work. As soon as it became apparent that the tunnel was in good hands and would probably be carried to completion at an early date, thus opening a parallel and rival line to the Boston & Albany Railroad, a persistent series of violent attacks was made upon the company and its contractors—and especially upon Mr. Haupt.

Articles were published in most of the leading papers to create an adverse public sentiment. In them the tunnel was described as a visionary and impracticable scheme, the contractors were denounced as swindlers, the subscribers to the stock were warned against liquidating their subscriptions and assured that the company had no power to enforce payment.

When the editors of papers which had made these attacks were summoned before investigating committees, the articles were almost invariably traced to Springfield, and to parties in the employ or under the influence of Chester W. Chapin, president of the Boston & Albany, then known as the Western Railroad Company. The articles had the effect, notwithstanding this exposure of their origin, of exciting hostile legislation, of embarrassing the tunnel company, of stopping the collection of subscriptions and of preventing the contractors from securing regularly the State payments for work upon which they had relied. The object of these movements was transparent; it was to kill the tunnel project by ruining the contractors.

But these unjust and wicked attacks only served to stimulate Mr. Haupt to increased exertions. Unable to secure any aid whatever from the railroad company of which the tunnel formed a part, he mortgaged his own large property in the State of Pennsylvania, sold stocks and borrowed money from personal friends and kept the work going until the financial crash occurred in 1857.

At this time he himself was carrying a floating debt of about $200,000. With the exception of $67,000, he had provided all the capital required to carry on the work. Not a dollar had been paid by the company, or any other party in Massachusetts; three of his partners had failed, and the remaining one could render no assistance.

Their failure impaired his hitherto gilt-edge credit. Discounts were refused, and he was forced to take up more than $20,000 of the paper of the discredited parties that already had been discounted.

2

In this emergency a friend in Philadelphia (Alexander J. Derbyshire) a director of the Pennsylvania Railroad, unsolicited and without security, providentially placed $30,000 to Mr. Haupt's credit, refusing to accept more than 6 per cent. interest, although money was worth $1\frac{1}{2}$ to 2 per cent. and even more per month.

This timely loan enabled him to so far complete the work required by the onerous conditions of the Massachusetts statute as to entitle him to the first payment of $100,000 from the State; and, after a severe contest, in which every obstacle, legal and otherwise, was interposed to prevent it, the Executive Council decided that the money had been fairly earned and ordered the payment to be made.

After this, the work progressed without embarrassment until 1860. The payments by the State had strengthened Mr. Haupt's credit, and he was again able to procure the necessary bank accommodations. When the Legislature met, an investigation was ordered at the suggestion of hostile parties, and a committee appointed, supposed to be unfriendly, with power to send for persons and papers.

After a protracted investigation the committee turned completely in his favor, and reported a bill, in the preparation of which he had largely assisted,* which placed the work on a sure basis, expunged the onerous and unnecessary features of the original loan act and, had it not been repealed subsequently, would have carried the tunnel to completion in about six years without costing the commonwealth one cent, either for principal or interest. The principal had been provided for by annual accretions to a sinking fund, and the interest was payable by the tunnel company.

The committee, after a thorough examination of the contractors and of their books, papers and superintendents, became convinced that the tunnel was actually costing only about $40 per running foot, and that an allowance of $50 per foot, or $1,250,000 for the whole tunnel, was sufficient to insure its completion with

---

* NOTE.—Amos B. Merrill, a lawyer of ability and a member of the committee, intimated to a mutual friend that he really wanted to know the exact truth in regard to the ceaseless charges that Haupt was a scoundrel and swindling the commonwealth. Haupt sent word to him that if he would come to his hotel he might see the record of every transaction pertaining to the contract. He went, with the result that he promptly changed front and, assisted by Haupt, drafted the bill above mentioned, which set the wheels of the great work to turning again.

the dimensions prescribed by statute, and they divided the loan (of $2,000,000) so as to apportion $750,000 to aid in the construction of the thirty miles of road between the tunnel and Greenfield.

These statements may seem very extraordinary in the face of the fact that, when the State of Massachusetts, in 1862, took possession of the work and undertook to finish it under direction of her commissioners, fourteen years of time and an expenditure of more than twenty millions in money were required for its completion, but they are literally true.

The bill of 1860 became a law with the approval of Governor N. P. Banks, and, had he remained in office one year more, the work would have been so far advanced that further efforts to hamper or destroy it would have had no prospect of success.

But, unfortunately for all, and especially for the commonwealth, Governor Banks declined a renomination and, upon leaving office in 1861, omitted by sheer accident to sign the order for the payment of the tunnel estimate. His successor, John A. Andrew, refused to sign the order, and expressed want of confidence in the State Engineer and dissatisfaction with the contractors.

As Mr. Haupt enjoyed the entire confidence of the Executive Council, the position of the Governor gave its members much embarrassment, but they passed the order for the payment of the estimate notwithstanding his objections. The Governor then asked the State Engineer to resign. He declined to do so, and was removed and a new engineer nominated to succeed him.

Mr. Haupt, being a member of the Board of Visitors, was at West Point at the time, where he received a telegram from a member of the Council informing him of the nomination and stating that, if unsatisfactory, the Council would refuse to confirm. He replied: "Make no opposition. I can get along with any engineer who is competent and honest."

The nomination of Engineer Whitwell was confirmed, but before proceeding to an examination of the work, he visited Springfield, where, as testimony subsequently proved, he remained for a day or two in conference with officers of the Boston & Albany Road, at whose suggestion, as was afterwards understood, he had been appointed.

Members of the Council had urgently requested the Governor,

before assuming a hostile attitude, to send for Mr. Haupt and ascertain the actual condition of affairs. This he refused to do. He desired no personal interview, wanted no new facts, and persistently adhered to what was really a position of unrelieved discredit.

Upon examining the estimates the new engineer could find no errors in the calculations. He then said that the questions at issue could not be decided by mere figures. He must "exercise judgment!" He must protect the State, he said, and arbitrarily deducted nearly $100,000 from the amount due for work done and materials delivered under his predecessor.

Mr. Haupt was then rapidly delivering rails under contract with the Rensselaer Iron Works, and deprivation of earned payments meant ruin. He therefore suspended work and appealed to the Governor and Council. A committee of three was appointed, who, after three weeks of thorough investigation, reported that the State Engineer had transcended his authority; that his acts had been in violation of the good faith of the State that had been pledged to the enterprise, and reported an order to require him to revise his estimates.

Governor Andrew refused to put the question on this order to vote. The Council then prepared a written protest against the arbitrary and absolutely unfair action of the Governor, signed by all of the members except one, and asked to have it inserted in the official minutes. The Governor refused to permit the protest to go into the minutes, and it reached the people as a part of a smudgy chapter in Massachusetts history by publication in *The Boston Post*.

Nothing more could be done until the meeting of the Legislature, when a joint special committee of investigation was appointed, consisting of seven members from the House and three from the Senate. The opponents of the tunnel made great efforts to secure an adverse report from the committee, employing ex-Governor Geo. S. Boutwell as counsel, but the report, after several months of protracted investigation, was unanimously in Haupt's favor.

It not only reaffirmed the decisions of the committee of the Executive Council and censured the State Engineer, but reported a bill which reinstated the contractors in possession of the work and appropriated $150,000 to compensate them for damages caused by the entirely wrongful suspension.

Governor Andrew was more than ever incensed at this sweeping report, and announced a determination to veto the bill if it passed, as well as any other tunnel bill, unless it should be one that would take the work out of Haupt's hands; but he signified a willingness to approve an act to put the work under charge of State commissioners.

This suggestion pleased those who wanted the tunnel. They begged Haupt to make no resistance to the wishes of the Governor; that justice would be done to him at some time, though not then. "Let the State get her foot into it," they said, "so that she cannot back out, and then we will see that your interests are protected."

He asked if the State could not then reimburse his personal expenditures with simple interest. The answer was: "No! If a single dollar is put into the bill for your relief, the Governor will veto it. We will put in a sum to pay the sub-contractors and land-owners, and we will extend the right of redemption to ten years, but that is all."

He replied that such extension would be valueless; that while he could finish the tunnel in six years, the State would not do it in ten, and the right would expire unused. Jonathan E. Field (brother to Cyrus W. Field and to Justice Stephen J. Field, of the United States Supreme Court), chairman of the Railroad Committee, said: "We will make the time sufficient. I will make it ten years from the completion of the tunnel," to which Haupt added, "and the opening of the same for use," which was accepted.

Haupt then stated that there was another condition of far greater importance, without which he could not accept the act. It had been proved that, in his hands, the two-million loan would be sufficient to complete the tunnel, but Haupt's experience with State work in Pennsylvania led him to apprehend that the cost under public management would be greatly increased, and might be extended to four or five millions, in which case he would be unable to redeem. A provision was therefore inserted that all expenditures made and to be made for which the company should be held responsible in the exercise of the right of redemption, should not exceed $2,000,000.

The bill passed and was accepted by the stockholders. Commissioners were appointed, and, after fourteen years of time and the expenditure of over $20,000,000 in cash, as already stated, the tunnel was completed and opened for use.

During this time Haupt made repeated efforts to secure the repayment of his advances, but the tunnel commissioners opposed any legislation to this end. All attempts were unavailing. The commissioners condemned the work generally, altered the plans, and missed no opportunity to inflict damage upon him, personally and professionally, apparently with a view to defend and justify the hostile action of Governor Andrew, although, at the same time, they were inflicting millions of losses upon the State.

At the time of the passage of the Act of 1862 no one questioned the existence of the Hoosac Tunnel Company's right of redemption under the general statute. No movement could be made, however, looking to redemption until the tunnel was complete. An application was made to the Legislature, after that event, for the appointment of a commission to determine the amount to be paid. The Attorney-General appeared in opposition and argued that no legislation was required, as "a perfect remedy existed in the courts."

The rejection of this petition forced Haupt to employ counsel and bring suit in the Supreme Judicial Court. He had the best lawyers in Pennsylvania, New York and Boston. Amongst them were Joseph H. Choate, E. Rockwood Hoar, John C. Bullitt, Samuel Dickson and D. W. Gooch, who considered the case perfect, both in law and equity, and regarded the jurisdiction of the court as unquestionable, and filed a bill.

The Attorney-General, to the surprise of all, now denied the jurisdiction of those courts, and, what was more astonishing, pleaded the sovereignty of the commonwealth as a bar to the enforcement of any judgment on a contract into which the State had deliberately entered.

Although such a course seemed impossible, the court sustained the demurrer of the commonwealth and dismissed the bill.

Thereafter for years all of Haupt's applications to the Legislature to obtain justice were unavailing. At last, however, the time arrived when the people of Massachusetts became dissatisfied with the annual losses of the Hoosac Tunnel under State management, and clamored for the sale of the property; but no purchaser could be found so long as the right of redemption remained unsatisfied.

If the property should pass out of the hands of the State to a party not protected by the shield of sovereignty which had been raised up to escheat her creditors, suit could be brought by Haupt and the property recovered. Necessity, therefore, compelled some settlement, and a bill was passed in 1884 authorizing the Governor and Council to liquidate the claims, if it could be done—not on a basis of justice, but on terms satisfactory to themselves.

Mr. Haupt had interviews with Governor Robinson and the State Treasurer, presenting statements showing that the expenditures of private parties in excess of the sums that had been advanced by the State, and including payments due for work done, amounted, with simple interest, to about $1,400,000. At the last interview the Governor said: "I will not deny that great injustice has been done to you; but it was not *my* administration that did it, and I am not responsible. Further, I may as well be perfectly frank, and say that I do not propose to make any settlement that I cannot justify as a good bargain for the people of Massachusetts!"

The Governor also stated that interest did not run against a State, and, whether Haupt had borrowed money at 6 or at 20 per cent. to carry on the tunnel work, no part of it should be refunded. He finally offered $300,000, to be paid to the Troy & Greenfield Railroad Company upon the transfer and surrender of all capital stock. If not accepted, he would refer the matter back to the Legislature and have no more to do with it.

There was therefore no redress. The ultimatum of the Governor had to be accepted. After paying counsel and some small debts of the company, only $200,000 remained. This was divided among all the stockholders, giving the contractors, H. Haupt & Co., eight cents on the dollar for stock they had been compelled to accept at par in payment for work done and materials furnished.

For twenty years Haupt paid interest on debts contracted in consequence of expenditures of which Massachusetts received the benefit, but he secured no reimbursement—absolutely not a cent—

and in consequence lost the fine coal lands and other property in Pennsylvania which he had mortgaged in order to prevent "the generous and opulent old commonwealth, whose honor is untarnished and whose financial credit is unsurpassed," from wrecking* her own enterprise!

Not only so, but at one period of the contest he became so straightened, financially, that Mrs. Haupt was compelled to pawn some of her jewels (though her husband was not aware of it) to help keep the family pot boiling.

A remarkable feature of this great tunnel controversy, so unprecedented in the history of any State, was the single-handed courage and ability with which Mr. Haupt fought his side of the battle during two-thirds of a generation, never losing a point before bodies in which integrity, intelligence, fairness and facts were permitted to control decisions. He never employed an attorney or was assisted by counsel until the end, when the matter was taken to the Supreme Court.

During the numerous and protracted hearings and investigations which characterized the contest, the enemies of the tunnel summoned nearly all of the engineers in Massachusetts and several from other States, who, of course, knew what was wanted of them. Haupt summoned none but, although strenuous efforts were made to deprive him of that privilege, he was permitted to cross-examine all witnesses.

Besides being confessedly one of the most learned and able engineers of his time, he had enjoyed practically the limit of engineering experience in canals, bridges, viaducts, railways, tunnels, highways and all forms of topographical and constructive work. He was thus able, almost invariably, to confuse his opponents, and sometimes to cover them with extreme ridicule.

At the time of the suspension of tunnel work in 1861, Mr. Haupt had made great progress in rock-drilling machinery, and

---

* NOTE.—"It affords me much gratification to be able to state," wrote General Haupt in 1889, "that a short time before his death Governor Andrew admitted to General William Raymond Lee, a mutual friend, that he had made a mistake in his Hoosac tunnel policy, and had done me personally great injustice. The acknowledgment disarmed the resentment I had felt for the long and unmerited persecution which followed me to Washington, disturbed my friendly relations with Secretary Stanton and led to my retirement in the fall of 1863 from the position of Director of Military Railroads, as the records will show."

had developed a machine that was far in advance of the perforator at work in the Mont Cenis tunnel at the same time. This drill was improved by a Mr. Taylor, in the employ of J. A. McKean, who represented Mr. Haupt in Europe, and accomplished more rapid progress at less expense for repair than any drill used in the St. Gothard tunnel or elsewhere in the Old World; but Haupt never received any royalties or other compensation for its use.

Mr. Haupt's supreme knowledge of engineering principles, his great energy and experience, his genius for inventing more efficient rock-drilling and other machinery, and his tact and economy in the management of men, if he had not been harassed and circumvented by Governor Andrew and other officials of Massachusetts, would have resulted in completing the tunnel without a cent of cost to the State. As it was, the State, in the end, sold to the Fitchburg Railroad for $7,000,000 a work which had cost $20,-000,000.

This somewhat extended notice of Mr. Haupt's long and disastrous battle with Massachusetts seems necessary, particularly because the contest was the means of depriving the Federal Government of the services, in the hour of her greatest peril during the civil war, of a military railway builder and transportation manager whose achievements stand in history unsurpassed to this day.

CALLED TO THE WAR DEPARTMENT.

In April, 1862, after the report of the investigating committee had been made and when the legislative contest was at a crisis, Mr. Haupt was called to Washington by an urgent telegram from Edwin M. Stanton, Secretary of War. Being promised by the chairman of the joint committee that his interests should be safeguarded, he proceeded at once to Washington and began, with that extraordinary energy which characterized all his movements, to rescue the railways and transportation service of the Federal armies from the apparently irretrievable chaos into which they had fallen.

Thus began the army career so modestly and concisely told in the story which forms the main body of this volume, and which gives to General Haupt his undying place in history.

Stanton, who was a man of enormous comprehension and

energy of action, well knew what he was doing when he sent for Haupt to take charge of the military railways of the United States. He had frequently met him and felt his powers in the long series of railway and canal litigation which he had conducted in Pennsylvania, when Haupt was Chief Engineer or General Superintendent and director of the Pennsylvania Railroad, and understood both his accomplishments and experience and his high order of native ability.

He knew that Haupt was among the very foremost engineers of his time—an organizer of large enterprises, a manager of big railroads and a man of probity, fearlessness and persistence, as well as an accomplished graduate of the Military Academy at West Point.

He therefore bestowed unlimited authority upon his new appointee, which was used with supreme energy, abundant success and the best of judgment.

In order to obey the call of his country, which he served with all his might without compensation, Mr. Haupt left his fortunes and professional reputation in jeopardy in Massachusetts, where he was not only plucked and skinned, but drawn and quartered.

TIRELESS AND SUPREME AT SECOND BULL RUN.

His financial and professional sacrifices on the altar of patriotism, great as they were, did not equal his services to the Union cause, and there are two pictures of his operations in the army which should be written in words of ever-living light on the most brilliant page of American history. At the second battle of Manassas (Bull Run), a few miles south of Washington, in August, 1862, in which General Pope and his handful of beleaguered fighters were left in the lurch before Stonewall Jackson's fiery army by McClellan and other Generals of the Army of the Potomac, who stood near in idleness with large bodies of veteran troops, Haupt for the time was President, Secretary of War, General-in-Chief, Chief Commissary and Chief of Transportation.

Night and day for several days, with little food and less sleep, he was going from place to place, and General to General, rebuilding bridges, forwarding refugees, telegraphing to the President, discovering the enemy, bringing away and caring for the wounded, advancing supplies and munitions and planning succor for Pope.

For days and nights he was among the chief men in the quaking republic, but he used all his authority and all his energies for no purpose except to prevent still greater disaster to the Union armies.

When he returned to Washington the Cabinet was in session in the War Office.

"Come in, Haupt," shouted Secretary Stanton.

As he entered Stanton rushed forward, held him with both hands, thanked him in the presence of the President and Cabinet, addressed him as General and, on the following day, sent him a brigadier's commission.

WONDERFUL SUCCESS AND FORESIGHT AT GETTYSBURG.

In the terrific crash at Gettysburg he was even more supreme, and his services were beyond the power of formal estimation. His old classmate, General George G. Meade, like himself a Pennsylvanian, had just been placed in command to fight in defense of his native soil. But Meade did not know how his own forces were distributed nor the whereabouts or movements of the enemy under Lee.

Haupt, as skilled in military strategy as any, perfectly familiar with every rood of ground in that section, and determined that Lee should be permitted to march no further into the North, came to the rescue. On foot, on horseback and on locomotive he raced about until he had located and counted the forces of the enemy; correctly divined the objects of the swift and sudden movements of Lee, which had been inexplicable to the Federal commanders; concluded that Gettysburg was to be the point of concentration of the enemy, and by courier and telegraph fully informed Meade and the authorities at Washington of the entire situation.

This had been barely accomplished when Lee opened the awful slaughter in which there were 55,000 killed, wounded and missing, with a dash and determination rarely equaled and never excelled.

The Confederates were met by a fire as deadly as their own, and while, for three days, the battle raged back and forth through Gettysburg, around the home which he had erected for his bride and where his children were born, Haupt was repairing bridges, restoring broken railways, removing the wounded and pouring stores and munitions upon the field at such a rate that at the close of the contest there was enough on hand, as stated by the Chief Quartermaster, General Rufus Ingalls, to supply the army for nearly a week in advance.

Not only so, but so ceaseless had been his energy day and night and so comprehensive his plans that, the second day after the close of the fight all the railway and telegraph lines which Lee had been continually destroying were restored and in working order to Washington and to Baltimore, although nineteen bridges had been broken on the Northern Central Railroad and several others on the branches.

Great as had been his usefulness, his important labors were not ended. Believing that Lee, out of forage and heavy ammunition, with his communications broken, was in a trap and could be captured with his shattered and hungry army en masse, Haupt, on the morning after Lee's retreat, sought Meade at headquarters to explain the situation and urge him to strike the final blow of the war.

When he found that Meade was afraid or unwilling to undertake to pursue his advantage over Lee, Haupt jumped on a locomotive at midnight of Sunday and rushed away to Washington. Before breakfast he had made known at the capital the true conditions at Gettysburg and urged the authorities to compel Meade to move, to pursue, to strike and capture Lee.

He then hastened his little engine back to Gettysburg, expecting the orders from Washington would be obeyed, and desiring to be there to help; but Meade did not move and Lee escaped, to the great disappointment of Lincoln, Stanton and Halleck, and the still greater disappointment and grief of General Haupt.

If Meade had acted, or if anyone had thought to place Haupt in command on Sunday, July 5, 1863, Lee would doubtless have been captured and the Rebellion ended.

GOVERNOR ANDREW'S HOSTILITY FINALLY SUCCESSFUL.

In the meantime, as opportunity offered, Haupt had been prodding away to save property tied up in the Hoosac tunnel, very much to the annoyance of Governor Andrew, who, apparently, had undertaken the entire destruction of the contractor, but who, thus far, had been worsted in every bout, even the committees which had been packed against Haupt turning and reporting in his favor.

Governor Andrew was intensely hostile to slavery and a furious and effective supporter of the war. He was ceaseless in his efforts to raise men and money; so, when he went to Washington and demanded that General Haupt be compelled to live up to the technical terms of his commission as Brigadier-General, which would have kept him away from Boston and the Massachusetts Legislature, Secretary Stanton was compelled to yield.

Stanton could do nothing without the active and hearty support of the loyal Governors of the North, of whom Andrew was a leader. It was Haupt or Massachusetts, and Stanton, of course, promptly chose Massachusetts.*

For some years subsequent to the war, General Haupt followed his profession of consulting engineer in Pennsylvania. In 1867 he visited Europe on the invitation of the Royal Polytechnic Society of Cornwall, to explain his system of mining and tunneling by power machinery.

One of the rock drills invented by him for use in the Hoosac tunnel, and which was the type of those used in driving through the great St. Gothard tunnel with so much rapidity, was on exhibition and received the highest honors awarded by the society.

---

* NOTE.—Inquiring minds may wonder whether Governor Andrew could assume, promptly on taking office and maintain for years, such an intense, special and officially active hostility against Haupt without some reason. There were reasons, of course, but they had no relation whatever to Haupt.

One of his closest and most influential friends was Frank Bird, a large paper manufacturer of Walpole. Bird was largely under the influence of Daniel Harris, President of the Connecticut Valley Railroad who, in turn, together with his little railroad, was dominated by Chester W. Chapin, President of the Western Railway.

As stated hereinbefore, Chapin was desperately anxious to kill the Hoosac tunnel project because, on its completion, it would open up the Troy & Greenfield Railway as a carrying line parallel and rival to his own. Besides, Andrew had a reason of his own for fighting Haupt—entirely personal. On leaving office, Governor N. P. Banks, his predecessor, delivered an elaborate valedictory. As valedictories were unusual, this unexpected performance, covering the leading features of the onsweeping rebellion, took nearly all the wind out of Governor Andrew's inaugural sails, at the very last moment, which embarrassed and angered him exceedingly.

Governor Banks, pressed by more duties than he could perform at the last moment, lost sight of Haupt & Company's order for $100,000, money previously earned and formally allowed, and failed to sign it.

Although such action was like "swearing a seal off the record," Andrew refused to sign the order, thus making a double play—hitting Banks, whom he disliked, and pleasing his friend Bird, the agent of Chapin, Harris and the Western Railway Company.

In 1870 he made an examination and report upon wood pavements, with experiments in Boston in preservative processes. The report was unfavorable and the processes were abandoned. During the same year he also reported upon and located the Shenandoah Valley Railroad, which was subsequently built.

In 1874 John Edgar Thomson, President of the Pennsylvania Railroad, urged the appointment of General Haupt as Vice-President of the Southern Railway Security Company, in which the Pennsylvania Company had a very large stock interest. That office was not created, but in lieu thereof he was appointed General Manager and director of the Richmond & Danville system, which extended from Richmond, Va., to Atlanta, Ga., with its connections and branches. In this position he prepared the plan for organizing the Southern Railway and Steamship Association, which was adopted. He was named as pool commissioner, but declined, when Albert Fink accepted the position. He continued as General Manager until the death of President Thomson.

HAUPT'S PROUDEST ACHIEVEMENT—A TIDE-WATER PIPELINE.

In 1878 he was employed by the Pennsylvania Transportation Company to investigate and report upon the practicability of constructing a pipe line for the transportation of crude petroleum from the wells in the Allegheny Valley to tidewater.

After procuring data from the various local pipe lines to determine the discharges under given pressures and thus obtain data for the main line, he concluded that the successful operation of a line hundreds of miles in length over high altitudes and through low valleys would require a number of pumping stations so located with reference to the topography of the country that the work of the plants would be equal, and that such governors or other mechanical devices must be introduced as would compel the pumps of the several stations to work synchronously and regulate each other automatically. Also, that provision must be made for expansion of so long a line of pipes over a rugged profile.

These apparently difficult problems were satisfactorily solved by him, a favorable report submitted, and the work begun.

This project naturally provoked the active hostility of the Standard Oil Company, and of all the trunk line railroads. Henry

Harley, the head of the pipe line enterprise, although a man of liberal means, was under heavy call obligations at the banks. The Standard Oil Company and some other corporations informed the banks that they must either cease carrying Harley or lose the company deposits.

The resulting pressure soon forced Harley into bankruptcy, and, as his company held the only charter in existence for a trunk pipe line, the project was supposed to have been killed.

At this juncture B. D. Benson and D. McKelvy, large producers of oil of Titusville, Pa., inquired of General Haupt whether a right-of-way could not be obtained by purchase and a pipe line built through the States of Pennsylvania and Maryland to tidewater, without a charter.

The great power of the hostile Standard Oil Company and of the trunk line railroad corporations, with their vast resources and numerous agents, together with the fact that there was no law authorizing the condemnation of land for this purpose, and that a single defect in title or a single break of even a foot in the line would be fatal, gave to the undertaking an extremely hazardous aspect.

There were hundreds of highways, one or two canals, many streams, several railways and thousands of farms to be crossed, but Haupt believed he could get through, under or over them all, and undertook the task. No one was to know or ever knew his plans, methods of procedure or route, but he was to have a carte blanche and unlimited credit.

He ran surveys through many counties and in numerous directions as a ruse to concentrate the operations of his enemies where they would be harmless, but quietly bought and paid for his right-of-way on routes where he had no surveyors, taking extreme caution in the preparation of all papers and contracts and the description of all lands, so that everything should be proof against injunctions and other processes of attack, always communicating with principals through third parties and by means of secret cipher.

He had succeeded everywhere and knew that his proceedings were secure, when, toward the end of the line, he was blocked in Maryland, where he was unable to get over the Baltimore & Ohio Railway tracks.

Finally he secured permission from the County Commissioners of Baltimore to lay his line on a county bridge, high over the tracks, thus defeating the railroad and reaching tidewater in safety.

Without the power of eminent domain to condemn rights-of-way for hundreds of miles through the property of those recalcitrant holders who are encountered in every great enterprise, and surrounded and watched everywhere by the hostile agents of the most powerful corporations in the United States, Haupt's pipe-line achievement stands as one of the most remarkable feats of its character in this country, and is the one in which, perhaps, he takes the greatest pride.

The Tidewater Pipeline, which Haupt's success rendered possible, is now, as it has been for many years, in successful operation, with offices on Broadway, New York, and is one of the decisive elements which combined to give cheap illuminating fluid to the people of the entire nation, while, at the same time, the members of its original enemy, the Standard Oil Company, have been able to accumulate fortunes that are really fabulous in size, due in part to the system of trunk pipe-lines like Haupt's now in general use under the general law subsequently passed.

In 1879 General Haupt was employed to examine and report upon Hardie's pneumatic motors, five of which were constructed and tested upon the Second Avenue Railroad in New York. A compression plant was erected in Harlem, from which air at a pressure of 360 pounds was introduced into cylinders placed under the car seats. The motors were entirely successful, but were never generally introduced.

Haupt demonstrated that the cost of transporting passengers by horse power, including general expenses and a 6 per cent. dividend, was 4.55 cents each, and by pneumatic motor 2.57 cents each.

Such a result was entirely revolutionary, but the projectors could not get their motors upon the roads.

In the same year (1879) General Haupt was appointed consulting engineer of the United States Hydrogen Company, a corporation engaged in developing processes for the anti-corrosive treatment of iron and steel. Many of the results were entirely satisfactory, and articles treated by these processes resisted even the attacks of aqua regia.

It is certain that the remarkable success which attended the treatment in some cases positively proved that equal success could have been secured in all other cases if the essential conditions had been carefully determined and duplicated; but in consequence of circumstances beyond his control they were not; the enterprise languished and died, though the process and General Haupt's knowledge still live.

GENERAL MANAGER OF THE NORTHERN PACIFIC.

In the spring of 1881 he was appointed General Manager of the Northern Pacific Railroad, which position he held until the fall of 1884. During this period the road was completed to the Pacific Ocean, and the various divisions and departments as reorganized by him were put in working order.

The management of the Villard gold-spike celebration at the opening of the road in Montana was attended with peculiar difficulties and many serious risks. There were four sections of about fifteen Pullman cars, each to be transported from St. Paul over two mountain ranges, with temporary grades of 240 feet per mile, and with a large number of inexperienced train hands to manage the brakes. It was an extremely anxious time for General Haupt, who alone knew and appreciated the full extent of the danger and responsibility; but he carried everything through without accident, and the gold-spike celebration marked an epoch in railway history.

In 1883 he prepared a pamphlet on the bane of constant legislative interference by States with railroad properties and management, which was so favorably received by the railroad companies of the Northwest that several thousand extra copies were printed for general distribution.

While General Manager he secured the great terminals at St. Paul, Minneapolis and elsewhere, which now form such an important part of the value of the Northern Pacific.

In 1884 he was elected President of the Dakota & Great Southern Railroad, and at about the same time became one of the ten proprietors of the town-site of West Superior, at the head of Lake Superior, which has since grown from a pine slashing to a place of between 30,000 and 40,000 people, and to be one of the very largest shipping ports on the Great Lakes.

3

During all these activities General Haupt has been a voluminous writer, especially upon technical and professional subjects. He has made investigations and prepared treatises and reports almost without number, some of them, unquestionably, of great and enduring value.

His report on the Meigs system of elevated railroads sustained the claims of the inventor.

One of his most elaborate reports relates to Birdsall Holly's system of steam-heating for cities. It introduced a series of direct experiments on the transmission of elastic fluids through pipes, made at the works of the Holly Manufacturing Company, at Lockport, N. Y., from which new and valuable formulæ were deduced for the calculation of discharges under pressure, with numerous tables of lasting and practical value.

The subject of improving the navigation of rivers had occupied his attention as far back as when he was Chief Engineer of the Pennsylvania Railroad. He then published a review of the plans proposed by Charles Ellett and others, with suggestions of his own especially applicable to the Ohio. Having been invited to attend a meeting of the Ohio River Commissioners in Washington in 1880, he prepared papers which, on being submitted to Congress, were published in H. R. Miscellaneous Doc. 33, 46th Congress, 2d Session.

His plans were well received by the committees of both Houses, and were referred to the Secretary of War, and by him to the Chief of Engineers, who appointed a board consisting of five of the highest officers of the Corps to investigate and report upon them. Several hearings were given, and the board finally reported, in substance, that, although they possessed the results of twenty-five consecutive years of observations on the flow of water in the Ohio, made by their own engineers, their data were insufficient; that more extended and careful examinations should be made and, if previous results should be confirmed, the plans of General Haupt would be worthy of careful consideration.

The report did not suggest whether the required "observations" should cover twenty-five years or twenty-five centuries.

The Haupt plan contemplated a navigation without locks or dams, that would not obstruct commerce in high water or at ordinary navigable stages, but would secure a depth of six feet at the lowest stages. All that he asked was permission to test his principle on one of the worst shoals in the river, not interfering with traffic and giving ample security to the effect that, if not successful, in the opinion of a mixed board of civil and military engineers, he would remove all the material placed in the stream and leave it precisely as it was before undertaking the experiment.

The cost of the improvement would have been about one-fourth that planned by the Government engineers, as illustrated at the Davis Island dam at Pittsburg.

James B. Eads characterized the proposed plans for retarding the velocity of discharge and increasing navigable depth as entirely new, but believed they would accomplish the desired end. Nevertheless, the Government, which could have done so without a cent of cost or risk, has never permitted them to be tested.

In 1893 he published a volume giving comparative estimates of cost of construction and operation of all the systems of city and suburban railways then known and used. As to power, he found that compressed air, used in a proper motor, was cheaper, better and safer than any other system and, with an honest capitalization, would earn fair dividends on $2\frac{1}{2}$-cent fares.

It was impossible to secure the adoption of compressed air on any prominent line in consequence of the opposition of capitalists who had many millions invested in electrical apparatus and who felt compelled to discourage and paralyze anything that promised to be a formidable competitor to electrical propulsion.

IN ACTIVE BUSINESS AT EIGHTY-FIVE.

Although in his eighty-fifth year, General Haupt has not retired from active business. In the enjoyment of perfect health, with all his faculties clear, strong and vigorous, he is President and the active head of the American Nutrient Company, of Jersey City, and travels back and forth between Washington (his home) and Philadelphia, and New York, and elsewhere, with all the eagerness and buoyancy of a man of forty.

He is a life-member of the American Philosophical Society, Pennsylvania Historical Society and Franklin Institute, and an honorary member of other associations. He takes an active interest in social, philosophical and public questions, and occasionally finds time to publish leaflets and pamphlets giving his views upon current topics.

The modesty of his Christian life, the generosity of his forgiving spirit, the fairness of his profound judgment and the integrity of all his thoughts and purposes form a rare supplement to his great abilities, his strong will, his fearless attacks, his ceaseless energy and his many, many splendid achievements.

FRANK ABIAL FLOWER.

POTOMAC CREEK BRIDGE, BUILT (AS LINCOLN SAID) OF CORNSTALKS AND BEANPOLES.

CHAPTER I.

CALLED BY SECRETARY STANTON.

ON April 22, 1862, while engaged in an exciting contest in
Boston over the Hoosac Tunnel bill, I received a telegram
from the Secretary of War requesting my immediate presence in
Washington, and, about the same time, one from Hon. John
Covode, of Pennsylvania, in these words: "Come here immedi-
ately; Secretary Stanton wants you."

I showed these telegrams to Hon. Jonathan E. Field and other
prominent members of the Massachusetts Senate and House, who
advised me to go, pledging themselves to protect my interests,
which pledge was fully redeemed.

A Joint Special Committee of ten had made a report unanimously endorsing my management of the Hoosac Tunnel construction, and had reported a bill to reinstate me in possession of
work, of which I had been deprived by Governor John A. Andrew,
with an appropriation to compensate for the damages caused by the
enforced suspension.

Governor Andrew had announced his determination to veto
this bill, or any other that would retain the work in my hands, but
was willing to assume the partially-completed tunnel as a State
work. After several conferences with members of the Legislature
and officers of the Company, I had agreed to surrender possession to
the State on certain very important conditions, and had the promise that these conditions should be inserted in a bill to be presented;
but the bill had not been drafted and the action of the Executive
was uncertain. The situation was critical, as fortune and reputation were at stake.

However, I immediately reported in Washington to the Secretary of War. At this interview I made inquiry as to the service to
be performed and the time probably required. Mr. Stanton stated
that General McClellan was on the Peninsula operating against
Richmond; that General McDowell was ordered to coöperate by a
forced march across the country, but could not move until the
Fredericksburg Railroad was put in order for transportation of
troops and supplies; that the bridges had been burned, the track
destroyed and the rails carried off; that so soon as the line could be

reconstructed, McDowell could move, Richmond would fall and the war would be ended. My services might be required for three or four weeks, and added: "If the war is not finished in three months, I will resign."

I desired the Secretary to put his orders in writing, and soon after received the following note:

WASHINGTON CITY, D. C., April 24, 1862.

Herman Haupt, Esq.

DEAR SIR: I desire you to proceed directly to the Headquarters of Major-General McDowell on the Rappahannock and receive his instructions respecting the engineering work which he desires to have executed for his advance. If, upon inspecting the operations, you can devote your time and abilities to the service of the Government in their completion, you will be regarded as rendering important and patriotic assistance to the country which will be cordially acknowledged by this Department.

Your obedient servant,

EDWIN M. STANTON,

Secretary of War.

To this communication the following reply was returned:

WASHINGTON, April 25, 1862.

Hon. E. M. Stanton, Secretary of War:

I have considered your request and will go immediately to General McDowell, ascertain the position of affairs and the precise character of the duties to be performed. If they shall appear to be such as imperatively to require my personal attention, it will be given, although the sacrifices in other important interests will be great. If I can suggest arrangements to dispense with my personal services, this may be done. In any event, I would expect to continue only so long as public exigencies demanded it.

I have no military or political aspirations, and am particularly averse to wearing the uniform; would prefer to perform the duties required without military rank, if possible, but if rank is essential as a means to aid in the performance of duty, I must acquiesce.

Pay I do not require or care about. If I take the position you have so kindly offered, it will be with the understanding that I can retire whenever, in my opinion, my services can be dispensed with, and that I will perform no duties on the Sabbath unless necessity imperatively requires it, and of that necessity I must be the judge, so far as may be consistent with military subordination.

Yours, with much respect,

H. HAUPT.

A small steamer having been placed at my disposal, I proceeded down the Potomac in search of General Irvin McDowell. I found him on a steamer lying at anchor near Belle Plain, presented my letter from the Secretary and remained about one hour in conversation, during which he gave me very full information as to the condition of the road and bridges and the work required to be executed.

As I was about to retire he remarked, much to my surprise:

"Why, Haupt, you don't seem to know me." I replied that I was not aware that I had ever met him before. "Well," said the General, "that hurts my feelings. Don't you remember when I came to West Point as a plebe in 1834, that you took me into your tent during my first encampment and extended to me your protection as an older cadet?"

I did remember that a fat boy from Ohio had been quartered in my tent, but had no idea that this boy was the General in command of the Department of the Rappahannock. However, the ice was broken; from that time we were friends. Our relations became most cordial and confidential, and there is no one for whom, as a gentleman and a soldier, I entertained a more profound respect.

On my return to Washington, April 27, I was appointed Aide-de-Camp on the staff of General McDowell with the rank of Colonel, and after collecting men and material, I proceeded to Acquia Creek and commenced the construction of the road to Fredericksburg, landing with my men at Acquia Creek Tuesday morning, April 29.

The following report to the Secretary of War, dated Fredericksburg, May 25, will give information in regard to operations in the reconstruction of the Fredericksburg Railroad:

OPERATIONS UNDER GENERAL M'DOWELL.

FREDERICKSBURG, VA., May 25, 1862.
Hon. E. M. Stanton, Secretary of War.

SIR: In compliance with your request that I should give a report of operations connected with the reconstruction and opening of the Military Railroad between Fredericksburg and Acquia Creek, I beg leave to state that on Tuesday, April 22, I received your telegram at Boston requesting an immediate interview at Washington. I started on Wednesday, called upon you on Thursday, saw General McDowell at the headquarters of his Division on Friday, learned from him the urgent necessities which required prompt action, returned on Saturday to Washington to make further arrangements with your Department, procured implements and supplies, and on Tuesday morning, in company with Daniel Stone, Esq., landed at Acquia Creek prepared to commence operations.

The condition of the road was briefly as follows:

The extensive wharf at Acquia Creek, covering a surface of more than an acre, or about 50,000 superficial feet, with all the buildings connected therewith, had been destroyed by fire. For a distance of three miles the track had been torn up, the rails carried south out of reach, the ties put in piles and burned. All the bridges were destroyed, the superstructures burned, and in several instances the abutments blown up.

The reconstruction of the roads and wharf demanded immediate attention. A commencement had been made at the wharf, and some ties had been cut in the woods, but there was no proper organization for work. We proceeded on Tuesday to organize and commenced to lay track. The road bed had been used by cavalry, the wet weather had converted the clay surface into tenacious mud, the cross ties were of all conceivable dimensions. The artificers were soldiers without experience in track-laying, the weather was rainy; yet, by taking some of the most intelligent young officers, using them as assistant engineers, making levelling instruments from sticks, working all night in the rain, spiking rails by the use of lanterns, the three miles of track were laid in three days so that engines could pass over and transport material for work further in advance. More than 3,000 cross ties were manufactured by soldiers from the stump during that time and delivered on the road.

On Saturday morning, May 3, the first load of bridge lumber was carried from Acquia Creek for the Ackakeek bridge. This opening was a single span of about 150 feet and elevation of 30 feet. About noon on Saturday we were honored by a visit from yourself in company with Secretaries Seward and Chase and General Moorhead. At that time no part of the bridge had been erected and only the framing commenced. The next afternoon General McDowell rode across the bridge on an engine.

The time occupied in erecting it was about 15 working hours.

The next and most serious obstruction was the deep chasm of Potomac Creek nearly 400 feet wide, which had been crossed by a deck bridge of about 80 feet elevation above the water. No work was done until the 3d of May, except cutting some logs in the woods at a point so distant that but few of them could be used. On Saturday, May 3d, some of the logs were laid for crib foundations, but it was not until Tuesday of the following week that any proper organization could be effected. Three companies of the 6th and 7th Wisconsin and of the 19th Indiana Regiments, under Lieutenants Harker, Pond and Ford, had been detailed as a construction force, but many of the men were sickly and inefficient, others were required for guard duty, and it was seldom that more than 100 to 120 men could be found fit for service, of whom a still smaller number were really efficient, and very few were able or willing to climb about on ropes and poles at an elevation of 80 feet. With soldiers unaccustomed to such work, with an insufficient supply of tools, with occasional scarcity of food and with several days of wet weather, the work was nevertheless advanced so rapidly that in nine days the bridge was crossed on foot, and in less than two weeks an engine was passed over, to the great delight of the soldiers whose labors had constructed it.

By a computation made by A. W. Hoyt, Esq., Civil Engineer, it appears that the number of lineal feet of timber in the bridge across Potomac Creek is 34,760, which, if placed in a straight line, would reach nearly seven miles. The equivalent in board measure is about two and a half millions of feet.

The bridge across the Rappahannock was constructed under the immediate supervision of Daniel Stone, Esq., who was placed by you in general charge of construction. The bridge was constructed in about the same time as that at Potomac Run. It is about 600 feet long and 43 feet above water, depth of water 10 feet.

The reconstruction of the road and bridges, under the circumstances, in so short a time, with an ordinary detail of troops taken promiscuously, without selection, with, for part of the time, an insufficient supply of tools and implements, is certainly a most extraordinary performance, and reflects the highest credit upon the officers and soldiers whose energy and perseverance have accomplished it.

The services of Captains Simon Barstow and Joseph C. Willard, of the staff, cannot be too highly estimated, but much credit is due also to Major Brown, of the staff, Captains Conrad, Shannon, Henry and Feaster, of the Pennsylvania Reserves. Colonel Biddle and his officers, especially Lieutenants Kennedy, of the 9th Pennsylvania Reserves; Lampman, of the 30th New York; Rogers, of the 6th Wisconsin; Upperdale, of the 14th New York; Sexton, of the 2d Wisconsin; Thomas, of the 6th Wisconsin; Harter, of the 19th Indiana; Ramsey, of the 8th Pennsylvania; Pennypacker, of the 4th Pennsylvania, and many non-commissioned officers and privates who, in consideration of valuable services, have been detailed permanently as members of a construction corps for future operations of a similar character. The services rendered by E. C. Smeed, W. W. Wright, I. B. Nevins, G. F. Spear, W. R. Fulton and Samuel Longmaid, civilians and foremen in the construction of the work, must not be overlooked.

The above report is very respectfully submitted by

H. HAUPT, A. D. C.,
Chief of Construction and Transportation,

Fredericksburg, Va.,
May 25, 1862.
Department of the Rappahannock.

During the reconstruction of this road, General McDowell came out almost daily to watch the progress and encourage the men by his presence. He said he had never heard sweeter music than the click of the hammers when we were working all night near his Headquarters, spiking rails by the aid of lanterns, the men soaked with rain and the ties laid in mud.

It was a hard-looking track when first laid, and when the General rode out next morning to inspect it, he expressed the opinion that an engine could never be run over it. I requested him to suspend judgment until next morning, and look at the road then. He came, as promised, and expressed surprise to find the track in good line and surface and ballasted with earth, but as the ties had been cut by soldiers and varied in thickness from four inches to a foot, the task of surfacing was not an easy one.

It was good work, under existing conditions, to lay three miles of track in three days.

The bridge across the Ackakeek was commenced on Saturday, May 3, and finished so that General McDowell crossed on an engine, Sunday, May 4. The length was 150 feet. Time of reconstruction, 15 hours.

The Potomac Run bridge was now taken in hand. Some work was commenced May 3, but no organization effected until May 6. The last trestle was raised on May 13, so that but seven days were occupied in this work, at which time the bridge could be crossed on foot. An engine passed over on the evening of May 15, and on Monday, May 19, trains were running to Fredericksburg.

The following statement was made by General McDowell before the Court of Inquiry:

The Potomac Run Bridge is a most remarkable structure. When it is considered that in the campaigns of Napoleon, trestle bridges of more than one story, even of moderate height, were regarded as impracticable, and that, too, for common military roads, it is not difficult to understand why distinguished Europeans should express surprise at so bold a specimen of American military engineering. It is a structure which ignores all the rules and precedents of military science as laid down in books. It is constructed chiefly of round sticks cut from the woods, and not even divested of bark; the legs of the trestles are braced with round poles. It is in four stories—three of trestle and one of crib work. The total height from the deepest part of the stream to the rail, is over 80 feet. It carries daily from 10 to 20 heavy railway trains in both directions, and has withstood several severe freshets and storms without injury.

The bridge was built in May, 1862, in nine working days, during which time the greater part of the material was cut and hauled. It contains more than two million feet of lumber. The original structure, which it replaced, required as many months as this did days. It was constructed by the common soldiers of the Army of the Rappahannock, command of Major-General McDowell, under the supervision of his aide-de-camp, Colonel, now Brigadier-General Herman Haupt, Chief of Railroad Construction and Transportation.

The Potomac Creek bridge [see illustration on page 41] was the first of the kind constructed, but it stood the test and served as a model for many others subsequently erected. It was practically a mistake to build the first story of crib-work, but as many of the men were accustomed to building log houses and were not carpenters, I put them at work at which I supposed they were familiar. Possibly a day or two might have been saved by using trestles or bents for the whole structure.

The most remarkable feature about this bridge is the fact that it was built by common soldiers, not by mechanics. After a permanent Construction Corps had been organized and the men properly drilled, a much larger bridge was erected by one of my former assistants, E. C. Smeed, in half the time.

The following telegram to General McDowell from Potomac Creek, May 14, 1863, reports some difficulties:

There are so few men here able or willing to climb about on the high trestles, that I fear the work of bracing will be extremely tedious. Out of twelve men selected to spike poles on top of bents, only one made his appearance. I must therefore resort to new expedients. I propose, as soon as I can get track timbers down and track closed, to pull over the engine, Washington, by means of ropes. If it goes into the creek, it will cease to trouble us for awhile; if it reaches the other side, it will have a good road and may keep the track. We can readily get cars over by planking between the tracks and pushing. The rain gives us much trouble, but I will spare no effort to get an engine to the Rappahannock by Saturday (17). Men are wet, dull and no life or activity in them.

With all these difficulties, the bridge was finished in ample time, as the army did not move until May 26, and then it was a retrograde and not an advance movement.

When Fredericksburg had been evacuated by the Confederates, a number of torpedoes with percussion fuses had been placed under the tracks about the depot grounds to blow up trains that might attempt to enter. The locations had been pointed out by friendly contrabands, and the soldiers had removed quite a number and placed them in a small brick building detached from the station, that had been used as a powder magazine by the railroad company. A sentinel on duty one day probably handled one of these torpedoes carelessly and caused an explosion of the whole number. The report was startling. The city was shaken and the building blown to atoms—not a brick left. Nothing was ever seen of the sentinel except a piece of his gun at a considerable distance from the spot.

As it was not certain that all the torpedoes had been removed, the first train was made up by putting the engine behind and a car very heavily loaded with scrap iron in front, so as to explode any torpedoes before the engine reached them; but none were found.

After completing the road to Fredericksburg, I removed my Headquarters to that city and took possession of a comfortable residence that had been abandoned by its former occupants. General Marcena R. Patrick was Provost Marshal-General. His administration gave great satisfaction to the citizens. Private property was protected, depredations by soldiers punished, and good order maintained.

On my first visit to the city I saw fifteen or twenty soldiers standing along the curbstone, with boards on their backs stating their offenses, such as "I stole a ham," "I broke into a private house," etc. On one occasion a General Officer had taken possession of a dwelling occupied by a widow and two daughters and required them to seek other quarters. When General McDowell heard of it, he reprimanded the officer, compelled him to vacate, and reinstated the former occupants.

On Friday, May 23, President Lincoln and most of the members of his Cabinet visited General McDowell at his Headquarters at the Lacy House, on the north side of the Rappahannock. I accompanied them from and to Acquia Creek. The President seemed to be much interested in the Potomac Creek bridge, and on his return to Washington remarked to members of the War Committee that he had "seen the most remarkable structure that human eyes ever rested upon. That man Haupt has built a bridge across Potomac Creek, about 400 feet long and nearly 100 feet high, over which loaded trains are running every hour, and, upon my word, gentlemen, there is nothing in it but beanpoles and cornstalks."

At this interview, after other matters had been considered, General McDowell turned to the President and said that Shields' command had come back from the Shenandoah valley out of shoes, clothing and, in fact, everything; that his supplies could not be issued before the next day (Saturday) and that he could not be ready to move before Sunday; but, knowing the President's disinclination to initiate movements on that day, he would defer to his judgment and allow him to name the time. The President reflected for a short time and then said: "I'll tell you what to do; take a *good ready* and start Monday morning."

Every preparation had been made for a very rapid movement towards Richmond on Monday, May 26. I had a profile of the line to Richmond, knew the size of every bridge, and was prepared for prompt reconstruction.

The Massaponix bridge, 6 miles from Fredericksburg, had been prepared for burning and, anticipating an advance, was burned Monday morning, but we had a new bridge ready, and although I was not personally present, the bridge was reconstructed by a portion of my force in half a day, much to the surprise of the contrabands, who said: "The Yankees can build bridges quicker than the Rebs can burn them down."

On Sunday morning, May 25, an Orderly rode to my quarters and delivered a note from General McDowell, who wished to see me immediately. I accordingly repaired to the Lacy House and found him in a state of great excitement. He placed in my hands a bundle of dispatches and told me to read them, and they would advise me of the situation.

I found that orders had been issued to move the army by forced marches to Front Royal to intercept Jackson. McDowell replied, substantially, that Washington was in no danger; that forces under Banks and Fremont were sufficient for the protection of the capital; that Jackson had only one-third the distance to retreat that he had to advance; that before he could reach Front Royal the enemy would be out of reach; that the move was only a diversion to break up the plan of the campaign; that if allowed to advance, Richmond would fall and the war would be substantially ended. If orders now received were insisted on, the war would be indefinitely prolonged.

The orders were insisted upon and, as the sequel proved, the war was indefinitely prolonged. For the failure to capture Jackson the public demanded a victim and, soon after, McDowell was relieved and Pope put in command.

So far as my observation and knowledge of the facts extended, General McDowell was rarely permitted to execute any movement that he recommended, but was compelled to do that which was contrary to his own judgment and against which he protested.

The next day, Monday, May 26, I was off with my corps for

Bridge Across the Chattahoochee River, Georgia, 780 Feet Long and 90 Feet High, Built in 4½ Days.

Alexandria to reconstruct the Manassas Gap Road and throw troops and supplies into Front Royal, leaving Daniel Stone with a part of the force to reconstruct the bridge across the Massaponix, for which the material was already loaded on the cars.

The following telegrams exhibit some of the difficulties I had to contend with:

POTOMAC CREEK, May 13, 1862.

General McDowell:

The last bent was raised at Potomac Creek this evening, and several persons have walked over it, but the day has been a miserable one, and with all my efforts I could scarcely get two hours' work out of the men. They soon became wet and worked without spirit or good will. I have sent for 50 laborers, and will be able to determine how many more will be required if I can get an idea of the number of contrabands available at Fredericksburg for warehouse purposes.

H. HAUPT.

May 19, 1862.

P. H. Watson, Assistant Secretary of War:

Accept my thanks for your prompt attention to my request. I have not yet been supplied with material as fast as I could use it; when I can draw upon the woods I am independent, but I cannot make planks and spikes with axes, so excuse the trouble I have given you.

H. HAUPT.

WAR DEPARTMENT, May 20, 1862.

Colonel H. Haupt:

I congratulate you on the success of your first attempt. Your foresight, energy and general good management will insure continual success. The news of the evacuation of Yorktown without either fight or bombardment is confirmed. The evacuation was completed last night, but had been going on for some days.

P. H. WATSON,
Assistant Secretary of War.

FREDERICKSBURG, May 26, 1862.

To Major-General McDowell.

SIR: After receiving your instructions this morning, to advance for the purpose of constructing the bridge across the Massaponix, I proceeded to make the necessary preparations, but found that the opinions of Mr. Stone and myself did not precisely coincide and that considerable confusion existed. Whilst giving some directions in regard to the movement Mr. Stone handed me his letter of instructions from the Secretary of War, which I had never before seen, and which is in the following words:

WAR DEPARTMENT,
WASHINGTON CITY, D. C., April 26, 1862.

This may certify that Daniel Stone is authorized to do anything he may deem expedient to open for use in the shortest possible time the Richmond & Acquia Creek Railroad, and all Government transports are required to transport free of charge any men or material he may require for that purpose.

EDWIN M. STANTON,
Secretary of War.

This letter gives Mr. Stone absolute and exclusive control, not only over the bridges, but over the construction of the road, leaving me absolutely nothing to do but play the part of superintendent of transportation, a position which no consideration but a sense of duty would for a moment induce me to accept, and which I would hold only until a successor could be found. By not showing me his instructions, Mr. Stone left me under wrong impressions in regard to his position, which led to hostile jurisdiction.

The Honorable Secretary of War stated to me verbally that I was placed in general charge of all matters pertaining to construction and transportation in your Division of the Rappahannock, at least I so understood him, but he could not at the time have remembered the character of the letter given to Mr. Stone, which admits of no such construction. I do not see under the general powers granted to Mr. Stone directly from the War Department, that even you can give him any directions; the language is explicit and comprehensive in an extraordinary degree: "Daniel Stone is authorized to do anything he may deem expedient;" it leaves nothing for any one else.

In the Department of Transportation there is also a conflict of authority in the general instructions given to Col. McCallum, as General Director of all the Military Railroads of the United States. In the exercise of his authority he has the exclusive right to appoint all employees, purchase all supplies, direct all operations. I can only act as his assistant and subordinate; there cannot be two co-existent and equal heads in one Department. Mr. McCallum is my personal friend. There is not, and will not be, any personal difficulty between us, but there is a serious defect in organization which interferes with successful operation.

I find no fault with the Secretary of War. I understand and appreciate his position. His extreme desire to secure the completion of this important communication induced him to summon others as well as myself to his aid. If I have rendered any services, the fact is a sufficient compensation for me, and if I have aided you in any way, it will ever afford me much gratification to remember the very flattering acknowledgment I have received from yourself and from the Honorable Secretary of War. It seems to me now that my mission here is ended, or will be as soon as the transportation shall have become better organized. But I wish to assure you that I shall carry with me a grateful recollection of your kindness and the highest appreciation of you as a soldier and a man. Your efforts to suppress disorder, punish crimes, enforce discipline, and do justice to all classes have done much to relieve war of its most odious features and have secured for you the esteem even of those whose sympathies are with the enemy.

Very respectfully submitted, H. HAUPT.

Immediately afterwards I received the following, which placed me in supreme command:

WASHINGTON CITY, D. C., May 28, 1862.

Colonel Haupt.

SIR: You are hereby appointed Chief of Construction and Transportation in the Department of the Rappahannock, with the rank of Colonel, and attached to the staff of Major-General McDowell.

You are authorized to do whatever you may deem expedient to open for use in the shortest possible time all Military Railroads now or hereafter required in said Department; to use the same for transportation under such rules and regulations as you may prescribe; to appoint such assistants and employes as you may deem necessary, define their duties, and fix their compensation; to make requisitions upon any of the military authorities, with the approval of the Commanding General, for such temporary or permanent details of men as may be required for the construction or protection of lines of communication; to use such Government steamers and transports as you may deem necessary; to pass free of charge in such steamers and transports, and on other military roads, all persons whose services may be required in construction or transportation; to purchase all such machinery, rolling stock and supplies as the proper use and operation of the said railroads may require, and certify the same to the Quartermaster General, who shall make payment therefor.

You are also authorized to form a permanent corps of artificers, organized, officered, and equipped in such manner as you may prescribe; to supply said corps with rations, transportation, tools and implements by requisitions upon the proper Departments; to employ civilians and foremen and assistants, under such rules and rates of compensation as you may deem expedient; to make such additions to ordinary rations when actually at work as you may deem necessary.

You are also authorized to take possession of and use all railroads, engines, cars, machinery and appurtenances within the geographical limits of the Department of the Rappahannock, and all authority granted or instructions heretofore given to other parties which may in any way conflict with the instructions herein contained are and will be without force or effect in the said Department of the Rappahannock from and after this date.

By order of the President, Commander-in-Chief of the Army and Navy of the United States.

EDWIN M. STANTON,
Secretary of War.

Manassas, May 29, 1862.

GENERAL ORDERS,
No. 17.

The following, received from the War Department, is published for the information and guidance of all concerned:

War Department,
Washington, May 28, 1862.

Ordered, That Colonel Herman Haupt be recognized as the Chief of the Railroad Construction and Transportation in the Department of the Rappahannock, and that all other persons connected with that Department be subordinate to him, under the Department command.
EDWIN M. STANTON,
Secretary of War.

Accordingly, all persons connected with the railroads, either in the Departments of Construction or Transportation, will receive the orders of Col. Haupt, A. D. C., as if they were given directly by the Major-General commanding the Department.

By command of Major-General McDowell.

SAM'L BRECK,
Official. A. A. *General.*

Notwithstanding the objections of General McDowell, the orders to march to Front Royal and capture Jackson were insisted upon, and on Monday, May 26, 1862, instead of the "on to Richmond" move that had been determined upon, and for which all things were ready, the army commenced its forced marches across the country, leaving baggage and knapsacks to be forwarded by river and rail. I left with my Construction Corps for Alexandria, and after making, as I supposed, satisfactory arrangements with the Superintendent at that point, Colonel J. H. Devereux, for the management of the transportation, proceeded to reconstruct the Manassas Gap Railroad.

The road was soon put in passable condition to Rectortown and Piedmont. About the middle of the week General McDowell reached, and established his Headquarters at, Rectortown, and a depot was formed at Piedmont. The equipment of the road was insufficient for the amount of transportation so suddenly thrown upon it, and to make requisitions upon other roads and secure rolling stock, required time. The difficulties of the situation were greatly increased by the usual military interference with the running of trains, and by the neglect or refusal of subordinates in the Commissary and Quartermaster Department to promptly unload and return cars.

On my arrival at Piedmont, four miles beyond Rectortown, I found a paymaster who had appropriated one of the box-cars standing on the main track, and was using it as his office. This gentleman had been appointed from civil life and was, as usual, greatly impressed with the importance and dignity of his position. He positively refused to vacate the car. I represented that the army could not be supplied unless we could have the use of the track; he expressed the opinion that the payment of the men was quite as important as supplying them with rations. To the representation that he could establish his office just as well in a house as in a car, he again decidedly declared his intention not to vacate.

As remonstrance was useless, I went off, procured a detail from the guard, ordered the men to remove the money chests, table, chairs and papers to a brick house near the track, and directed the paymaster to follow, which he did without further opposition.

At Piedmont a blockade occurred by failure to unload trains. The fact was reported to General McDowell, who sent for his chief Quartermaster and chief Commissary and ordered them to repair immediately to Piedmont and superintend personally the unloading of cars. This was an unpleasant duty. The night was dark, the distance four miles, and the rain poured down in torrents.

Expected trains next morning did not come forward. I waited for hours in suspense and anxiety. Concluding that my orders about the schedule had been disobeyed, I wrote a letter of censure to the Superintendent and proposed to remove him.

It was fortunate that I waited for explanations. J. H. Devereux was one of the best men in the service, but I did not then know him. When we did know each other, our relations became almost fraternal. His ability was recognized also by others, and after the war he became one of the leading railroad managers of the country.

The letter from Colonel Devereux will explain the situation:

ALEXANDRIA, June 3, 1862.

H. Haupt, Colonel and Chief Construction and Transportation, Department of Rappahannock.

SIR: I beg most respectfully to answer more in detail your telegram of to-night.

You say "the road has been opened and track clear since Sunday morning, but not a pound of supplies had reached Front Royal at noon."

I answer: All my power save engines Rapidan, Fairfax, Delaware, Ferguson and Indiana were on the Gap Road. The Fairfax was (and is yet) too much out of order to run. Still, we press her as a switch engine, and are forced to use her on main line, where she broke down on Saturday, delaying for hours all business. She switches and brings up cars from Quartermaster and Commissary Department. The Rapidan is the only engine we can trust to do the daily heavy work between Washington and Alexandria. She has to be here, and nevertheless she has been sent with heavy trains to Manassas to be forwarded on Gap Road by your return power.

The Indiana is an old machine, only used as a switching engine in this yard, poor at that, but has been forced (with our engines off), to take part in the Washington work. The Delaware and Ferguson have had all they could do in forwarding Quartermaster and Commissary stores from here to Manassas to meet there the return power, and in distributing stores to troops guarding our road.

I, therefore, could not send through trains to Front Royal, but I knew well Stone, at Manassas, and Irish, at Rectortown, representing me, would do *all* they could do. And I beg to say they act for me, and I am responsible for their shortcomings. But *they* could not get other engines, or the use of the telegraph.

Knowing the need of the stores (telegraphed about it from Washington and spurned by the Commissary and Quartermaster), I advised and posted Irish and Stone daily about it. But generally in their reply was the fact the military were holding the trains somewhere, or the military were using the wire. I could not myself get anything from Irish without a long delay—in one case for an entire day, and I was rapped over the knuckles by the War Department in endeavoring to get an important order to him and was told to "hold on." In my dispatches to you, sir, I stated the condition of the stores, and how they would have to be moved, and this not only one time, but several, as I remember, and in your one reply you said the power should be "returned promptly."

June 1st, Irish telegraphs he had sent trains all forward to Markham, and Col. Haupt may send further, and he (Irish) cannot say when a train will return. And this "return" was about these stores. Again, Irish tells me he sent troops on the trains from Rectortown in the morning, and at 5 P. M. they were ordered by you to Front Royal, and that then, 11 at night, they had not returned, and would not probably return, as the road at night was not safe to run.

I could not satisfy myself with every possible inquiry that the trains were moved to the best advantage. But in all cases I did find that Stone and Irish were doing everything they could and were permitted to do, and I fell back on the satisfaction of knowing that Col. Haupt, my commanding officer, was there in person, and that he would have my requests to himself and to my men properly carried out. Stone and Irish, sir, as well as yourself, I advised that the return power from the

4

Gap Road must take the stores I forwarded there, and if no stores or supplies had reached Front Royal at the time you state, I think I have shown that it was through no fault of the Transportation Department.

You say "no excuse can be made for this (lack of supplies) that will satisfy the public," if coal is out. The question is, "why was not all procured in season?"

Because, sir, I respectfully state that to the public no such excuse will be made. We have only one coal light engine, *never* used for freight. On Monday week, Col. McCallum seized from Baltimore & Ohio Road three heavy coal burners for the special purpose of aiding me in sending forward Ord's Division. They were on the road when you came, but had done the duty they were procured for and I still kept them, and to meet the demands that might occur by keeping them, I ordered coal. This was last week. The engines did not get out of coal till yesterday, Monday.

Col. McCallum telegraphed me this A. M.: "I ordered a car load of soft coal for you on Friday from Georgetown, and the party agreed to deliver it at Alexandria by Saturday night. He has had some trouble in getting vessel to take it, but has succeeded in getting vessel this morning, and promises to have the coal in Alexandria some time to-night."

I therefore must say that neither I nor my men could have done more, and, moreover, more than three-quarters of your locomotives on Gap Road are wood burners. Coal burner 70 being broken, leaves only *two* coal engines in use. The 70 has her steam chest perforated and her cylinders out of order, and is of no use. And I did not propose to do anything to her, as on our own broken machines we have plenty of work day and night.

The telegraph officers are not enough in number and have only one operator to work the 24 hours through. A man must sleep and eat.

Irish telegraphed me Glasscut was used up, and it was useless to try to work the road as it should be until more operators were obtained. I at once referred him to you and to have you ask Col. Stager for the help needed.

About this I stated to you at Rectortown, and you said if I telegraphed you a list of officers and operators you would at once apply to Col. Stager for them. I sent this telegraph, designating stations, within ten minutes after reaching Alexandria on Saturday morning.

As I write, my operator comes to my desk and tells me he can't get my train business off, being ordered out of circuit by the War Department.

Since I have been in charge here, sir, matters have worked well and smoothly. So say at least the powers above me. You make the first complaint against me, and I beg to say that day and night I have been at my post, and in action and planning could do no better. But I have *not* control of my trains, my telegraph, neither have my men, and we could only do what we have been allowed to do.

Any arrangement you suggest or tell me to do, I will carry out cheerfully and with all my energy, but please do not hold me responsible for the effects of such plans or for any military interference with them, at least when you are there on the ground.

You instruct me to run without reference to telegraph and I at once proceed on your order, using all the engines that can come to us, but of course, the trains must remain on the sidings until I can obtain the power.

And in this very hurried letter (to go with an officer expected momentarily) I beg to add, in conclusion, that I have said nothing, sir, that must be construed into any lack of esteem for your well-known abilities or my appreciation of your kindness to me, a stranger.

And I am, most respectfully, your obedient servant,

J. H. DEVEREUX,
Superintendent Government Railroads.

In consequence of my arrangements for the operation of the road by schedule having been interfered with by the approval of the War Department, the schedule suspended, and the use of the telegraph resumed, a report was made to the Secretary of War giving reasons for the action that had been taken:

MANASSAS GAP R. R., June 6, 1862.

Hon. E. M. Stanton, Secretary of War.

SIR: As much difficulty has been experienced in the transportation over the Manassas Gap Railroad, I consider it of importance that the position of affairs should be reported to and understood by you.

The road has been operated heretofore exclusively by the use of telegraph without any schedule or time-table for running the trains. This system of operating a road may answer if the telegraph is always in order, operators always at their posts and the line exclusively appropriated to railroad purposes, but in the present case the line has not been in operation from Alexandria to Front Royal for a single hour since I came here until yesterday. When in operation it was appropriated for military purposes. I have been compelled to go eighteen miles to put myself in telegraphic communication with the Superintendent to learn the cause of the detention of trains, and have been compelled, after waiting for hours, to leave without answer, the line being occupied or out of order.

A system which admits of such irregularities is not safe and reliable. To require trains to lie for hours, perhaps for days, upon sidings waiting for instructions, when there is no possibility of communicating with them, I cannot approve of, and it was under the pressure of such an exigency that I assumed the responsibility of suspending the use of the telegraph and issued Order No. 2 directing trains with supplies to continue on to Front Royal as rapidly as was consistent with safety, and requiring empty trains returning to give the right of way and send flagmen in advance. There was no other way of getting supply trains in. In one instance I walked eight miles to order trains forward. This order I withdrew this morning, having received information last evening that the line was working better. I directed the trains to be run as formerly under the direction of the Superintendent, whose duties I have no wish or intention to interfere with, except when an imperative necessity requires it.

As soon as the bridge can be rebuilt across Bull Run and the power properly distributed, a suitable time-table must go into operation. Until that is done, I am satisfied that the operation of the road cannot be carried on with regularity and despatch. Even if a wire and operators should be provided for the exclusive use of the road, the line would be liable to derangement from storms and other causes, and generally at the time when most urgently required. With a good schedule strictly adhered to the line can be operated with regularity without any telegraph. The telegraph is a convenience in railroad operations. If it should chance to be in order when an accident occurs, it may be highly useful, but it is not a necessity. As a principal or sole means of operations I consider the telegraph very unreliable; as an auxiliary, highly useful. On this line and during the last week a dependence upon it has been a cause of derangement and delay to an extraordinary degree.

Another serious difficulty which arises from the operation of a line by telegraph alone without a schedule, is the fact that there is no fixed time for starting or stopping trains at any point.

If officers on business, sick or wounded are to be sent, a special extra train must be dispatched with them, or they must wait for hours in uncertainty. I have been asked repeatedly when the next train would start, and to the surprise of those who asked the question, I have been compelled to answer "I do not know."

I respectfully request a perusal of the following extracts from my diary for the last week.   Respectfully submitted,

H. HAUPT, A. D. C.,

Chief of Construction and Transportation,
Department of the Rappahannock.

As the telegraph could never be relied upon in the operation of the Military Railroads, my policy was to run trains in sections by schedule, to use the telegraph to give orders for train movements only in case of derangement, and if the telegraph could not be used then, even at some risk, to keep the trains moving by sending runners ahead with flags and relieving the runners where fatigued until expected trains were met, then side-track empty return trains, and let eastward-bound supply trains proceed. I considered anything preferable to standing still for hours or for days waiting for telegraph orders that could not be transmitted.

This system worked well after the trainmen understood it, and by it we were subsequently enabled to pass thirty trains per day during the battle of Gettysburg over a road that had capacity for only three or four under ordinary conditions.

By Saturday, May 31, 1862, we were engaged on the last bridge across Goose Creek. Five of these bridges had been destroyed, and they were reconstructed in about a day and a half. In the afternoon I received a note from General McDowell, then at Front Royal, stating that an engineer officer had reported a bad break on a high embankment west of the summit; track torn up, rails and ties thrown several hundred feet down the side of the mountain, and a pile of wrecked cars at the east end of the break; also that two days or more would be required to repair the damage. I sent back word by the messenger that the General should not be uneasy. If the rails and ties were within reach and no more bridges broken, a few hours would repair the damages.

Next morning, Sunday, June 1, we reached the summit soon after daylight and found that a dozen or more cars, side tracked at that point, had been turned loose and pushed over the grade. They had run as far as the high bank, where the rails had been removed, and then capsized, making a bad wreck.

Bridge Trusses Made of Boards, Prepared for Hooker's Campaign. Span 60 Feet.

The first thing to be done was to tumble the broken cars over the bank. With the strong force at hand, this was soon accomplished. The track gang was then divided into two parties, working towards each other from the ends of the break. The rails and ties were hauled up by ropes, and before 10 A. M. I had passed over the break on an engine, and reported to General McDowell, who was on horseback in the streets of Front Royal.

After expressing much surprise at the rapid reconstruction of the road, I was requested by him to return and hurry forward General Augur's command. This was done, and a few hours later found it also at Front Royal.

But it was too late; Jackson had escaped. McDowell's predictions had been verified. Nothing remained but to send some troops, as McDowell said, skedaddling after them up the valley with no hope of catching them, but, on the contrary, a good chance of catching a Tartar by the enemy suddenly turning on their pursuers, if found without support.

The move had been a horrible one; rain, mud and no shelter, army demoralized, the public clamorous, critics numerous, the President discouraged, a victim demanded. McDowell must be relieved, and about three weeks later General John Pope was in command, but it is some satisfaction to know that the Court of Inquiry did McDowell justice, and declared in their official report, Vol. I, Part I, p. 336 of Records, "His conduct at Fredericksburg should receive unqualified commendation."

The early weeks of June were employed in the return of the army from the Shenandoah Valley and the re-occupation of the line of the Orange & Alexandria Railroad. General McDowell established his Headquarters near Manassas. In a review of some of his troops one day, his horse reared and fell over backward on his rider, injuring him severely and rendering him unconscious. I was with him while still in this condition. His staff surgeon endeavored to get some brandy into his mouth, but his teeth were rigidly set and the effort was unsuccessful. On mentioning the circumstance to the General after his recovery, he remarked that it was a gratification to know that even when unconscious brandy could not be forced down his throat.

During the occupancy of the Manassas Gap Road efficient military protection was afforded by the command of General Geary, who had been ordered to confer with me as to the proper disposition of the forces.

The lull in active operations gave time for a more efficient organization of the Construction Corps, which was still composed of details of soldiers. Afterwards the Corps was composed chiefly of contrabands, selected from the thousands of refugees in Washington, directed by civilians as foremen and superintendents of gangs. No language is too strong to commend the efficiency of this Corps, or the importance of the service it rendered under the following regulations:

June 11, 1862.

1. The Construction Corps of the Department of the Rappahannock will consist of such commissioned and non-commissioned officers, privates and civilians as may be detailed from the force under the orders of the Department Commander, or especially enlisted or employed for the service of the Corps.

2. The duties of the Corps will consist in the construction and reconstruction of roads and bridges, the erection of buildings required for transportation purposes, the preparation of materials for structures, and generally the performance of any duties that may be assigned to them by the Chief of the Department.

3. The Corps will be organized into squads of ten men each. Each squad will be under the command of a non-commissioned officer, each two squads under command of a lieutenant, and the whole under command of an officer designated for the purpose by the Department Commander.

4. The Adjutant of the Corps will keep a register, in which shall be entered the names of the men, their residence, the companies from which they have been detailed, their former occupations, the kind of work in which they are most expert, the number of the squad to which they belong, and any other facts or particulars that may be worthy of note. Transfers from one squad to another will be made when required.

5. The Adjutant of the Corps will also act as Commissary and Quartermaster, and·it will be his duty to see that the Corps is, at all times, provided with rations, suitable in quality and sufficient in quantity; also, that the cooks and cooking utensils, tents, and transportation have been provided. The Adjutant shall also publish all orders and keep a record of all reports; he shall be allowed one or more time-keepers or clerks, who shall report to and receive instructions from him; he shall prepare pay-rolls and receive time-reports from officers of squads, and shall perform such other duties as may be, from time to time, prescribed by the officer in command of the Corps.

6. It shall be the duty of a clerk, acting under the orders of the Adjutant, to keep a correct record of all tools, implements, and public property of every kind belonging to or used by the Construction Corps. Each tool or implement will be marked with the words "Construction Corps, Rappahannock," branded upon the handle, and also numbered both upon the handle and upon the iron, by means of stamps. Each squad should have a separate tool-box, which will be under the care of the non-commissioned officer in charge of the squad. Each individual will be charged with the tool furnished him. He will be responsible for its condition, and will retain and use the same as designated by its number. To one of the squads shall be assigned the duty of taking care of ropes, pulleys, blocks, tackling, and hoisting apparatus generally. Another squad shall take care of all materials, lumber, iron, spikes, nails, etc., used in construction, and see that no waste is permitted. To another will be assigned the duty of taking care of and collecting together tools used in common and not chargeable to individuals, such as sledges, mauls, crow-bars, rammers, etc., but, as far as practicable, individuals must use

the same tools and be responsible for them. At regular periods the tools will be inspected by the officer in command.

7. When on active duty, so urgent as to require that every hour of day-light shall be employed, the time for breakfast will be at the dawn of day, and will be preceded by reveille and roll-call, at which all who are late or absent will be reported. Cooks must rise sufficiently early to prepare the meals in time. Immediately after breakfast the Corps will be assembled by call of bugle, squads called out by their numbers, and marched to their work. Those who are not employed in the immediate vicinity of the camp must take dinners with them, and all will be expected to work, if necessary, as long as day-light continues, and also at night, if required so to do. Periods of excessive exertion will generally be of short duration, and will often be succeeded by long intervals of repose. Men who are not willing to work, even for 16 hours continuously, when required, are not wanted in the Construction Corps of the Rappahannock, and are requested to leave it and return to their regiments at once.

8. Extra pay will be given for all time actually engaged in construction or other work. Officers in charge of squads will keep time by the hour, and return the same weekly by the Adjutant of the Corps.

9. Officers are particularly requested to make constant observations, and report to the Adjutant in regard to the skill, industry, habits, and general deportment of the members of the Corps; and the Adjutant will keep a record of the same. All who habitually use profane or obscene language; who are immoral, vicious, indolent, or insubordinate, and especially those who commit depredations upon the property of citizens, will be sent to their regiments with a statement of the offense committed, and will be otherwise punished as circumstances may require. The members of the Construction Corps are not authorized to investigate and decide upon the loyalty of the inhabitants of the country, much less to condemn them as rebels and appropriate their property to themselves. Such assumption of authority will not be permitted in any one. All who are not in arms against the Government are entitled to protection against injury or insult.

10. Each squad will occupy its own tent, and will be responsible for the care of it, as also for the tool-box, cooking utensils, and other property appropriated to its use. Each tent, tool-box, and utensil shall be numbered to correspond with the number of the squad.

11. No member of the Corps shall discharge fire-arms without the orders of a commissioned officer, except where imperative necessity requires it.

12. Civilians, who may be employed as superintendents in charge of construction, will be considered as having, while so employed, the rank of a captain, and foremen as having the rank of lieutenant, and will be obeyed and respected accordingly.

13. Civilians, who may be employed as ordinary mechanics and laborers, will be entitled to the same pay and rations as enlisted men detailed for service in the Construction Corps, and must conform to the rules, regulations, and discipline of the Corps in every particular. In case of dismissal for improper conduct, neglect of duty, or other cause, the officer in command may require the forfeiture of any back pay that may at the time be due, which may be given to others as premiums for good conduct, or extra services, or otherwise appropriated at the discretion of the officer in command.

14. A diary shall be kept by the Adjutant, and a quarterly report compiled from the diary shall be submitted to the Department Commander, in which shall be given the names of all who have been distinguished by efficient services, and also the names of those who have been sent to their regiments in consequence of misconduct or inefficiency.

15. It is expected that all who have volunteered in defense of their country in the present eventful crisis are, and will show themselves to be, gentlemen as well as soldiers. No one whose deportment and conversation prove that he is not such, can remain a member of the Construction Corps of the Rappahannock for a longer time than may be necessary to procure a substitute.

H. HAUPT, A. D. C.,
Colonel of Staff,
Chief of Construction and Transportation,
Department of Rappahannock.

Considering, in June, that I had performed the duties for which I had been summoned to Washington, and, with a view to retirement, I sent this letter to the Secretary of War:

ALEXANDRIA, June 20, 1862.

Hon. E. M. Stanton, Secretary of War.

DEAR SIR: It is now two months since I was summoned to Washington by your telegram, and was informed that the service required of me was the prompt reconstruction of the railroad from Acquia Creek to Fredericksburg, to facilitate a movement against Richmond. I consented to perform the service in the belief that the time required would not exceed two or three weeks, and that necessity for my continuance would then be at an end; but when the Fredericksburg line was opened and put in successful operation, it became an urgent military necessity that the injured portion of the line to Front Royal should be reconstructed.

This was promptly done by the Construction Corps under my direction. I then found that the transportation was in a state of great confusion, and required reorganization; this duty has occupied my time since the opening of the road to Front Royal, but now I am able to announce that the communications are all open, the roads in good condition, the trains running regularly to schedule, abundant supplies of stores for a week or more in advance already transported, and no probability of any new work for the Construction Corps for several weeks. Under these circumstances no imperative necessity exists for my personal presence, and I propose to return to Massachusetts and give some attention to my financial affairs, which are in much confusion, consequent upon my long and unexpected absence.

In the way of compensation, I desire nothing. I cannot draw pay as Colonel, because I have not complied with the forms and cannot subscribe to the certificates. All I ask is that cash I have actually paid out since my connection with the service shall be returned to me from the contingent or other fund. If acceptable to the Department, I will continue for a time to give my services in the same way; that is, by the repayment of actual expenditures, but the condition of my pecuniary and domestic affairs, and my business engagements are such as to prevent me from accepting any permanent position in connection with the army that will remove me from the vicinity of Boston.

I find that my pay and commutations as Colonel would amount, for the time employed, to over $500, while my expenditures, portions of which have been for supplies used by assistants and foremen, do not much exceed $300, including traveling expenses. This is all I ask to be repaid.

With many thanks for your kindness, and with a grateful sense of obligation for the consideration I have received at your hands, I remain,

Yours very respectfully,

H. HAUPT.

To this letter no answer was returned.

To prevent certain abuses by officers, I was compelled to issue the following in reference to the use of Military Railroads:

GENERAL ORDERS,   June 25, 1862.
    No. 7.

The following regulations are published for the information and government of all concerned:

Assistant Quartermasters and Commissaries are positively forbidden to load cars, or parts of cars, on any of the Military Railroads of the Department of the Rappahannock with any freights which are not strictly and properly included in Quartermaster and Commissary stores. They shall not load, or permit to be loaded by any employee, any articles for the private use of officers, whatever may be their rank or position, or for sutlers or individuals.

Sutlers will be allowed transportation on the railroads of the Department only on a permit from the Quartermaster-General. They shall certify the quantity and kind of goods, and the contents and marks of all boxes, barrels, and packages for which transportation is desired. Sutlers' goods shall be carried only at the convenience of the Transportation Department, and must not, in any case, be allowed to interfere with army supplies. They shall at any time, and in any place, be subject to examination so long as they are under the control of the Transportation Department; and for any false statement or concealment of facts, all the goods of said sutler will be liable to seizure and confiscation, and he will forfeit all right to transportation in future.

The use of the names of officers upon boxes, trunks, or packages, shall not shield them from examination, or confiscation, if found to contain improper articles; and if the name of an officer shall have been used without his consent, the goods shall be confiscated, and the party using it deprived of the right of transportation.

Hospital stores must be directed to the senior medical officer at the place of destination, and to the care of the Superintendent of the road, who will use his discretion as to examination.

Any officer who shall allow his name to be used by sutlers or others to secure transportation for that which is not his own personal property, will be considered as guilty of conduct unbecoming an officer and a gentleman.

Articles intended for private use of officers and soldiers, may be sent by Adams' Express Company; but all such articles will be subject to examination by the Provost Marshal.

Freights for individuals residing on the line of any Military Railroad shall not be carried if the parties are known to be disloyal; all other individual freights which it may be proper to transport over the Military Railroads of the Department shall be carried by Adams' Express Company, subject to such rules, to such charges, and to such examination as the Chief of Transportation may approve.

By order of Major-General McDowell.

H. HAUPT, A. D. C.,
Colonel of Staff,
Chief of Construction and Transportation,
Department of the Rappahannock.

The within regulations have been submitted to me, and meet with my approval.

JAS. S. WADSWORTH,
Brigadier-General.

CHAPTER II.

SECOND BATTLE OF BULL RUN.

NOTWITHSTANDING my letter to the Secretary of War of June 20, 1862, I was not relieved. So long as General McDowell remained in command, he was not willing that my services should be dispensed with, but on June 26, 1862, General Pope took command and McDowell assumed the position of a subordinate.

General Pope did not recognize me in any way, and gave me no instructions. After this state of things had continued for some time, I asked McDowell for an explanation. He said that the subject had been frequently discussed, but that General Pope considered that a separate and independent department for the construction and operation of the railroads was unnecessary. Railroads, he contended, were used for the transportation of army supplies and should be under the direction, control and management of the Quartermaster's Department.

McDowell said all he could to convince Pope of his error; had told him that under the old regime his army had never been properly supplied; that if he had relied entirely upon his wagon trains, his movements could have been made with more celerity and certainty than when dependent upon the railroads, but that under my administration there had been no deficiencies that it would have been possible for the railroads to supply; but all his efforts were futile to change Pope's opinion.

I thanked General McDowell for his frank explanation and said that, as I was no longer needed, I would return to Massachusetts. I called at the War Department and explained to Assistant Secretary Peter H. Watson the condition of affairs, and then returned to my residence in Cambridge, having said to Watson that if I was again needed he could send for me, and requesting him to keep me posted occasionally as to movements.

The first letter, received a few days after my return to Cambridge, stated that things were still working smoothly, and remarked that if other departments had been as well organized and managed as the Military Railroads, "the war chariots would not have been so frequently off the track;" but soon after I received from Assistant Secretary Watson a telegram in these words:

"Come back immediately; cannot get along without you; not a wheel moving on any of the roads."

I returned as requested, and, after an interview with Watson, took an engine and rode to the nearest point to Pope's Headquarters, which was at a farm house near Cedar Mountain, where the battle had occurred a few days before. During my absence, July 23, General Halleck had been placed in command as General-in-Chief of all the armies.

I arrived at Headquarters at Cedar Mountain August 18, and found Generals Pope and McDowell with members of the staff in a farm house. I was cordially welcomed back, especially by McDowell, and General Pope was quite civil. After a brief conversation, he turned to his chief of staff, Colonel Geo. D. Ruggles, and directed him to issue any orders I might dictate, and then told me to dictate such orders as I considered necessary. They were as follows:

CEDAR MOUNTAIN, August 18, 1862.

GENERAL ORDERS,
No. 23.

All railroads, and especially the Orange & Alexandria Railroad, within the limits of the Army of Virginia, are placed under the exclusive charge of Colonel Herman Haupt.

No other officer, whatever be his rank, shall give any orders to any employe of the road, whether conductor, engineer, or other agent. No orders respecting the running of the trains, construction or repair of the roads, transportation of supplies or troops, shall be given, except by authority of these Headquarters through Colonel Haupt.

All persons now employed in any way on these railroads will immediately report to him, and will hereafter receive instructions from him only.

All requisitions for transportation, and all applications for construction or repair of roads, will be made directly to him at Alexandria, Va.

All passes given by him to employes will be respected **as if** issued from these Headquarters.

By command of Major-General Pope.

GEO. D. RUGGLES,
Colonel and Chief of Staff.

WASHINGTON CITY, D. C., August 19, 1862.

Ordered: That the Department of Colonel Herman Haupt, formerly Aide-de-Camp to Major-General McDowell, and Chief of Construction and Transportation in the Army of the Rappahannock, is hereby extended to embrace all the railroads which are or may hereafter be included within the lines of operation of the Army of Virginia; and the instructions of May 28, 1862 [see page 54], are continued in full force.

EDWIN M. STANTON,
Secretary of War.

After giving orders to Colonel Ruggles, General Pope mounted his horse and rode off to review one of the Corps, but returned

BRIDGE OF BOARD TRUSSES BEING TESTED FOR DEFLECTIONS.

in haste in about an hour with the information that the enemy was in full force in front and advancing rapidly. He ordered an immediate retreat, and turning to me requested that I would do all in my power to remove the stores at Culpepper, where a large amount had been collected.

I immediately took an ambulance, and, in company with General B. S. Roberts, Chief of Cavalry, rode to Culpepper and succeeded in reloading all the stores and sending them to a safe distance in the rear. I then turned my attention to reorganizing the transportation, which had again been thrown into confusion from the usual causes—military interference, neglect to unload and return cars, too many heads, and, as a consequence, conflicting orders. General Pope had at last discovered that a railroad could not be run successfully with more than one person to give orders.

The retrograde movement commenced August 18, and was so expeditious that, as General Pope reported the next day (August 19), his whole army was posted behind the Rappahannock.

On the 21st and 22d the enemy made unsuccessful attempts to force a passage in front, and then commenced a flank movement.

On the afternoon of the 22d I returned to the front to ascertain the condition of affairs and the requirements of the army in the way of transportation. I found General Pope at some distance from the railroad, seated under a tree on a hill which overlooked the valley and the country beyond. I remained perhaps two hours, during which reports were made to the General to the effect that the enemy's wagons had for some time been moving up the river.

This appeared to me to indicate a flank movement, and I asked General Pope how far he had his scouts up the river. The distance named was not great, and I then asked: "Is that far enough? What is to prevent the enemy from going even as far as Thoroughfare Gap and getting behind you?"

He replied: "There is no danger." I did not wish to press him with further questions, thinking he might consider me impertinent and that his sources of information were better than mine; but I felt uneasy, and soon after returned to the railroad, and started towards Alexandria.

I had passed Catlett's and reached Manassas when the operator handed me a telegram from General Pope: "The enemy in largely superior force has turned my right flank," and requesting me to retire the rolling stock to a safe distance.

The next train following me had been fired into and captured, and about the same time Pope's Headquarters was raided by Stuart's cavalry.

I could not withdraw the rolling stock, as General Pope had

ordered a large amount to the front, and between it and myself there was a large force of the enemy. I should myself have been captured had I been half an hour later.

At Burkes Station I met General Philip Kearney moving in cars to the front with part of his command. I told him I had important information, and asked him to come to the office where I could have a private conversation. I then showed him the telegram from General Pope, and explained the situation. He asked me to let him have a pilot engine and two flat cars to send with a guard in advance of his trains. This was certainly a very hazardous duty for train men, but they never hesitated on this, or on any other occasion, where the danger was as great as if they had been in line of battle. In fact, several of my men were killed and others captured during the war.

The engine and cars were furnished, and that was the last I saw of General Kearney. He was killed at Chantilly.

Neither did I see Generals Pope or McDowell again until after the battle. A few telegrams passed between us, when the wires were cut and all communication interrupted.

From General Pope's report, I make a few extracts:

On the night of the 24th a dispatch was received from Colonel Haupt that 30,000 men had demanded transportation and would be shipped this afternoon and next day. * * *

On the night of the 25th I sent an order to Colonel Haupt to direct one of the strongest Corps to take part at Manassas Junction, and Gen. Franklin to march, as he could move as rapidly as by rail with the limited transportation.* * *

At 8 P. M., on the night of the 26th, Jackson's force had passed Thoroughfare Gap. Had Franklin been at Centreville, or Cox and Sturgis even as far as Bull Run, this move of Jackson's would have been impracticable.

From August 18 to the morning of the 27th, my troops had been continuously marching and fighting night and day.

August 31, there were not five horses to a company that could be forced into a trot. * * *

September 1st, near sunset, Kearney and Stevens were killed.

The forces that joined General Pope were Reynolds' Pennsylvania Reserves, 2,500, August 23; Heintzelman and Porter, August 26 and 27. The Pennsylvania Reserves and Heintzelman's Corps, consisting of Hooker's and Kearney's commands, rendered efficient service. Porter's Corps took no part except in the action of August 30. "This small fraction of 20,500 men was all that drew trigger of the 91,000 veteran troops from Harrison's Landing."

September 1 General Pope reported to General Halleck that the Army of the Potomac was demoralized owing to a change of commanders, and added: "Where there is no heart in the leaders and every disposition to hang back, much cannot be expected from the men."

There seemed to be good reasons for this complaint. The distance from Alexandria to Bull Run is not twenty miles, and as most of the camps were four miles south of Alexandria, it would have been but a short day's march to join General Pope; but troops were in camp several days demanding transportation by rail which could not be furnished.

As General Pope says, less than one-fourth of the Army of the Potomac rendered him any assistance. Had they marched, nearly all could have rendered good service in the action, and the result would probably have been changed.

It does not admit of question that, if the Army of the Potomac was ready to ride into action on railroad trains, it would have been in a better position for action after one day's march. To wait three or four days, as was the case, demanding rail transportation, seems to have been only an excuse. The trouble seems to have been an indisposition on the part of McClellan to assist Pope in gaining a victory. In one case where I furnished them, cars remained for hours unused, and were then withdrawn and used to forward supplies.

The successful flank movements of Lee's Army cut off all telegraphic communication with General Pope, and no further instruction could be received from him. I was compelled to use my own judgment and to assume much responsibility. I sent out operators with pocket instruments to push their way to the front, climb trees, make observations, and report all they saw and heard, and for some time all the information received at Washington came through my office.

During this time the President was in a state of great anxiety, and frequently telegraphed to know if any further information had been received.

The following letters and telegrams, many of which are not found in the records of the office, will throw light upon the operations of the campaign:

RAPPAHANNOCK CROSSING, August 20, 1862.
Col. Herman Haupt, Superintendent of Railroads, Alexandria:

I wish a train of 20 cars for subsistence to be kept constantly at the order of E. G. Beckwith, Chief of Commissary, at these Headquarters.

This train is required to keep the troops supplied with rations, as I am about to send back all my wagons and wish no depot. I wish you would see that this train runs regularly according to its orders, as we depend upon it for the daily bread of this command. I desire also that you send nearly the whole of the rolling stock of the road to be switched off on the side-tracks, either at Catlett's or Warrenton Junction, so that in case of necessity I can carry off all the baggage and material of the army by railroad at the shortest notice. I shall have no wagons left here for that purpose.

Inform General Halleck whether you station the trains at Catlett's or Warrenton Junction. JOHN POPE,
Major-General Commanding.

August 20, 1862.

Major-General Pope:
I am sending to Manassas to-night all cars loaded with stores not immediately required. We will have 60 cars sent to Warrenton Junction to-morrow. Forage has all been sent forward, and, taking it for granted that you will want more, I have ordered a part of the 60 cars to be loaded with forage. I have informed General Halleck that 60 cars will be at Warrenton Junction to-morrow for use in case of need. You will understand that this will concentrate our power at this end, and we will be short at Alexandria if troops are to be forwarded.
H. HAUPT.

August 20, 1862.

Major-General Halleck:
I have ordered the siding at Rappahannock to be immediately extended to hold 20 cars of commissary stores. 20 cars more will be kept back at next station to replace the first when empty. Stores not immediately required, I have sent and am sending to Manassas. To-morrow morning 60 empty cars will be at Warrenton Junction to use in case of necessity. If you intend to order Sturgis' command forward, please let me know, as there will be some trouble in arranging transportation; all our power may be at this, the south end.
H. HAUPT.

August 21, 1862.

Colonel Geo. D. Ruggles:
Sixty empty cars await your orders at Warrenton Junction. I have stationed J. D. Irish at Rappahannock Station, who will receive and carry out your directions about cars. Do you wish to move the baggage of the whole command? If so, how far—to Catlett's, to Manassas, or where? I am coming back this morning; where will I find you?
H. HAUPT.

August 21, 1862.

Major-General Pope:
Troops under command of General Kearney are understood to be lying in transports at Alexandria. No applications for transportation, and no replies to my inquiries about destination. Only orders received have been to remove the 34th Massachusetts to Banks this afternoon. At what point shall they leave the cars? I am returning to Rappahannock.
H. HAUPT.

August 21, 1862.

P. H. Watson, Washington, D. C.:
Please request the proper officer to keep me advised of troops that are coming, who is in command, what are their numbers, what their destination, and other particulars required to arrange transportation. 20,000 men have just been thrown upon us when we require another day of regular movement to remove those previously on our hands.
H. HAUPT.

August 21, 1862.

Major-General Halleck, Washington, D. C.:

General Pope has this day informed me that he expects reinforcements from the West and from other sources. Will you please inform me as early in advance as practicable, what will be the probable demands for transportation, and at what time, as it will be necessary to return power from the south end of the line, where it is held in reserve to meet the demand when it arises.

H. HAUPT.

August 21, 1862.

D. C. McCallum, Washington:

I received your telegram on the field with General Pope; referred it at once to him. The condition of affairs is such that no reliable information can be given in regard to the permanent demands of transportation. At present all the capacity of cars and engines is taxed to the utmost. Nothing is unloaded; no depots made; forage and commissary stores delivered from cars—a large number; 60 empty cars held at Warrenton Junction to meet a sudden demand. Cars also required at Alexandria to forward troops expected to arrive as reinforcements. General Pope says send no rolling stock away at present.

H. HAUPT.

RAPPAHANNOCK, 11:40 P. M., August 21, 1862.

Colonel Haupt:

I wish you to send engines enough to take away all the cars here early in the morning, should it become necessary.

JOHN POPE,
Major-General.

WASHINGTON, D. C., August 22, 1862.

Colonel Haupt:

Troops will be arriving to-day or to-morrow at Alexandria for the line of the Rappahannock, probably in the next forty-eight (48) hours from ten to fifteen thousand (15,000).

H. W. HALLECK,
General-in-Chief.

ALEXANDRIA, August 22.

Colonel Haupt:

General Kearney is here, and Major Keyes with orders from General Halleck to send the soldiers, now waiting here, forthwith. They will insist on getting them off without regard to schedule.

J. H. DEVEREUX.

August 22, 1862.

J. H. Devereux:

We must conform to your present arrangement, but it is all wrong. Neither General Halleck or anyone else has any right to give orders in regard to trains in opposition to my instructions. I want the schedule restored to-morrow. You can run extras between, but the regulars must run, or I will decline all responsibility. The doctors have been assured that the schedule would be conformed to, and they must have their sick and wounded ready. I hope to reach Alexandria some time or other, when I will ascertain particulars.

H. HAUPT.

RAPPAHANNOCK CROSSING, 10:30 P. M.

Colonel Haupt:

Push forward the troops to Catlett's at daybreak in the morning. Halt all troops coming up at Catlett's. Keep the road open.

By command of Major-General Pope.

GEO. D. RUGGLES,
Colonel and Chief of Staff.

August 22, 1862.

Geo. D. Ruggles, Chief of Staff:

I had made arrangements to use all the power necessary before the receipt of your telegram, leaving only two engines at lower end to supply forage and commissary stores. My arrangements have been interfered with by orders, which the Superintendent says came from General Halleck, to forward troops as fast as they could be loaded. The schedule has been set aside, and everything is in confusion; trains are on the road, and we cannot tell where, and cars cannot be sent in.

I have censured the Superintendent in strong terms, and would suspend him if I had any one else capable of performing his duties. So long as I am responsible for the management, no orders except from myself or through me must be respected.

I will investigate this matter, if I can succeed in reaching Alexandria. The train which left Rappahannock before noon is still detained here, as well as three others that came after it; all of them waiting orders. I fear much trouble, but will do all I can to keep things moving.

H. HAUPT.

August 22.

J. H. Devereux:

General Pope orders all the rolling stock to Alexandria to bring up troops. You can order it forward as you can use it. We have several engines and cars at Manassas waiting orders to go to Alexandria. Is it probable that they will be received before morning? If not, do not keep train hands waiting all night.

H. HAUPT.

August 22, 1862.

McCrickett:

Forward such troops as General Robinson may wish to send immediately; send light engine in advance as pilot; examine well the bridges and the cut near Bristoe. Send flat car with engine.

H. HAUPT.

August 22, 1862.

Major-General Pope:

The 34th Massachusetts were not in a condition for immediate service, and I did not consider it proper to send them up. They were without caps and without cooked rations. By 9 A. M. 5,400 men in all will have reached Manassas. We will continue to send forward as rapidly as cars can be returned. We have sent all who have applied for transportation, except the 34th Massachusetts, and they will go at noon. I have made inquiries, but cannot find General Heintzelman; will send again. The troops sent, I understand, belong to General Kearney. Do you wish the instructions given to Colonel Wells, 34th Massachusetts, changed?

H. HAUPT.

August 22, 1862.

Major-General Pope:

The whole number of men sent to Catlett's at 9 A. M. was 6,600. Watson telegraphs that Cox's Division will reach the Avenue in two hours, and engines will be sent to bring the cars without unloading; this will help some. If we can get our engines back, we will be in shape to rush troops ahead with great rapidity, but none have as yet been returned. I have a messenger out in search of General Heintzelman, but he has not yet been found.

H. HAUPT.

WASHINGTON, August 22, 1862.

Colonel Haupt:

If you cannot move the trains beyond Catlett's Station, land all the troops at that place, and keep your rolling stock this side and out of danger. Expect large arrivals at Alexandria to-morrow, and make preparations to take them forward to General Pope.

H. W. HALLECK,
General-in-Chief.

August 22, 1862.

Major-General Halleck:

What you order in regard to subsistence is precisely in accordance with my directions. What is needed for subsistence must take precedence of everything else, but no accumulation of stores in front to be permitted.

H. HAUPT.

RAPPAHANNOCK CROSSING, 11:20 P. M.
August 22, 1862.

Colonel Haupt:

Let no train pass Manassas except those containing troops. Trains containing troops will be sent forward to Catlett's at once. You had best send down to get the cars that are here, if there are no locomotives here; otherwise, telegraph to the proper person here to have them sent immediately to Catlett's. Everything that has to be transported by cars must be loaded before they leave here.

JOHN POPE,
Major-General Commanding.

RAPPAHANNOCK CROSSING, 11:40 P. M.
August 22, 1862.

Colonel Haupt:

Say to Generals Heintzelman, Cox and Sturgis, as they come forward with their troops, to halt them at Warrenton Junction, or on Cedar Creek, and take up a position there against any force of the enemy advancing in the direction of Warrenton. The enemy has succeeded, in greatly superior numbers, in turning our right in the direction of Sulphur Spring and Warrenton. Ask General Heintzelman to endeavor to keep open the railroad communication between Cedar Creek and Rappahannock Station. I have ordered a force back to Catlett's Station. Send forward the provision trains to this point.

JOHN POPE,
Major-General Commanding.

August 22, 1862.

P. H. Watson:
    I have not been able to find General Heintzelman, and am now told
that he is in Washington.   You can possibly give him the message.
                                                    H. HAUPT.

August 22.

Major-General Pope:
    Conductor of train No. 6 from Catlett's just in; reports train fired
into by rebels at Catlett's.   He says they opened throttle, ran through
rebels at full speed, and have just arrived.   The train hands laid down
to escape bullets.   I will hold trains here for instructions.   I can only
explain the occurrence by supposing it to be a cavalry dash.   We have
2,100 troops here in cars.
    The fire was from both sides, but most heavy from the east side of
the track.   H. HAUPT.

August 22, 1862.

P. H. Watson, Assistant Secretary of War:
    I fear that I may be compelled to-night to do that which may ap-
pear inhuman—turn out the sick in the street.   Doctors will persist in
sending sick, often without papers, to get them off their hands, and we
cannot send forward the troops if we must run our trains to Washington
with sick, to stand for hours unloaded.   My first care is to send forward
troops, next forage and subsistence.   I hope to start forage to-morrow
noon.   Have you any suggestions?   H. HAUPT.

About midnight I had been waiting in much anxiety for the
arrival of four trains, then some hours overdue, when a conductor
came in with a lantern in hand and reported that the trains had
been stopped four miles out of town by order of General Sturgis,
who had assumed control, and would not permit them to be moved.
I immediately reported the situation to General Halleck, and then
started, in company with Superintendent J. H. Devereux, to see
the officer personally.

    When I reached his Headquarters, the General was seated in
an arm-chair surrounded by his staff.   His salutation was, "Well!
I am glad you have come, for I have just sent a guard to your office
to put you in arrest for disobedience of my orders in failing to
transport my command."

    I replied that I was acting under the orders of General Hal-
leck; that so far as my personal comfort was concerned, the arrest
would be quite a relief, if he could lend me a blanket and allow me
a corner of the floor, as I had not been able to sleep for a considerable time, and a few hours of rest would be quite refreshing, but
he must understand that he was assuming a very grave responsibility; the trains were loaded with wounded; the surgeons with ambulances were waiting for them at the depot; the engines would
soon be out of wood and water, and serious delays would be caused
in the forwarding of troops to General Pope.

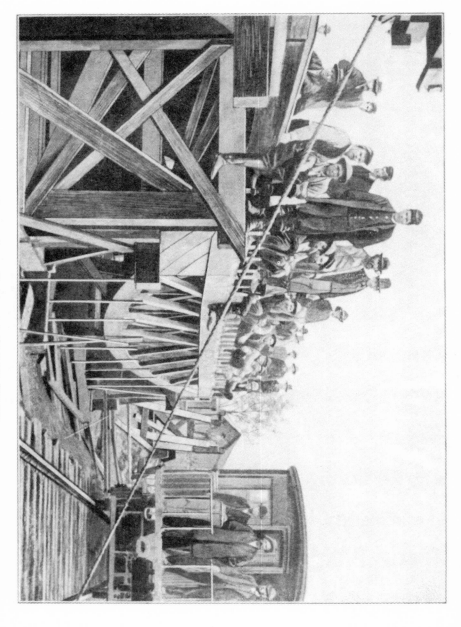

TESTING BOARD TRUSSES FOR MILITARY BRIDGES.

The General exclaimed in an excited tone: "I don't care for John Pope a pinch of owl dung!"

He then called one of his staff and whispered something which I did not hear, but learned subsequently that he had sent an order to the engineers to cut loose from their trains, run to Alexandria for wood and water and then return. As there was but a single track and no one capable of performing the Munchausen feat of picking up the engines and carrying them around the trains, the order could not be executed.

Soon after, an Orderly rode up and delivered to me a dispatch from General Halleck in these words: "No military officer has any authority to interfere with your control over railroads. Show this to General Sturgis, and if he attempts to interfere, I will arrest him."

I tried to make the General comprehend this, but he seemed to think that the dispatch was from General Pope, and several times repeated his former declaration: "I don't care for John Pope a pinch," etc.

At last Devereux took the paper from my hands and gave it to the Chief of Staff with the request that he try to make his chief acquainted with the contents.

He was successful at length in conveying the information that the telegram was not from General Pope but from General Halleck. "Who did you say, General Halleck? Yes, I respect his authority. What does he say?"

"He says if you interfere with the railroads he will put you in arrest."

"He does, does he? Well, then, take your d——d railroad!"

This interference deranged the trains for some time and kept at least 10,000 men out of the battle. Assistant Secretary Watson wished me to prefer charges and have the General court-martialed, but as he was not in his normal condition at the time, and was afterwards willing to carry out instructions and acknowledged that the delay had been his own fault, I let the matter drop.

There were doubtless others who entertained the same feelings towards General Pope, and who remained in camp demanding railroad transportation, knowing they could march to the field in one-third of the time required to furnish it.

The road was but a single track, with a limited equipment of cars and engines, and these were detained for long periods at the front by failure of the proper officers to unload and return cars. As a consequence it was impossible to forward troops with the rapidity that would otherwise have been practicable; besides, it was simply absurd to wait for days to secure rail transportation when a march of a single day would have carried them to the battlefield, particularly when it is considered that in marching they would have been in position for prompt action, while in cars they were defenseless.

These official telegrams are instructive:

August 23, 1862.

McCrickett:

General Pope orders to push forward all troops at Catlett's at daybreak. Have everything ready, that there is no delay. Start before daylight rather than later.

H. HAUPT.

August 23, 1862.

McCrickett:

As it is now day there seems to be no necessity for the pilot engine. The troops should all go forward as far as the track is in order, then march; there should be no delay. See General Kearney immediately. Let engine return and report the condition of affairs, which you will please telegraph immediately.

H. HAUPT.

August 23, 1862.

P. H. Watson, Washington, D. C.:

We have forwarded up to this time, since yesterday afternoon, 6,600 men to Catlett's. This throws our power at the other end. Until it can be returned our capacity is very limited. We will send an engine over to bring troops of Cox's Division to Alexandria and make up train in readiness to send forward when engines return. Devereux is active and efficient. Being compelled to hold rolling stock in readiness to remove supplies in case of an attack in front, this flank movement puts us in bad shape. I have not been able as yet to hear from Catlett's this morning. The confusion there last night must have been awful. Nearly all our wagons are there. Your offer to send cars will expedite matters some. I will keep you advised of everything of importance.

H. HAUPT.

War Department,
August 23, 1862, 9:45 A. M.

Colonel H. Haupt:

Is it not of the utmost importance to prevent a great accumulation of power and rolling stock at the outer end of the road? If the enemy should, by sudden dash, burn a bridge or set the trains on fire, it would for the time being put it out of our power to send forward either regiments or supplies.

P. H. WATSON,
Assistant Secretary.

August 24, 1862, 10:20 A. M.

P. H. Watson:

You are, as usual, perfectly right. It is not my intention to accumulate power at the other end. The orders are, run up, unload and return immediately to Manassas; there pass trains and proceed to Alexandria. None of the power has yet been returned, and I have not to this time been able to get an answer why.

H. HAUPT.

WAR DEPARTMENT,
August 23, 1862, 10:45 A. M.

Colonel Haupt:

Can you manage in some way to make it understood at the other end of the road that cars can be used either for transportation or for warehouses, but not for both; that they can receive reinforcements and supplies only by returning the cars?

P. H. WATSON,
Assistant Secretary of War.

August 23, 1862.

General Pope:

The number of troops now sent forward is 6,600; 1,500 more now marching up and transportation ready for them. After repeated attempts for hours to get answer, I learned that the track is clear, the bridges safe, and that six engines and trains are now ready to return to Alexandria. There must have been great delay somewhere. Please order some competent officer to see that the cars are unloaded and returned. There will be no relaxation of effort on our part so long as we can hold out. Shall the place of unloading be Warrenton or Catlett's for the remainder? Nine trains will be returned in three hours, if no accident occurs.

H. HAUPT.

August 23, 1862.

Major-General Pope:

After consulting with General Kearney I have ordered one regiment to be sent to Catlett's immediately with a small engine, one flat car, and fifty men in advance. The other troops will be advanced as rapidly as possible.

H. HAUPT.

August 23, 1862.

McCrickett:

After reaching Catlett's General Robinson will send back a pilot engine to give you notice, when, if the coast is clear, send forward the whole force to Warrenton, or as near it as they can get.

H. HAUPT.

August 23, 1862.

P. H. Watson:

If General Hooker is in Washington, please ask him if it will suit him to start in the morning instead of this night. Calls have been made on transportation, which were not expected, and delays from various causes make returns of power slow. We keep running day and night, eat little and sleep almost none. 20,000 more troops just arrived.

H. HAUPT.

August 23, 1862.

Colonel Haupt:

Where is General Heintzelman's command? Have any of his troops passed Manassas Junction? What troops and whose are on the way?

JOHN POPE,
Major-General.

RAPPAHANNOCK, August 23, 1862, 1:11 A. M.

Colonel H. Haupt:

Run all the trains here back till they meet the first troops at Warrenton Junction or Catlett's. Unload them there and then send all the cars and locomotives back to Alexandria to bring up troops.

By command of Major-General Pope.

GEO. D. RUGGLES,
Colonel and Chief of Staff.

August 23, 1862, M.

Colonel Haupt:

Brought all the cars and stores away excepting about three loads forage which were unloaded last night and burned this P. M. General Pope is, I think, going towards Warrenton with his army; has given instructions for train of wagons to be unloaded here with C. S., and then sent there under a strong escort; will do what we can to work empty cars back promptly.

J. D. IRISH.

RAPPAHANNOCK STATION, August 23, 1862.

Colonel Haupt:

Hurry forward those troops from Catlett's to Warrenton to-night as fast as you possibly can.

JOHN POPE,
Major-General.

MANASSAS, August 23, 1862.

H. Haupt and J. H. Devereux:

It is expected that an attack will be made on this place to-night by strong cavalry force, and that an attempt will be made to burn the commissary and destroy the stores lying at this place. I have one loaded and a few empty cars here. Colonel Pierce has telegraphed to General Sturgis for reinforcements. I do not know how reliable this may be, but consider it a duty to advise you.

McCRICKETT.

August 23, 1862, 11:30 P. M.

McCrickett:

You are not right in holding trains at Junction. You cannot be at a loss for sidings when you have the Gap and Centreville Roads to stand cars upon. The Gap intersection is at some distance, but it would be very easy to order trains forward by a preconcerted signal with light. A very moderate amount of ingenuity should devise expedients to avoid delay which is excessive.

H. HAUPT.

WAR DEPARTMENT,
August 23, 1862.

Colonel H. Haupt:

Two (2) regiments of Cox's Division will reach here within an hour or two. Can they be sent forward to Manassas, or such other point as they are required, in the same cars in which they came here? Do you find any difficulty in managing the railroad? If Quartermaster or other officers refuse or neglect to obey your orders, report them immediately, and a prompt and effectual remedy will be applied. Answer immediately.

P. H. WATSON,
Assistant Secretary of War.

HEADQUARTERS, August 23, 1862.

Colonel Haupt:

Hurry forward with all possible despatch the trains of troops, or our trains will be in danger.   JOHN POPE,

Major-General Commanding.

ALEXANDRIA, VA., August 23, 1862.

Colonel H. Haupt:

I have very peremptory orders from the General-in-Chief to get my Division off by railroad to-night. The General hoped that I would be able to get in behind Kearney and ahead of Hooker. The greater part of my Division is now lying along the road waiting for transportation, and I trust you will enable me to report to the General that I have left.

S. STURGIS,

Major-General.

ALEXANDRIA, August 23, 1862.

General S. Sturgis:

If ordered by either General Halleck or General Pope, I will be most happy to comply with your wishes, and give your command precedence of all others, but until so ordered, or until I have reason to believe that these officers desire General Hooker's command to be separated and carried forward at intervals, I see no propriety in the course you wish me to pursue. I beg leave respectfully to direct your attention to the enclosed copy of General Halleck's order forbidding interference. We will be able to load your troops at daylight to-morrow morning.

Very respectfully yours,   H. HAUPT,

Colonel and Chief of Transportation.

ALEXANDRIA, VA., August 23, 1862.

Colonel:

In order to get my Division off to the field and to relieve you of any responsibility in the matter, I hereby assume military control of such cars as may arrive from whatever direction, as far as placing my Division on board may go. I trust, therefore, that you will, regardless of what troops may arrive, place a sufficient number of cars near Clouds Mills to transport eight regiments to Warrenton Junction.

I am, Colonel, very respectfully yours,   S. STURGIS,

Major-General.

Colonel Haupt, Superintendent Railroads.

No communications were received on August 24 or afterwards from General Pope; my reports were made and instructions received until the close of the campaign from the President, Secretary Stanton, Assistant Secretary Watson and Generals Halleck and McClellan.

WASHINGTON, August 23, 1862.

Colonel H. Haupt:

No military officer will give any orders to your subordinates, except through you; nor will any of them attempt to interfere with the running of trains. Your orders must come from General Pope, or myself, except in case of an attack on the road, when you will consult with the Commander of the nearest forces.   H. W. HALLECK,

Commander-in-Chief.

WASHINGTON, August 24, 1862.

Colonel H. Haupt:

The railroad is entirely under your control. No military officer has any right to interfere with it. You were notified to this effect this morning. Your orders are supreme. By order

MAJOR-GENERAL HALLECK.

August 24, 1862, 4:35 A. M.

Major-General Halleck:

As I receive no answer to telegrams to General Pope, I will ask if all the troops are to be sent to Warrenton Junction. Is not Catlett's preferable? The shorter the distance the less will be the time required to unload and return cars. The number of trains is so large that Manassas is the only place at which they can be passed.

We have advices of ten trains now returning, but none are in yet. As soon as they are in, we can return 10,000 men. We are just starting 1,000 men, 38th Ohio, in Baltimore & Ohio cars. I suppose it is your wish that commands should go as much as possible together.

Have you directed that Sturgis' command should take precedence of all others? It is so stated, but the orders should be sent to me.

The agent at Manassas reports that it is expected that an attack will be made on that place to-night by a strong cavalry force. I report the statement, but attach no importance to it. I do not learn that it rests on any good foundation.

A note from General Sturgis has just been received; he says you gave peremptory orders that he should be sent after Kearney's batteries. Whatever you direct will be carried out. In the absence of instructions we will finish Hooker and Kearney before commencing on Sturgis. We can get all away by to-morrow morning if no accident occurs.

H. HAUPT.

WAR DEPARTMENT,
August 24, 1862, 6:30 A. M.

Colonel Haupt:

It is thought probable that not only cannon, but also infantry will have to march out to Warrenton Junction. It is obvious that the capacity of the railroad is unequal to the transportation of one-half the troops that will have to go out.

P. H. WATSON,
Assistant Secretary of War.

August 24, 10:20 A. M.

P. H. Watson:

Just received answer from Manassas that none of the engines sent to Catlett's with troops have returned. I have ordered an empty engine to go forward cautiously, ascertain cause of detention and report.

H. HAUPT.

August 24, 1862, 10:35 A. M.

Major-General Pope:

We expect to clear out all the troops now here and all that are expected to-day as at present advised. Forage and commissary also will be sent. No trains were dispatched since yesterday afternoon in consequence of interference of General Sturgis, who took military possession of the railroads and ordered me in arrest. I appealed to General Halleck, who ordered General Sturgis to cease further interference, or he would be placed in arrest himself. Details when I see you.

H. HAUPT.

August 24, 1862, 11:07 A. M.

P. H. Watson:

If you can find General Hooker, who is said to be in Washington, please say to him that we expect to carry his whole force to-morrow; but, to do it, the trains must be loaded in 15 minutes, and everything should be beside the track. To-night we carry supplies, ammunition and forage; four or five trains. I have informed General Sturgis that he has forfeited all claim for transportation until others are supplied and can have no more cars; he says, all right. I will try to see General Halleck to-morrow. H. HAUPT.

August 24, 1862, 11:15 A. M.

P. H. Watson:

I am waiting in intense anxiety to know what has become of return trains. I ordered, some time ago, a reconnoitering engine to go forward; no report as yet. If power is returned we can forward large numbers—10,000 per day. Until I can get answer I can give no information. Not an engine has yet returned of all that went up the road. I learn that some reached Warrenton Junction, which is very favorable intelligence thus far, but why they are not sent back I am as yet unable to ascertain.

H. HAUPT.

August 24, 1862, 11:25 A. M.

General Kearney:

You telegraphed to-day for another battery; it cannot be sent in morning, as it is not unloaded from boats. H. HAUPT.

August 24, 1862, 1:05 P. M.

Major-General Pope:

None of the engines sent from Manassas to Catlett's have returned to Manassas. I have ordered an engine to go forward to reconnoiter, return and report cause of detention.

Sturgis asks transportation for 10,000 men, horses and baggage. It is clear that his command should march to Manassas, 18 miles, and leave the transportation to those who need it more.

Hooker's advance, 2,000 men, is now in transports.

H. HAUPT.

August 24, 1862, 1:15 P. M.

Major-General Halleck:

Your dispatch enables me to resume operations on the road this morning. The blockade, consequent upon the interference, continued half a day. I have commenced sending forward General Sturgis' Division, as General Hooker informed me that all of his troops had not arrived, and he would be satisfied to get off this evening. We expect during the day and night to clear out all the troops here except the fresh arrivals, and take also some forage and stores, two trains of which are now going forward. The Quartermaster informs me of 20,000 more troops by transport, and also a lot by rail. Our capacity, under favorable circumstances, is 20,000 troops per day, but accidents and detentions will greatly reduce it. If the troops are to go by rail, I should know the order in which they are to go, and the points of destination. Please direct that the information be communicated to me so that I may arrange for it.   H. HAUPT.

WAR DEPARTMENT,
August 24, 1862, 1:25 P. M.

Colonel Haupt:
General Hooker was in Alexandria last night, but I will send to Willard's and see if he is there. I do not know any other place that he frequents. Be patient as possible with the Generals; some of them will trouble you more than they will the enemy.

You can accomplish more than I expected you could under the adverse circumstances against which you have had to work.

If General Hooker is not heard from within an hour, give direction to the next officer under him, or to the Colonels of the regiments, who, wherever they are, must have their men ready to embark. If they refuse to go, report the fact, and load up the train with other troops and send them forward. There must be no stop to the movement of the troops outward, except to send supplies.   P. H. WATSON,
Assistant Secretary.

August 24, 1862, 3:30 P. M.

McCrickett:
We are, of course, perfectly powerless to send a man until you can return us the power now up the road. We have been waiting all day for it in a state of the greatest anxiety and impatience. Cannot you contrive in some way to return it sooner? Not a train yet back, and some out 24 hours. The trains are run on your orders. Where do you get your information about the enemy?   H. HAUPT.

August 24, 1862, 7:30 P. M.

P. H. Watson:
Please inform Secretary Stanton and General Halleck that another day is lost in our transportation by the neglect of General Sturgis' officers to load the cars furnished to them. Hearing nothing from the trains, I went in search of them and found them still unloaded and no possibility of moving anything until they are out of the way. I have seen General Sturgis and informed him that no more cars can be furnished him until others are supplied.

He frankly admitted that the fault was in his men; he ordered them to unload, but they did not.

I ordered back nearly all the trains, and will load them to-night with supplies and ammunition, and send forward as fast as possible in preference to troops. I must go to the Department and explain position of affairs, but have been incessantly engaged day and night for a week. Will try to come to-morrow.   H. HAUPT.

August 25, 1862, 5:05 A. M.

Major-General Pope:
We will get off Hooker's command during the day and night. Sturgis has been the cause, directly and indirectly, of more than 24 hours' delay in transportation of troops and supplies.

BRIDGE OF BOARD TRUSSES LOADED UNTIL IT BROKE AT TWO TONS PER FOOT.

A Baltimore & Ohio engine, sent forward, blocked the track six hours by getting out of order on the road. When cleared, an engine got off the track; this caused more delay. I have now ordered that no more cars shall be loaded on track south of Alexandria. The loading of troops must all be done on Washington track, so as to keep main track clear.

We have just dispatched six trains for Hooker. General Heintzelman and staff are in car just moving off. Cox will go forward in morning.

Long bridge broke with Baltimore engine yesterday; it is now repaired.

Transportation will be furnished in the following order: Subsistence for men, forage, ammunition, hospital stores, troops, artillery, horses, wagons.

Artillery and some of the infantry should march; horses should be driven.

I have requested General Halleck to detail Major Keyes to settle question of priority of troops, and say in what order they shall be forwarded. There is a constant contest for priority of transportation. We will keep moving night and day. All stores have been forwarded as fast as delivered to us; the yard is quite clear of any forage and subsistence.

H. HAUPT.

August 25, 1862, 9:45 A. M.

Major-General Pope:

I have not only sent forward every car loaded with forage and commissary stores that has been delivered to us, but I have gone personally late at night to the Commissary and Quartermaster to urge them to load cars, even beyond their requisitions, that there should be no deficiency.

The trouble is that Ferguson has not the grain to send. We are this moment advised of the arrival of some in Washington. An engine is already there to bring it. It shall have precedence over all other transportation.

All of Hooker's command did not get off last night. The number of men was not correctly reported at this office, and the cars sent were not fully loaded. This will detain Cox's command perhaps until evening. We will keep moving and do all we can.

H. HAUPT.

WAR DEPARTMENT,
August 25, 1862, 10:40 A. M.

Colonel Haupt:

When you cannot get orders from General Pope, land the troops where you deem most convenient, but as near to General Pope's army as you can.

H. W. HALLECK,
General-in-Chief.

August 25, 1862, 11:36 P. M.

Major-General Pope:

Your servant Anderson has not reported at this hour, 11:20 P. M. We can send him at 6. A. M. If he is not here, then he can go at 11 A. M. We have arranged to resume schedule to-morrow. Some of General Hooker's command, I am just informed, are still here. He had 5,600 men to forward, and we sent cars for 6,000. They could not have been properly loaded. I will ask General Halleck to send Major Keyes to superintend the loading hereafter, and insist on a proper number to each car. Our conductors can do nothing; they are not obeyed. Cars have carried 60 each, but I estimate capacity at 50 only.

H. HAUPT.

I find but few telegrams throwing light upon important movements this day. Many of my papers have been lost in consequence of handling by other parties in my absence. It appears, however, that I sent a communication to General Halleck making suggestions as to certain movements, which were approved, and I was directed to call upon Generals Smith, Sturgis, Slocum or any other General Officer I could find for forces necessary to carry out the suggestions. I find a copy of a telegram from General Hancock to General Halleck which refers to this order.

August 26, 1862, 8:50 A. M.

Major-General Halleck:

In addition to the transportation for 1,200 men, some other trains are coming and are this side of Manassas. We may have in a few hours transportation for 3,000 or 4,000. They can be advanced as far as possible by rail, then marched forward.

I am just informed that the four trains following the engine Secretary are captured, and that the rebels are approaching Manassas with artillery. These may be exaggerations, but the operator and agent are leaving, and prompt action is required.

It is unfortunate that a portion of our forces did not march. I await instructions.

H. HAUPT.

August 26, 1862.

Major-General Halleck:

Two soldiers just arrived from Manassas at Fairfax; report bridges all right between these points. Good, very good so far. This was my greatest source of anxiety.

H. HAUPT.

August 26, 1862.

Major-General Halleck:

The following telegram has just been received from Manassas:

The engine Secretary was being followed by four other trains, which are in great danger, as there is no communication. The wire is cut between Manassas and Warrenton. We have transportation for 1,200 men; this number might be sent to Manassas to protect the road while we repair it. I suppose the bridge at Bristoe will be destroyed.

H. HAUPT.

WAR DEPARTMENT,
August 26, 1862, 9:25 A. M.

Colonel H. Haupt:

General Smith, General Slocum, General Sturgis, or any other General Officer you can find, will immediately send all the men you can transport to Bristoe Bridge or Manassas Junction. Show this order.

H. W. HALLECK,
General-in-Chief.

August 26, 1862.

General Halleck:

Operator at Manassas just says: "I am off now sure." I directed the agent to run the two engines at Manassas forward, wait until the last moment, and then escape on the engine if a real necessity existed. Operator had just commenced message to Headquarters of General Pope when wire was cut. It is clear now that the railroad can be relied upon only for supplies. No more troops can be forwarded; by marching they will protect communication; in cars they are helpless. Our capacity by this raid will be much reduced. H. HAUPT.

HEADQUARTERS, August 26, 1862.

General Halleck.

SIR: I have just received your dispatch addressed to Generals Smith, Sturgis and Slocum, or any General Officers you can find, and being senior officer here, will send forward all the infantry the railroad can furnish transportation for, and as much artillery as can be moved to the point or points designated. Colonel Haupt has requested a force to protect the bridge at Bull Run, which I will furnish unless otherwise instructed by you. W. S. HANCOCK,
Brigadier-General Commanding Sixth Army Corps.

The above telegram appears to have been forwarded by General Hancock at 12:15 A. M. on the morning of the 26th, received at 2:40 A. M. and copy sent to me from War Department and received at Alexandria 11:30 P. M.

August 26, 1862, 11 A. M.

D. C. McCallum:

So far Bull Run is safe. Four trains empty cars lost at Bristoe. Rebels have possession of Manassas. Some of our artillery taken and used against us. Damage at Manassas not known. Sent out 3,000 men last night, also a large wrecking and construction force to Union Mills, where track is blocked by a collision in rear. H. HAUPT.

August 26, 1862.

J. H. Devereux:

No. 6 train, engine Secretary, was fired into by a party of Secesh cavalry, some say about 500 strong. Ties were piled on track, but engine took good run at them and scattered them from track. Engine well riddled by bullets. McC.

NOTICE.

ALEXANDRIA, August 26, 1862.

Transportation on the Military Railroads of Virginia will be furnished in the following order:

1. Subsistence for men in the field.
2. Forage for horses.
3. Ammunition.
4. Hospital stores.
5. Infantry regiments that have seen service, with Staff horses.
6. Infantry regiments composed of raw troops.

7. Batteries, except in cases of urgent necessity, will march.
8. Cavalry will march.
9. Mules and wagon-horses will be driven.
10. Wagons, ambulances and other vehicles will be hauled over the common roads.

It must be understood distinctly, that nothing required for the use of the Army will ever be refused transportation when it can be afforded without excluding other transportation entitled to priority.

The proper duty of the railroad is to forward supplies. It cannot, in addition thereto, transport large armies on short notice, but it can, with present facilities, remove ten thousand men per day if no accident occurs, and if there is no delay in loading and unloading.

No cars will hereafter be loaded on the main track south of Alexandria. The proper place of shipment is on the Washington track west of Alexandria.

H. HAUPT,
Colonel and Chief of Construction and Transportation,
Army of Virginia.

August 27 was a very eventful day, and the telegrams are of much interest. Unfortunately the operators neglected, in most cases, to record on the face of the dispatch the hour of forwarding and receiving.

It appears that in consequence of orders from General Halleck I made search for some General Officer to whom his instructions could be communicated, but could find none. The attractions of Washington kept most of the General Officers in that city.

Colonel Scammon, of Cox's brigade, was sent out after midnight. In Colonel Scammon's report he states that, in obedience to the orders of the General commanding the Army, received through Colonel Haupt, he went, on the morning of the 27th, to Bull Run bridge with the 11th and 12th Ohio Volunteers. General Taylor was found severely wounded and turned over the command to Colonel Scammon.

Fight was maintained by Colonel Scammon from 8:30 A. M. until 3:30 P. M., when he was forced to retire, marching to Alexandria, which he reached next day 10 A. M., August 28.

He reported the force of the enemy actually engaged to be six regiments of infantry, six pieces of artillery, and also a stray force of cavalry of from 1,000 to 5,000.

The conduct of the New Jersey brigade, after General Taylor's fall, was reported to be discreditable. They retreated in disorder along the railroad; only one lieutenant and twelve or fourteen men remained to help fight the enemy.

At 4:25 A. M. a telegram was sent to President Lincoln informing him that the forces sent out the previous night had held Bull Run bridge until twenty minutes of the time of filing the message, but if not then destroyed, it probably would be, which elicited in reply the inquiry:

"What became of our forces which held the bridge until 20 minutes ago, as you say?"

At 6:35 A. M. General Halleck was notified of the situation, and complaint made of the indisposition of troops to go forward. Several other telegrams were sent to the President and to General Halleck advising them of the situation, and at 11 A. M. I ventured to suggest a movement of considerable importance, with a view to protect the communication and force supplies forward. At 11:50 A. M. General Halleck replied: "If you can see General McClellan, consult him. If not, go ahead as you propose."

The situation in which I was placed at this time was one which compelled me to assume responsibilities. I was cut off from all communication with General Pope, and the only information that could be received at Washington was through operators and assistants connected with my department, who were directed to advance as far as possible under cover of the brush, climb trees, and report observations. General Halleck took no offense at what might have been considered an impertinence in suggesting military movements.

CHAPTER III.

RESULTS OF McCLELLAN'S CONDUCT.

AFTER receiving instructions to consult General McClellan, of whose expected arrival I had not been advised, I repaired to the wharf, procured a row-boat and searched for him amongst the transports that had arrived. I found the General in the cabin of a steamer some distance below Alexandria, surrounded by members of his staff. I showed him the telegrams, and he came with me in my boat to the office. Here I explained fully the situation. Taylor's brigade had been cut up; Colonel Scammon had been holding the bridge at Bull Run and was in great danger; Pope's army was out of forage for horses and rations for men, and to relieve them was an imperative necessity. I explained my plans for giving them relief, but a strong force was necessary to protect the trains.

General McClellan listened, and, when I ceased, remarked that he could not approve the plan; that it "would be attended with risk."

I reminded the General that military operations were usually attended with risk, but that I did not consider the risk in this case excessive. The railroad was in our possession nearly to Bull Run. We could go as far as it was quite safe on the trains, then dismount skirmishers to advance and feel their way, keeping the trains in rear. If the enemy was found in force, they could retire, take the trains and be run back to a safe distance.

My representations and arguments availed nothing; the General would not give his consent, or assume any responsibility, and would give no orders, instructions, or suggestions of any kind!!!

After a time the General had a sudden attack of indisposition, became very pale, and asked if I had any brandy.

I replied that I did not use it, but would send for some.

On its arrival he drank a portion, which revived him. He then wrote a dispatch to General Halleck, which original dispatch, in his own handwriting, is now before me, forwarded at 2 P. M. In it he reports, from information I had given him, that Taylor's brigade is either cut to pieces or captured, and that some of Cox's troops were engaged with the enemy. He recommended the defense around Washington be made secure; that some cavalry be sent out towards Gainesville to mobilize a couple of corps as soon as possible, but not to advance there until they could have artillery and cavalry.

I do not wish to criticise General McClellan or any one else. There have been too many critics, but it is worthy of note that in this dispatch, the first sent after landing, there is no suggestion of any relief for the army fighting in the field against superior numbers and out of supplies.

If General Pope's report is reliable, there were over 90,000 troops returned from the Peninsula, and only about 20,000 in the fight, leaving the balance to be protected by the forts around Washington.

After sending this telegram, General McClellan mounted his horse and rode off, leaving me in a condition of great dissatisfaction and uncertainty. I had been directed to consult with him, and the consultation had resulted in no decision whatever.

Had I been so fortunate as not to have found General McClellan I could have acted, but my hands were tied. The army was suffering and in danger. I could not remain quiet. I determined to assume responsibility, but as I considered it proper to notify General McClellan, I sent him, at 9:50 P. M., a notice that at 4 A. M. I proposed to start a wrecking and construction train bound for Bull Run; also train with forage and subsistence. I asked for 200 sharpshooters only as train guard to report at 4 A. M., and stated that if the troops did not report, *we would go without them.*

No answer was received to this dispatch, and near midnight I took a lantern and visited the camps four miles down the road to see if I could not get a guard. I found General Hancock in bed in his tent. He arose immediately and cheerfully agreed to give me the force I required, promising that they should be on hand at 4 A. M. punctually. They were there on time and performed good service in the operations of the next day.

August 27, 1862.

Major-General Halleck:

I have been on the search for some general officers, but can find none. Cox is in Washington; Sturgis is in the field; Smith I can learn nothing about. I have found Colonels Scammon and White, of Cox's command, who will be ready in an hour. I will now go to other camps and endeavor to drum up more. The engine Secretary, two miles this side of Bull Run bridge, ran into the rear end of another train, doing serious damage. The track is blocked. I will send out 3,000 or 4,000 troops, but they can do no more to-night than hold Bull Run bridge. The damage at Manassas cannot now be helped. Whatever it is, has been already done.

H. HAUPT.

August 27, 1862, 4:25 A. M.
A. Lincoln, President:
    Intelligence received within twenty minutes informs me that the
enemy are advancing and have crossed Bull Run bridge; if it is not
destroyed, it probably will be. The forces sent by us last night held it
until that time.   H. HAUPT.

August 27, 1862.
Colonel Haupt:
    What became of our forces which held the bridge till twenty
minutes ago, as you say?*   A. LINCOLN.

August 27, 1862, 6:35 A. M.
Major-General Halleck:
    I have been using incessant exertions all night to get the 3,000
troops off, but the last did not leave until daylight.
    There appeared to be a disposition to use up the night before get-
ting to the scene of action.
    Three thousand men, with abundance of ammunition, have gone
forward. Information from Fairfax during the night stated that two pieces
of one of our batteries were taken at Manassas, our men cut up, number
not stated. They were surrounded, one man escaping wounded to Fairfax. The enemy had scouts out in every direction. A party appeared to
be moving toward Union Mills, where our track is blocked; if so, Bull
Run bridge may be destroyed. I give the information as I received it.
As intelligence comes in, I will transmit it to you.
                                                    H. HAUPT.

August 27, 1862, 10:05 A. M.
General Halleck:
    I ordered troop trains to proceed to Union Mills, four miles north
of Manassas, where collision occurred, then march troops to Bull Run;
leave 500 men to protect bridge, and balance, 2,500, to proceed to
Manassas. The last of the troop trains was unloaded at Union Mills and
returned to Fairfax Station, six miles; report fighting two miles beyond
Bull Run bridge, and cannonading in direction of Manassas. Further
information as soon as received.   H. HAUPT.

August 26, 1862.
President Lincoln:
    Two operators from Manassas have gone up the Gap road towards
Gainesville, with instruments, to get as near as possible to the scene of
action, make connection with the wire and report. You are probably advised of this fact, but if you are, there is no harm in repeating, and if
you are not, it will be of interest to you.   H. HAUPT.

August 27, 1862, 11 A. M.
Major-General Halleck:
    I venture the suggestion: As soon as the cars return which carried
troops to Union Mills, I propose to load the whole with subsistence, put
on top and inside 1,500 or 2,000 more men, and endeavor by all means to
work the trains through.

---

* NOTE.—See answer August 28, page 107.

HAUPT'S TORPEDO FOR QUICKLY WRECKING WOODEN BRIDGES.

The most serious matter, if true, is the capture of some pieces of our artillery, which, if turned against our train, would render our advance impossible.

I am told that a battery left here yesterday, and should this morning be near Manassas, but I fear it has no infantry support.

I am not advised of any movements except those made under my direction by rail.

Do you approve sending forward the subsistence train in the manner proposed? If so, please answer.

I would suggest that artillery with a good infantry support should be sent forward immediately. I propose this plan: Load a battery, or part of a battery, on cars; carry with it a sufficient infantry support. Let this precede the supply trains to some point where the battery can be unloaded and advanced by common road to Manassas to recapture, if possible, the pieces taken and prevent them from being used against the train. I have a strong force, one wrecking and one construction train, now on the ground, with very efficient men. The track will be cleared and reconstructed in the shortest possible time, so as to advance trains.

H. HAUPT.

WAR DEPARTMENT,
August 27, 1862, 11:50 A. M.

Colonel Haupt:

If you can see General McClellan, consult him. If not, go ahead as you propose.

H. W. HALLECK.
General-in-Chief.

General Halleck, Alexandria:

I learn that Taylor's brigade, sent this morning to Bull Run bridge, is either cut to pieces or captured; that the force against them had many guns and about five thousand (5,000) infantry, receiving reinforcements every moment; also that Gainesville is in possession of the enemy. Please send some cavalry out towards Dranesville via Chain Bridge to watch Lewinsville and Dranesville, and go as far as they can. If you can give me even one squadron of good cavalry, then I will ascertain state of case. I think our policy now is to make these works perfectly safe, and mobilize a couple of corps as soon as possible, but not to advance them until they can have their artillery and cavalry. I have sent for Colonel Tyler to place his artillery men in the works. Is Fort Harney securely held? Some of Cox's troops are also engaged with another force of enemy.

McCLELLAN.

August 27, 1862, 9:50 P. M.

Major-General McClellan:

I propose to start at 4 o'clock precisely, a wrecking and construction train bound for Bull Run; also a forage train and a subsistence train. It is perhaps proper that 200 good skirmishers should be sent with the trains, who should be at the depot at Alexandria before 4 A. M. to-morrow morning. General Pope will be notified by courier to-night to have his wagons at Sangster's Station by daylight to-morrow. If the troops are not here by 4 A. M., we propose to go ahead without them.

H. HAUPT.

BURKES, August 27, 1862.
J. H. Devereux:
 Engine Dover here waiting; cannot go to Fairfax; was fired into one and a half or two miles west of here by cavalry or band of guerrillas.
               McCRICKETT.

August 27, 1862, 6:50 P. M.
Major-General McClellan:
 General Taylor is on his way to Alexandria, having been brought to Burkes on hand-car. I sent construction train forward with orders, if possible, to bring off wounded from Fairfax. The engine was fired upon two miles west of Burkes and compelled to return; firing by cavalry or guerrillas. Burkes Station abruptly closed this moment. Operator leaving indicates approach of the enemy.   H. HAUPT.

August 27, 1862.
Colonel Stager:
 We are about to send out a railroad reconnoissance, with an operator and men to repair the line. Will you permit Conway, Bickford and Boyle to accompany it at their request? An immediate answer is desired.   H. HAUPT.

August 27, 1862.
Major-General Halleck:
 General Taylor was sent to Burkes on hand-car, and is now on his way to Alexandria. I sent engine and cars of construction train with orders to proceed to Fairfax and bring off wounded if possible. The engine was fired into by cavalry two miles west of Burkes and compelled to return without wounded. Operator at Burkes has this moment, 6:50, broken off suddenly; probably compelled to evacuate.

              H. HAUPT.

FAIRFAX, August 27, 1862.
Colonel Haupt:
 We have a number of wounded. General Taylor wishes you to send a train immediately.   S. HUDSON,
          Assistant Surgeon 11th O. V. I.

WAR DEPARTMENT,
August 27, 1862.
Colonel Haupt:
 Is the railroad bridge over Bull Run destroyed?
             A. LINCOLN.

August 27.
J. J. Moore, Burkes:
 If you can reconstruct the bridge so as to pass over the train, reach Fairfax, and bring off the wounded before night, do so; if not, return immediately. Bull Run bridge is burned and the enemy had 20,000 men in and about Manassas last night. At least one of the bridges beyond Fairfax is destroyed, perhaps others. It is not probable that we can use the road again for some time, and the army must cut its way through.   H. HAUPT.

FAIRFAX, August 27, 1862.

J. H. Devereux:

Jersey brigade reported to be cut up and surrounded; 200 or 300 soldiers have left field and all coming down road. Rebel position on hill commanding Bull Run bridge. It is reported that rebel cavalry are trying to cut us off. I have returned here for orders to know if you think it advisable to go up to wreck and clear track. I have just arrived from Manassas, and cannot say how reliable these reports are.

McCRICKETT.

FAIRFAX STATION, August 27, 1862.

J. H. Devereux:

Fairfax office opened for business; news favorable; holding position this side Bull Run bridge until reinforcements arrive. General Taylor and number of others are here wounded. Can we take engine and run to Bull Run for further information? Mr. Moore is still here and was about walking to Bull Run.

McCRICKETT.

August 27, 1862.

McCrickett:

To run an engine may attract too much attention if there is an enemy in the vicinity, but if you deem it safe, you might take an instrument, go part way on an engine, make a connection at some point in the woods and communicate with me as soon as possible.

H. HAUPT.

August 27, 1862.

McCrickett:

If we send reinforcements, the wounded can return in same cars. We have asked instructions from General McClellan.

H. HAUPT.

NOTICE.

ALEXANDRIA, August 27, 1862.

The demands for transportation at the present time greatly exceed the capacity of the road and rolling stock, even with regularity of operation. Without regularity, the duty of the road cannot be performed, and the army cannot receive its regular supplies.

The schedule, which has been interrupted by derangement of train movements, will be resumed to-day, and must be rigidly adhered to. No detention will be permitted from any cause. Agents will inform Medical Directors and others of the hours of starting of trains, and impress upon them the importance of having sick and wounded loaded in time; that, whether they are in the cars or not, the orders are peremptory to start trains at schedule time, and these orders must be obeyed under penalty of dismissal.

H. HAUPT,

Colonel and Chief of Construction and Transportation,
Army of Virginia.

Having received, as stated, no reply from General McClellan to the request to send a train guard for the proposed expedition to Bull Run, application was made to General Hancock, who responded promptly and promised that the required force should be ready at 4 A. M., at which time the train started. The train movements were under the charge of an experienced conductor, C. M. Strein; the construction force under James J. Moore, assistant engineer; the military under Lieutenant-Colonel Chandler, and accompanied by three telegraph operators who had volunteered for the same. The instructions were as follows:

August 28, 1862.

Conductor Strein:

The expedition for railroad reconnoissance this morning, so far as concerns the advance or return of the train and rate of speed, will be under direction of the officer in command of skirmishers. I would recommend that the train proceed at the usual speed to a point near Burkes Station, being careful, however, not to run too fast, as the cars will be in advance of the engine. Beyond Burkes the train will proceed with great caution, the skirmishers advanced on both sides and particularly in the woods. The officer in charge, or some other detailed for that purpose, to signal the conductor as to the movements of the train. Proceed in this way, if possible, as far as Bull Run bridge; ascertain its condition, and also the position and condition of Colonel Scammon's force. If an enemy be found in superior numbers, retire and telegraph the fact. If no enemy be found when Bull Run is reached, and the bridge is safe, proceed at the discretion of the officer to Manassas and ascertain condition of property. Report every observation of importance by telegraph. An operator will be sent with the expedition, and also men to repair the line.

H. HAUPT.

Lieutenant-Colonel Chandler will coöperate with the conductor in carrying out the within instructions.

WM. F. SMITH,
Major-General Commanding Division.

The train proceeded without interruption as far as Burkes Station, thirteen miles from Alexandria, when a telegram was sent by Moore with the information that a bridge of twenty-four feet span across Pohick Creek, one mile west, was destroyed, and that there was no lumber to repair it. He was ordered to reconstruct the bridge, even if it should be necessary to tear down buildings to get material, and proceed, if possible, to Fairfax, sixteen miles, and bring off the wounded before night.

By 10 A. M. the bridge had been rebuilt, and the wounded at Fairfax brought off safely. Important information was also obtained and reports made to the President and to Generals McClellan and Halleck. This movement was made by men who knew that 20,000 of the enemy were in front of them!

On the receipt of my dispatch, General McClellan sent a note stating that "he was very glad that I had sent out the reconnoissance." He had not given his approval to the movement, but he claimed to be glad that it had been successful.

The history of the subsequent operations for the day will be found in the telegrams and reports hereto annexed:

August 28, 1862.

Major-General Halleck:

Having had no instructions since the telegram from you yesterday morning directing me to consult with General McClellan, and having had no word from General McClellan since my interview with him last night, I went this morning to the camp and made some suggestions to Generals Franklin and Hancock, which, having been approved, are now being carried into effect. The following instructions [see page 106] to the conductor will give you particulars. H. HAUPT.

August 28, 1862, 1:15 A. M.

General Halleck:

I found General Hancock in his camp; he will send 1,500 men, and 1,500 of Cox's command will go forward immediately. I have recommended that 500 men be left at Bull Run, and the balance go forward to Manassas and await orders. A wrecking and construction train will proceed at same time to clear track and repair damages. Should not orders be given to march forward forces to Manassas to-morrow?

H. HAUPT.

BURKES, August 28, 1862.

Colonel Haupt:

Bridge across Pohick, one mile west, is destroyed. The clear span is 24 feet. We have no lumber here to repair it.

J. J. MOORE.

August 28, 1862.

Major-General Halleck:

The train sent out to reconnoiter found a bridge of 24 feet span destroyed one mile beyond Burkes Station. Operator sent with train made connection and telegraphed for instructions. I replied: "Reconstruct the bridge, even if you must tear down buildings to get material, and proceed. If you can, reach Fairfax and bring off wounded before night." I have just received the announcement, "We are at Fairfax." This was done by our men with a knowledge of the fact that a force of 20,000 rebels were probably in front of them. H. HAUPT.

August 28, 1862.

Haupt:

Have you heard anything since I saw you last night?

McCLELLAN.

August 28, 1862.

Major-General McClellan:

I have just sent a messenger to you with dispatches. We have no intelligence from the front, except through General Clough, that a company, Co. A, 16th Virginia, acting as guards on the road, has been captured. H. HAUPT.

August 28, 1862.

President Lincoln:

I am much gratified to be able to inform you that Colonel Scammon is safe and has returned to Alexandria. I went out on an engine to meet him and bring him in. He held Bull Run bridge a long time against a very superior force, retired at last in perfect order, eluded the efforts of the enemy to surround him, and brought off his whole command with but little loss. I have advised General McClellan of his presence; he has important information to communicate.

The rebel forces at Manassas were large and several of their best Generals were in command. I have sent out a reconnoitering party of 200 sharpshooters by rail, with operators and wire to repair telegraph, make communication and report observations.   H. HAUPT.

WAR DEPARTMENT,
August 28, 1862, 2:40 P. M.

Colonel Haupt:
    Yours received. How do you learn that the rebel forces at Manassas are large, and commanded by several of their best Generals?
                                                                A. LINCOLN.

August 28, 1862.

President Lincoln:
    One of Colonel Scammon's surgeons was captured and released; he communicated the information. One of our firemen was captured and escaped; he confirms it, and gives important details. General McClellan has just seen him; also Colonel Scammon.
                                                                H. HAUPT.

August 28, 1862.

General McClellan:
    I have brought back Colonel Scammon; am getting him something to eat. He can communicate important intelligence as to the number and position of the enemy. He is at my quarters near my office, where an interview will be quiet and undisturbed. He can see you in half an hour, or at your convenience.   H. HAUPT.

August 28, 1862.

President Lincoln and General Halleck:
    One of our men who is just in, left Bristoe yesterday noon, says our carpenters had nearly finished repairing Kettle Run bridge. A large number of cars with four engines were the other side of Kettle Run bridge ready to come over as soon as possible. One of the engines, the one in advance, had 12 cars of ammunition and more behind.

After the completion of Kettle Run, the train can advance to Bristoe; they are probably there now. This intelligence is extremely gratifying. I learn, too, that Broad Run bridge has been attempted to be destroyed by cutting off the legs of all the trestles. The rebels could not have done mischief in a way that would render it more easy and expeditious for us to repair the damage. A very few hours should make Broad Run passable, and then Bull Run will remain the only obstacle.
                                                                H. HAUPT.

August 28, 1862.

    Enemy is advancing with 120,000 men, via Arlington and Chain Bridge, to attack Washington and Baltimore. General Barnard telegraphs me to-night that the length of line on fortifications this side Potomac requires 2,000 artillerymen and additional troops to defend intervals according to circumstances. At all events, he says an old regiment should be added to the force at Chain Bridge, and few regiments distributed along the lines to give confidence to our new troops. I agree with him fully, and think our fortifications along the upper part of our line on this side of river unsafe with their present garrisons, and the movements of the enemy seem to indicate an attack upon those works.

G. B. McCLELLAN.

This dispatch was probably sent to General Halleck and a copy to me. It is quite characteristic of General McClellan. With 70,000 of his own men from the Peninsula not in action, he was asking for reinforcements to put in the fortifications around Washington, and over-estimating the forces of the enemy.

He knew, or should have known, that the only forces available for any purpose were his own. Most of them were lying in camp, apparently indisposed to aid Pope to gain a victory.

August 28, 1862.

J. J. Moore:

You have done yourselves infinite credit. Bring the wounded and return immediately. How many wounded are there? Please answer.

H. HAUPT.

ALEXANDRIA, August 28, 1862, 11 A. M.

Major-General Halleck:

The result of our railway reconnoissance to-day was extremely gratifying. The Construction Corps reconstructed the bridge across Pohick, the operators repaired telegraph lines, and wounded at Fairfax were all brought off safely.

Important intelligence was obtained from a soldier who came on foot from Warrenton Junction. He confirms the statements of the burning of Bull Run bridge, and of the other bridges between Warrenton Junction and Bull Run. He says that Generals Siegel and Hooker occupy Manassas.

From a chaplain captured and released on parole, our Superintendent Devereux elicited the information that the enemy became alarmed last night at Manassas, and went off. He saw General Lee to-day at Fairfax about 1 o'clock, who took the road towards Vienna with a large force, accompanied by artillery. I am now sending the chaplain to General McClellan; also copy of report of conductor.

I have arranged with General McClellan to send out to-morrow a strong reconnoissance by rail to Bull Run, accompanied by artillery and cavalry, with a wrecking and construction party, to clear the way and open communication with Bull Run, into which, if our forces occupy Manassas, I will endeavor to pour supplies without delay; will reconstruct Bull Run bridge in the shortest time possible.

H. HAUPT.

ALEXANDRIA, August 28, 1862, 10:45 A. M.

My Dear Colonel:

Your note with enclosure is just received. I am very glad you have sent out the reconnoissance. I hope to collect sufficient cavalry and artillery to-day to send at least a portion of the forces to the front. As soon as I can communicate with my cavalry, I will send some Orderlies to your office. Will probably call there myself on way to camp.

Very truly yours,

GENERAL GEO. B. McCLELLAN.

Colonel Haupt, Chief of Construction, etc.

August 28, 1862.

General McClellan:

I just learn that Colonel Scammon has returned with his command, and is at this moment at General Franklin's Headquarters. I will go immediately on engine to see him and report.   H. HAUPT.

August 28, 1862, 4:40 P. M.

President Lincoln:

The latest news is that our men are busy reconstructing bridges beyond Bull Run. One of my assistants, just returning from Bristoe to Manassas, reports bridges across Kettle Run finished, a good force at work at Broad Run and another at Bull Run, one train of supplies sent out and unloaded, another of thirteen cars of bread and meat just starting. The track to Bull Run should be clear by this time, but I have no advices of the fact. Major Fifield has this moment arrived on return train, and gives it as his opinion, from the position of affairs when he left, that Jackson has by this time surrendered; this is doubtful, as we can still hear firing.   H. HAUPT.

August 28, 1862.

Major-General McClellan.

SIR: I have just received through General Clough the following items of information:

A private of Company C, 68th Illinois, employed on picket duty in guarding the telegraph line between Washington and Acquia Creek, came to Alexandria yesterday. Was returning last night to join his squad, about 16 miles from Alexandria on telegraph line; reached a point one mile from his squad. On the way he passed cavalry, citizens and contrabands fleeing towards Alexandria. Being unarmed and seeing a man near the road who had just been killed, he returned. The fugitives reported that rebel cavalry in considerable force was behind.

This is probably the Prince William Cavalry, of which a scout gave information last night. I have just ascertained that the telegraph is not cut yet.

Colonel Close reports to General Clough this morning, on the authority of three men who escaped, that Company A, 16th Virginia, sent on guard duty at some point on the railroad between this place and Manassas, were all captured some time last night.

H. HAUPT.

ALEXANDRIA, August 28, 1862.

J. H. Devereux.

DEAR SIR: In accordance with orders from Colonel Haupt, I proceeded west with engine Vulcan and a detachment of soldiers this A. M., finding the road in good order and unobstructed to Burkes. One mile west of Burkes the bridge across Pohick Run we found burned. The construction force on my train proceeded at once to repair this, and we

STEEL HOOKS, AND PIECE OF RAIL TWISTED BY THEIR USE.

proceeded to Fairfax. From here to Fairfax the road was in good order. The telegraph being cut about midway between Burkes and Fairfax, the repairer on my train put this in order. At Fairfax I proceeded and placed on my train the wounded of yesterday's engagement. I have brought them to Alexandria. A soldier came to Fairfax, who reports that he left Warrenton Junction this morning and came on foot to Fairfax; that the bridges over Broad Run, between Bristoe and Manassas, and over Bull Run were burned, and the engines and cars at Bristoe were burned and destroyed, and that the cars at the scene of the collision of night before last were burned. The engines Maryland and Waterford are still uninjured. He states also that Generals Hooker and Siegel occupy Manassas. This soldier, whose name and company, from a press of business, I could not learn, was taken charge of, I think, by the Colonel commanding the force on my train.

Respectfully,   C. M. STREIN,
Conductor.

P. S.—The soldier referred to reports heavy firing during the time he was in hearing, in the direction of Gainesville, west from Manassas.

C. M. S.

Edwin M. Markham, brakeman Orange & Alexandria Railroad, states:

Left Warrenton on Engine 136, with empty train, on Tuesday, August 26, about 5 o'clock. On reaching Catlett's, met engine McCallum, which had backed up from Bristoe with the report that the trains ahead of her had been thrown off track, and fired into by the rebels. Stayed at Catlett's all night, and next morning, August 27, went back to Warrenton.

But on Tuesday night Engine 136 added to her train the empty cars of the McCallum, and went to Warrenton, taking a regiment of Kearney's Division, with which it proceeded nearly to Bristoe, or to Kettle Run bridge. The said regiment did *not* disembark at all, but after challenging the rebels, and getting for answer: "By G—d, come on, and we'll show you who we are," the said regiment returned to Catlett's, getting there about daylight.

From Warrenton, on morning of August 27, after getting trains ready, came down on train of McCallum, and got to Catlett's about noon; walked down track and saw fighting. Saw Hooker's battery get into position and causing the rebel battery, opposing, to skedaddle from two positions, and finally to take off towards Thoroughfare Gap.

P. H. Watson, Assistant Secretary of War, sent me an armorclad, bullet-proof car mounting a cannon. The kindness was appreciated, but the present was an elephant. I could not use it and, being in the way, it was finally side-tracked on an old siding in Alexandria. The bullet-proof cabs on locomotives were very useful; in fact, indispensable. I had a number of them made and put on engines, and they afforded protection to engineers and firemen against the fire from guerrillas from the bushes that lined the roads.

General McClellan sent word to General Pope that he would

have all the available wagons and cars loaded with rations for his troops when he (Pope) should send a cavalry escort as guard to the trains. General Pope had not five horses to a company able to trot, and could not understand of what use cavalry could be to railroad trains.

WASHINGTON, August 29, 1862, 12:15 P. M.

Colonel Haupt:

An armor-clad car, bullet proof, and mounting a cannon, has arrived here, and will be sent down to Alexandria. P. H. WATSON.

WASHINGTON, August 29, 1862, 12:15 P. M.

Colonel Haupt:

After you see the bullet-proof car, let me know what you think of it. I think you ought at once to have a locomotive protected by armor. Can you have the work done expeditiously and well at Alexandria, or shall I get it done at Philadelphia or Wilmington?

P. H. WATSON,
Assistant Secretary of War.

August 29, 1862.

Colonel:

General McClellan has received an order from General Halleck to have construction trains sent out at once to repair the railroad to Manassas.

General Tyler has been ordered to furnish you such guards as you may think necessary. Please see General Tyler and arrange with him, so as to start off the construction parties as soon as possible. General Pope's troops are at Centreville, and he says that the enemy has for the most part retreated, so that I do not think that you will meet with much, if any, opposition.

Please have your trains with supplies for General Pope ready to push out as soon as the road is clear.

Very respectfully, R. B. MARCY,
Chief of Staff.

Colonel Haupt, Railroad Superintendent.

August 29, 1862, 3:40 P. M.

Major-General McClellan:

I think that about 200 men should ride in and out on top of the cars, and that 200 more should protect the depot where we unload ammunition and supplies. This is in addition to the 200 sent out by General Tyler this morning to act as scouts and protect construction parties. We will be sending out trains constantly during the day and night. Where are the men, and where can they be loaded? General Tyler has just come into the office and says he can give us all the men we want, except the sharpshooters. H. HAUPT.

WAR DEPARTMENT,
August 29, 1862.

Colonel Haupt:

What news from direction of Manassas Junction? What generally? A. LINCOLN.

August 29, 1862.

President Lincoln and General Halleck:

General Pope was at Centreville this morning at 6 o'clock; seemed to be in good spirits; Hooker driving the enemy before him, McDowell and Siegel cutting off his retreat; army out of forage and subsistence; force of enemy 60,000. This is the substance of information communicated by two ambulance drivers who came from Centreville, and who also gave many particulars confirming previous statements. I have ordered a train of forage and another of subsistence to be got ready to start before daylight, and will notify General Pope to-night by courier that he can have wagons to receive it at Sangster's Station by daylight to-morrow morning.

H. HAUPT.

The ambulance driver mentioned made the following statement :

August 29, 7 P. M.

Robert I. Johnson, ambulance driver, went a week ago, August 22, with 75 ambulances to Pope's Headquarters, delivered them to Colonel Cleary Tuesday, and stopped at Warrenton Junction Tuesday night, the night of the raid on Catlett's. On Wednesday night came on foot to where the battle was near Bristoe. Forces engaged, Sickles and Hooker; about 30 men killed, rebels about the same; don't know how many wounded. Thursday morning went on battlefield and stayed at Bristoe until 1 P. M. Came on to Bull Run at the bridge on the road between Manassas and Centreville; heard firing in direction of Gainesville. Judge from the shells and ammunition that the guns of the rebels were not heavy. Heard firing in direction of Centreville from 5 P. M. to dark. Saw General Pope at Bristoe, and he came down railroad towards Manassas.

Came to Centreville at 6 A. M.; saw General Pope at Centreville. Fighting towards the mountains; had fifty prisoners. Hooker was in rear of rebels; appeared to be driving them, and heard from some of Pope's aides-de-camp that Siegel and McDowell were heading them off. Saw some of the wounded, who said they came in by Manassas Gap; they said the force might be fifty or sixty thousand, commanded by Jackson, Longstreet, Ewell and A. P. Hill.

We came through Fairfax C. H. to-day. We saw a lady who said Generals Lee and Stuart were at her house yesterday; they had 500 cavalry; they came close to the 14th Massachusetts, but were not seen by them, a small hill screening them. When we got to Fairfax C. H., about 10 or 12, we still heard firing in direction of Centreville and beyond. Met Smith's Division seven or eight miles from Alexandria.

CHAPTER IV.

TWO PERILOUS DAYS AT BULL RUN.

ONE of the prominent incidents of this day's operations was an invitation by the Secretary of War to clerks in the department, citizens of Washington and citizens of Baltimore to volunteer as nurses to assist in caring for the wounded on the battlefield.

It was an impulsive and kind-hearted but ill-advised act. At a time when passes were refused to every applicant, when communication with the enemy was rigorously guarded, the gates were opened and trains required for military supplies and reinforcements were ordered to Washington to bring forward a promiscuous rabble, and scatter them broadcast over the country.

Upon receiving orders through Assistant Secretary Watson to send trains to Washington for this purpose, I protested against it, and begged him to use his influence to have the invitations recalled. This could not be done; they had gone out and the Secretary felt that he could not rescind the order, even though it might be a mistake.

I sent on a train, and when it reached Alexandria it was packed full, inside and on top. Some women even had forced themselves into the cars, which were ordinary freight cars without seats. It was night. Superintendent Devereux came to me, after inspecting the train, and begged to have it side-tracked; that it would not do to send it forward; that half the men were drunk and nearly every one had a couple of bottles of whisky.

I replied that we were not responsible for results; we must obey orders, which were peremptory, but I would delay the train as long as possible, and he should send a conductor to announce to its passengers that the enemy was near Fairfax, where they were to be unloaded, and that a proper regard for their safety required that a train with troops should be sent in advance. This quieted them and they were very patient.

When sent forward, I telegraphed the officer in command at Fairfax to arrest all who were drunk and put a guard over them. Those who were sober enough straggled off as soon as it was light enough to see and wandered around until whisky and provisions became exhausted, when they returned to the station to get transportation back. In this, most of them were disappointed. The

116

orders had been to take them out, but none to bring them back, and although it seemed cruel to compel them to walk, cold, hungry and wet with rain, it would have been far more cruel to let the wounded lie on the ground to perish in order to furnish transportation to those whose necessities were not so great.

No doubt some were induced to volunteer from proper motives, but generally it was a hard crowd, and of no use whatever on the field. In fact, I was told that in some instances parties who had money bribed ambulance drivers to take them back to the station, thus compelling the wounded to lie longer upon the field. Telegrams came in from officers, "don't send out any more civilians."

August 30, 1862.

Colonel H. Haupt:

J. W. Garret, President Baltimore & Ohio Railroad Company, came in this moment, by direction of the Secretary of War, for the purpose of having arrangements made for the prompt transportation by rail, from Washington to Bull Run, of surgeons and volunteers who go to care for the wounded of General Pope's army.

P. S.—A notice is posted by the Secretary of War in the hotels, calling on all able-bodied men to volunteer as nurses, and go out to the battlefield, saying that transportation will be furnished to them. You may have a large number to go, and the arrangements you make I will have posted on the hotel bulletins.

D. C. McCALLUM.

August 30, 1862.

P. H. Watson:

Surgeons must be accommodated by all means, but I would ask whether the several hundred volunteers who propose to go are needed, and whether they will not be in the way, and possibly help to produce a stampede. I fear if we send a train it will be filled with a rush, and possibly the surgeons excluded.

Our trains sent out this morning at daylight have not yet returned; until they do, we are in the dark, as we have no operators at intermediate points. An operator will go in next train. Washington track is encumbered with Richardson's baggage and must be cleared before we can send train to Washington; in the meantime, while getting ready the trains, you can give your opinion whether it would not be best to send the doctors to Alexandria for shipment, and leave all the rest at home.

H. HAUPT.

August 30, 1862.

P. H. Watson:

We obey orders and will send train to Washington as soon as track is clear, but there should be some way of keeping back those who are impelled by mere curiosity, and sending only those who will be useful. I think time would be saved by sending to Alexandria. The hour of sending trains from this place will depend on the time of return trains, which is uncertain. We will be running out and in all night. I suppose the wounded will soon be pouring in, and the removal of them must be carefully managed, so as not to interfere with supplies. It seems to me that if the battle is over, we have men enough to act as nurses; if it is not over, we do not want any citizens to skedaddle and create a panic.

                                        H. HAUPT.

                                        August 30, 1862, 10 P. M.
P. H. Watson:
       A train of 16 cars, containing about 800 persons, has arrived. I do not wish them to go ahead of the ammunition train, as they will be very much in the way, so I have told them that a proper regard for their safety, and a desire to protect them against attack, induces me to delay them, to send an ammunition train with troops, and to place guards on top of each of their cars. They are very patient with this information. I hope to forward General Couch's regiment without special train, by placing the men on top of the cars. Abundance of commissary stores have been sent forward—18 carloads commissary and 36 of forage.

                                        H. HAUPT.

                                        August 30, 1862, 11:15 P. M.
P. H. Watson:
       A large portion of the nurses who came on last night were drunk and very disorderly. I sent them off with written directions to the officer in command at Fairfax, to arrest every one who was drunk and return him by the next train. I understand that a large number are on their way back. They are much in the way. Can you not place a guard on Long Bridge? We are now using care to bring back nurses who are satisfied with the experience of one night and are skedaddling back again.

                                        H. HAUPT.

                                        August 30, 1862, 9 A. M.
Colonel Haupt:
       What news?   A. LINCOLN.

                                        August 30, 1862.
President Lincoln:
       Firing this morning is heard in direction of Centreville. I have sent out four trains. The first left at 4:30 A. M., the others following immediately—a wrecking train to clear track, a construction train to repair bridges, a train of forage and one of bread and meat.
       A courier returning to General Pope last night was to convey the information that the trains would be at Sangster's Station soon after daylight with supplies. This point is four miles only from Centreville. I have directed that when a party arrives .at Bull Run, a detachment shall be sent forward on foot with such tools as they can carry to reach the engines and cars now cut off from communication at Catlett's, with instructions to work towards Bull Run, repair bridges, and telegraph call upon General Banks or any other officer for assistance and protection, and work along opening communications with Bull Run. When this is done, we can forward supplies by carrying them across Bull Run and reshipping.
       I have also sent wire, operator and instrument with the expedition, and a force of 200 riflemen, with directions to keep with the working party in the advance, send out scouts and report everything.

The intelligence last evening was that Hooker and Pope were pushing the enemy towards the Gaps in the mountains through which they had advanced, and that McDowell and Siegel were heading them off. This morning the direction of the firing seemed to be changing, and it is not impossible that the enemy's forces may be changing direction and trying to escape towards Fredericksburg. In this case my trains will be in great danger. I await intelligence with some anxiety, and will communicate anything of importance that I hear.

H. HAUPT.

August 30, 1862, 8:50 P. M.

Colonel Haupt:

Please send me the latest news. A. LINCOLN.

August 30, 1862.

A. Lincoln, President:

Our operator has reached Manassas; hears no firing of importance. I have directed part of the 200 riflemen to go out as scouts, make observations and report constantly. Two or three flashes just seen from Manassas in direction of Centreville.

Our expedition this morning appears to have been completely successful. We have re-established telegraphic communications with Manassas, will soon have cars running, but the military authorities heretofore have never extended to us the protection that was necessary, and we have assumed the responsibility of going ahead without it.

Our telegraph operators and railway employes are entitled to great credit. They have been advanced pioneers, occupying the posts of danger, and the exploit of penetrating to Fairfax and bringing off the wounded when they supposed that 20,000 rebels were on their front and flanks, was one of the boldest performances I have ever heard of.

H. HAUPT.

August 30, 1862.

President Lincoln:

We escaped any injury to the track and bridges last night. We sent forward trains until 2 A. M. They all reached their destination, which affords, I think, an ample present supply of subsistence and ammunition. We sent 88 cars. The trains were all guarded, the tops filled with riflemen and strong guards at all the bridges. We asked Manassas a short time ago if firing was heard; he said no. Fairfax just answers no firing heard. I sent out one of General Couch's regiments about 12 last night; the other reported for duty after 2 A. M. It was of no use to send it at that hour, and no train was ready.

H. HAUPT.

August 30, 1862.

Colonel Haupt:

There has been heavy and rapid firing in the direction of Fairfax for some time. I have sent out to ascertain what it is. I thought perhaps you might learn something by telegraphing to the front.

G. B. McCLELLAN,
Major-General.

August 30, 1862.

Colonel Haupt:
    Do you know what that firing is?

GEO. B. McCLELLAN,
Major-General.

MANASSAS, August 30, 1862.

General McClellan:
    There was a camp rumor as I came in from Bristoe that Jackson had moved towards Alexandria. Colonel J. C. Clarke, one of my aides, who has been out to the front, reports that Jackson has fallen back about five (5) miles towards the mountains. He judges mainly by the sounds of the guns. There has been an entire change of position, I judge. A scout reports at ten (10) A. M. that Jackson was at Gainesville with about 30,000. He said that he saw and knew him. My corps is moving up from Bristoe; no enemy near.

N. P. BANKS,
Major-General.

August 30, 1862.

Colonel Stager:
    Please order Flagg, Graham, and Waterhouse to return and reopen Burkes and Fairfax Stations, and ask General Halleck to direct that a company of riflemen and a few cavalry be sent to each station for information and protection. When we are sending supplies to Sangster's Station, I consider it very important that we should have a temporary connection and operator at that point. Please send some one for that purpose.

H. HAUPT.

WAR DEPARTMENT,
August 30, 1862.

Colonel Haupt:
    Have telegraphed Flagg to go immediately to Fairfax Station.
    Our advices are that fighting is still going on. The firing has been rapid and heavy during the last two hours.

A. STAGER.

WAR DEPARTMENT,
August 30, 1862.

Colonel Haupt:
    I have directed operators to resume their places at Burkes and Fairfax. Will have temporary office at Sangster's, as you request.
    Pope fought enemy all day yesterday and drove them in every instance, and has more prisoners than he can count. He was to resume the fight this morning. Pope's loss heavy, 8,000; enemy much larger. This comes by courier from General Pope. General Halleck directed me to give you all information I can, which I shall cheerfully do.

A. STAGER.

August 30, 1862, 5:48 P. M.

McCrickett and Major Haller:
    You are in much less danger of any attack than you were last night. The guards are strengthened by Carroll's brigade, and General Tyler will have skirmishers out in every direction. We must send sup-

Destroying Track, by Corkscrew Twist, With Levers and Steel Hooks.

plies as long and as fast as there are wagons to take them away. If you have any information from any source that is really reliable, it may change our plans. What do you know? We cannot act on surmises.

H. HAUPT.

MANASSAS, August 30, 1862.

Colonel Haupt:
I left force to work at Bull Run, and walked to Bristoe Station. Churchill and the force of contrabands finished Kettle Run bridge last night, and will be working at Broad Run this afternoon. The track stringers are destroyed and most of the posts cut off. Will do the best to repair it until we get lumber. They attempted to burn Conner's Run, but did little injury. Can be repaired soon. I return to Bull Run bridge this evening. I can hear nothing of the Construction Corps.

J. J. MOORE.

August 30, 1862, 12:25 P. M.

General Halleck:
The chief danger to our trains and construction forces arises from the cavalry companies of Prince William. I would be pleased if you could order some cavalry immediately to patrol the country east of the railroad towards the Occoquan; also to have a force of not less than 200 sharpshooters to ride on top of the cars and assist in unloading the trains.

H. HAUPT.

August 30, 1862, 3 P. M.

Colonel Haupt:
I have just received the following from General Halleck: "Send some sharpshooters and trains to Bull Run; the bridges and property are threatened by band of Prince William Cavalry. Give Colonel Haupt all the assistance you can; the sharpshooters on top of the cars can assist in unloading trains."

What trains are you to send, and how many men do you want to carry out General Halleck's order? I have 300 good men, including about fifty sharpshooters, armed with Sharp's rifles. At what time do you want these men? If you require any more, they will have to be taken from raw troops armed at once.

G. B. McCLELLAN,
Major-General.

August 30, 1862.

Colonel Haupt:
The General-in-Chief considers the protection of the railroad to-night as one of the most importance. General McClellan, therefore, desires that you will throw forward to the exposed front General Couch's Division, just arrived at Alexandria, as rapidly as the capability of the road will permit. General Couch has been instructed to confer with you.

S. WILLIAMS,
Assistant Adjutant General.

August 30, 1862.

Colonel Haupt:
Major-General Couch has been ordered, by direction of the General-in-Chief, to send the regiment of his command, which is now dis-

embarking, at once to Sangster's and other exposed stations by rail. General Couch is ordered to confer with you as to the points to be guarded and the strength of the guard.

General Halleck fears that the marauders may attempt the destruction of the road to-night. No time, therefore, is to be lost. Please acknowledge.

By command Major-General McClellan.

S. WILLIAMS,
Assistant Adjutant General.

August 30, 1862, 5:15 P. M.

P. H. Watson:

Please direct General Clough, Military Governor of Alexandria, to arrest and hold for examination until exigencies of the service will permit it, William Hook, a workman in machine shop, believed, from recent developments, to be a rebel, and charged with secreting parts of engines to render them unfit for service.

H. HAUPT.

August 30, 1862, 11:45 A. M.

P. H. Watson:

I have just had a conversation with M. P. Wood, Master Machinist, who has had charge of the machine shop in Fredericksburg. He says that after having used the forges two days, it was discovered that a loaded shell had been placed in each. I think the proprietor, John Scott, now under arrest, should not be released. His is an aggravated case.

H. HAUPT.

August 30, 1862.

General Halleck:

From the conductor of the wrecking and construction trains, I learn that the wreck at Bull Run is nearly cleared. The bridges will be commenced to-morrow and probably finished next day. I have just stationed 200 men at the bridges as a protection. The track is clear to Bull Run.

H. HAUPT.

War Department,
August 31, 1862, 7:10 A. M.

Colonel Haupt:

What news? Did you hear any firing this morning?

A. LINCOLN.

August 31, 1862.

President Lincoln:

No news received as yet this morning; firing heard distinctly in direction of Bristoe at 6 o'clock.

H. HAUPT.

August 31, 1862.

McCrickett:

Please send telegraph operator to Bull Run to make connection and report all that he learns; let him go on first train.

H. HAUPT.

August 31, 1862.

Generals Halleck and McClellan:

I am just informed that Manassas is being evacuated again by our men, and that Banks' forces are moving towards Centreville. I know very little of what is going on, but this movement would seem to indicate large reinforcements of the enemy from the direction of the Rappahannock, particularly as our own cars and engines at and near Bristoe were destroyed by our own men this morning.

As our forces occupy Centreville, Fairfax, Vienna and, in fact, the whole line north of the railroad, there should be but little difficulty in our retaining possession of the triangle formed by the line of railroads from Bull Run to Alexandria, the streams of Bull Run and Occoquan and the Potomac. If the bridges and fords on the Occoquan and Bull Run are guarded and cavalry scouts patrolling this triangle, no enemy could approach the line of road. A stronger force is required at Bull Run.

Our men are at work and expect to have Bull Run bridge passable to-morrow morning. Without artillery we cannot defend the bridge against artillery. If the crossings of the Occoquan are guarded, Bull Run bridge is our most exposed point.

Please give a thought to these suggestions.

H. HAUPT.

August 31, 1862.

Major-General Halleck:

Your telegram in regard to orders of General Couch has been received. As soon as the officer reports I will make the arrangement. We have already stationed 200 men at Bull Run, 150 at Fairfax, and 150 more will be sent by next train. 200 travel with trains as guards. The regiments of General Couch will be placed at bridges along the road between Alexandria and Fairfax, beyond which points trains will not run to-night. To-morrow there should be a better organization of guards than now exists. The attacks are usually made before midnight, and guards to be of use should be already posted.

H. HAUPT.

August 31, 1862.

Major-General McClellan:

We have been waiting perhaps an hour and a half for General Couch's regiment, and they have not been heard from. They are assigned to duty as follows:

3 companies to strengthen guards at Fairfax.
3 at Accotink bridge.
1 at bridge at Springfield.
2 seven miles from Alexandria.
1 at bridge near Burkes.

It is now so late that these guards will be of little use for to-night, and if they do not report soon, I must send off trains now waiting without them. The ammunition must go forward immediately. We have 200 men at Bull Run, and I consider it inexpedient to send any more beyond Fairfax to-night. At this point all supplies will be unloaded.

H. HAUPT.

August 31, 1862, 10:30.
Colonel Haupt:
Was ordered out of my car this morning with the word that our cars and engine were to be burned, and before I had picked up my traps the trains were on fire. Am now trying to come to Alexandria.

J. D. IRISH.

August 31, 1862.
President Lincoln and Generals Halleck and McClellan:
One of our train dispatchers reports from Manassas that he was ordered out of his car at Bristoe this morning by our troops with the information that they were ordered to destroy the cars and engines, and they have been burned. I suppose that this was done by command of General Banks.

H. HAUPT.

August 31, 1862, 11 A. M.
General Tyler, care Colonel Haupt:
The Commanding General directs that you furnish such guards for railroad and trains as Colonel Haupt may call for.

R. B. MARCY,
Chief of Staff.

August 31, 1862, 11 A. M.
Colonel Haupt:
Should you require any more troops to guard railroad or trains, please call upon General Tyler for them. He will be directed to furnish them. Can you send out any troops to Fairfax Station to-day and not interfere with the transit of subsistence? If so, how many?

R. B. MARCY,
Chief of Staff.

August 31, 1862.
General G. B. McClellan:
I have arranged with General Tyler for guards to roads and stations. He will strengthen the force at Bull Run bridge, and add a section of artillery. We still need about 500 cavalry between the railroad and the Occoquan. The troops asked transportation for, have not yet been sent. A regiment has just reported.

H. HAUPT.

August 31, 1862.
General R. B. Marcy:
I do not think that any additional force to guard the roads will be required. We have enough to protect against small parties, and we cannot be furnished enough to defend the road against an army. Cavalry scouts would be very useful if we could get them.

As to troops, our means of transportation depend entirely on the rapidity with which cars are unloaded and returned. We can probably send out 5,000 men in five hours.

We are annoyed by a drunken rabble who came out as nurses, by permission of the War Department. I telegraphed that if the battle was over, the companions of the wounded could attend to them. If it was not over, the presence of citizens was highly objectionable. I have requested that guards be placed at end of Long Bridge to keep any but physicians from coming over.

H. HAUPT.

August 31, 1862.

Colonel H. Haupt:

Confusion worse confounded. Here are hundreds of men who want to go to the battlefield. No passes being required, all claim the right. We have in the train five passenger cars and two freight cars full. I fear there are more persons going to satisfy a morbid curiosity than for any other purpose.

D. C. McCALLUM.

August 31, 1862.

D. C. McCallum:

Can you not get an order from the Secretary of War to prevent any more people from coming over? Near a thousand came last night, half of them drunk. We do not want any more of them. I said to Watson that if the battle was over, the companions of the wounded could attend to them. If it was not over, the presence of such a crowd might create a panic and do immense harm; in either case they were worse than useless. Have guards placed to keep them away, if possible.

H. HAUPT.

FAIRFAX, August 31, 1862.

Colonel Haupt:
Send no more citizens.

G. O. HALLER,
Major Seventh Infantry, Commanding.

FAIRFAX, August 31, 1862.

Colonel Haupt:

Recent news induces me to ask whether it would not be better to send all our wounded rapidly to Alexandria, and not ship here supplies until further notice. I can send the unfortunate far more rapidly and there may be yet a better reason for not sending citizens. They have overwhelmed us, and they retard, instead of, as they intended, assisting us.

G. O. HALLER,
Major Seventh Infantry.

WAR DEPARTMENT,
August 31, 1862, 12:55.

Colonel Haupt:

I placed your telegrams in the hands of the Secretary and General Halleck for answer early this morning. I gave an order to the Military Governor, General Wadsworth, to place guards at the bridges and wharves, and stop and turn back all nurses who might attempt to cross; also to stop and turn back all other civilians who have no proper passes. Let the drunken and other nurses in Alexandria be sent back by cars or steamers as may suit or be most convenient.

P. H. WATSON,
Assistant Secretary of War.

FAIRFAX, August 31, 1862.

Colonel Haupt and J. H. Devereux:

A slight misunderstanding existed for a short time between Major Haller and myself. He was going to take military control of everything here. Told him he must make an exception of railroad. We now understand each other and it is settled all right.

Told him we were here to do all in our power to advance the business of the Government, and that I will do anything that does not conflict with your orders. There has been awful confusion here this morning; unloading was progressing very slowly. Major has set to work and will have cars unloaded promptly. He has ordered all citizens back to Alexandria who refuse to go to Bull Run with train. They are in Devereux's train; eight or ten wounded are in same train; 277 wagons of wounded are just in. They are now being loaded.

This misunderstanding took place before Major received your message about unloading cars.

McCRICKETT.

WAR DEPARTMENT,
August 31, 1862, 6 P. M.

Colonel Haupt:

I have directed General Clough to arrest Hook, as you requested. You or General Clough are both authorized to arrest and send to the Old Capitol Prison, in Washington, any person whom you may deem dangerous to remain at large. You will report any such arrest, and the cause thereof, to this Department.

P. H. WATSON,
Assistant Secretary of War.

August 31, 1862, 11:05 P. M.

Major-General Halleck:

A young man has just returned from the battlefield who gives information of the position of affairs which, it seems to me, may influence your movements. I feel it to be my duty to send him to you, and am getting an engine ready for that purpose. I will send him to the War Office. Please direct the door-keeper to admit him, or direct where he can see you. He will be on hand before 1 A. M.

H. HAUPT.

CHAPTER V.

GENERAL POPE POUNDED TO PIECES.

THE oncoming disaster to Pope and his army, which General McClellan was doing nothing to avert, was already discernible, though the authorities at Washington were not yet without hope.

Major-General McClellan: About September 1, 1862.

Have you ordered Major Haller's command to be withdrawn from Fairfax? If you have, do you wish them to be transported on cars this afternoon, or can they remain until to-morrow? I would prefer, if you can spare them, that no part of the force at Fairfax be removed while the depot continues at that point.   H. HAUPT.

Colonel Haupt: September 1, 1862.

I have reason to believe, from reports received, that the enemy were to-night in possession of Fairfax Court House, and I very much fear that they will try to take possession of Fairfax Station. Please look at the instructions I have just sent over the wire to Major Haller, commanding at Fairfax Station. I think all the supplies that can be withdrawn from there should be withdrawn at once. Provide, if possible, the means for the retirement of Major Haller's command by rail; at least, to facilitate it.   GEO. B. McCLELLAN,
Major-General.

Major Haller, Fairfax: September 1, 1862, 12:30 A. M.

It is reported that a large force of cavalry and three light batteries of the enemy were this afternoon near Fairfax Court House. They may visit you to-night. Be ready for them. Infantry ought to handle cavalry anywhere in such a country as this. Be careful to secure your retreat, and in God's name do not be captured. Keep me constantly posted. If you find your communication with Fairfax Court House irretrievably cut off, destroy the stores and make good your retreat to Alexandria. Communicate the same orders to the detachment near you and personally in your front. If possible, fall back by the railroad, retreating only step by step, as you are forced to do so. Don't allow a mere cavalry raid to drive you off. Give ground only when you are absolutely forced to do so. Communicate by telegraph with Colonel Haupt, Superintendent Railroads.

By order General McClellan.   A. V. COLBURN,
Assistant Adjutant General.

Colonel Colburn: September 1, 1862.

Will you please continue to send out scouts at short intervals and report observations?   H. HAUPT.

September 1, 1862.

McCrickett:

We are informed that an attack may be made upon you to-night by cavalry. Send down immediately any cars that are at the station as fast as they can be loaded with wounded. We cannot send back any more cars and engines, because it would attract too much attention. Major Haller's command can retire much more safely on foot than they can in cars.

Send some one on foot to Bull Run to warn our railroad men and guards to retire if you are compelled to retire from Fairfax. Burn any stores, and particularly any ammunition that you may find it necessary to leave.

Do not communicate this intelligence to any of the nurses, or a rush will be made and a panic created. Get the wounded off first.

Keep cool and trust your legs and the bushes for escape.

H. HAUPT.

FAIRFAX, September 1, 1862.

J. H. Devereux:

All right; I feel perfectly cool and wet; have been fording streams and wading ditches since 4 A. M.

McC.

FAIRFAX, September 1, 1862, 4:30 A. M.

Colonel Haupt:

Then I may expect no engine to haul away the 13 cars still loaded with forage. It will be almost impossible to send messenger to Bull Run to-night. Will it answer about daylight?

McCRICKETT.

September 1, 1862.

McCrickett:

Take care of your wounded in preference to forage; destroy all that you cannot bring away. You cannot now stop to reload forage; you may risk the capture of the party; the forage is not worth it.

H. HAUPT.

September 1, 1862, 2:30 A. M.

Major-General McClellan:

If the enemy are at Fairfax Court House it will not answer to send any more engines from Alexandria to Fairfax Station. The noise made in going out would attract so much attention that they would be sure to be captured in coming in. I think it imprudent also to put the command of Major Haller in the cars, where they would be defenseless. I have therefore directed that empty cars shall be loaded with wounded and returned; that stores and ammunition, if any remain, shall be burned in case of attack, and that men who have legs shall depend on them and the bushes for escape.

H. HAUPT.

September 1, 1862, 2:40 A. M.

Generals Tyler and Clough:

I am advised by telegram from General McClellan that Fairfax Court House is probably in possession of the enemy. I have ordered the cars and engines with wounded to be withdrawn from Fairfax

DESTROYING TRACK, BY CORKSCREW TWIST, WITH LEVERS AND STEEL HOOKS.

Station and no more trains to be sent out. In case of attack by cavalry, which is expected, destroy the stores and retire. It is not impossible that a dash may be made in the direction of Alexandria, and you should be advised of the position of affairs.

H. HAUPT.

Major Haller, in command at Fairfax Station, marched his command towards Alexandria, thus withdrawing all protection. McCrickett remained until after 5 P. M., having succeeded in sending to Alexandria all the wounded and all the stores, except a few loads of forage, and then, in obedience to instructions, set fire to the building, and made his escape as the enemy was approaching, his last telegram being: "Have fired it. Good by."

FAIRFAX, September 2, 1862, 1:05 P. M.

General McClellan:

Major Haller's command just marching towards Alexandria.

H. HAUPT.

September 2, 1862.

S. Williams, A. A. G.:

We have ordered all cars forward immediately from Fairfax Station. Major Haller's command started some time ago. Your information comes too late to send additional cars from Alexandria to Fairfax. We are just advised that the last of our army has passed, and the depot is already in the rear. I have directed that, in case this information is correct, to start with all the cars at Fairfax, put in the wounded as rapidly as possible, and return to Alexandria. To send trains now from here to Fairfax would be certain capture.

H. HAUPT.

September 2, 1862.

McCrickett:

If the last of our army has already passed, and you are now in the rear, it would be folly to send more cars and engines with a certainty of destruction. If the position of affairs be as you represent it, all you have to do is to load the cars you have, pile in the wounded on top, inside, anywhere, as you best can, destroy any stores you cannot load, and come on to Burkes and Alexandria.

H. HAUPT.

September 2, 1862.

Colonel Colburn, Fairfax:

I do not know from whom you should receive instructions, but it will certainly be proper for you immediately to withdraw your command. If our troops have all passed, your position will be much exposed. If I can reach you with cars, I will do so. Leave no supplies, destroy what you cannot bring; let the road guards fall in and retire with you as you meet them.

H. HAUPT.

September 2, 1862.

McCrickett:

What property is left at station destroy it and retire immediately. It is too late to send up a train.

H. HAUPT.

September 2, 1862.

McCrickett:
After destroying Fairfax, come on foot to Burkes, and in the train there come to Alexandria.

H. HAUPT.

FAIRFAX, September 2, 1862.

J. H. Devereux:
Have fired it.   Good-by.   McC.*

The record of the campaign of the Army of Virginia, so far as the operations of the Military Railroad Department are concerned, ends with the evacuation of Fairfax September 2, 1862; and on the same day the Army of Virginia was merged into the Army of the Potomac, under General McClellan.

From June 26, 1862, to August 9, when the battle of Cedar Mountain was fought, I was not an active participant in military operations.   The experiment of a hydra-headed management of the railroads had been tried and failed.   I was recalled from Cambridge with the information that not a wheel was moving on any of the roads, and was reinstated with the official distinction from the General-in-Chief that my authority was to be supreme.

The brief intervening period until September 2, was one of intense activity and anxiety.   The operations of the railroad were subject to constant interruption from guerrilla bands, some of them mounted; bridges were destroyed, rails removed, track obstructed, every possible impediment placed in the way of successful operation.

The flank movement of Lee placed him in a very critical position, and I have always been of the opinion that if Pope had been properly supported by McClellan's Army of the Potomac, Lee would have been crushed between the upper and nether millstones.

It would not have required a very large portion of the force to defend the fortifications around Washington, and Lee would have been insane to have made an attack upon them with the Army of the Potomac on his flank and the Army of Virginia in his rear.

The veterans of the Potomac Army could have been mobilized, and one day's march would have brought them to the battlefield. Some of them, a very small proportion, did perform efficient service; but as Pope reported, more than 60,000 never drew a trigger in the battles.

I do not consider myself a competent military critic, but no man who reasons can avoid forming opinions.   It is claimed, in excuse for inactivity, that the commands lying in camp south of Alexandria were waiting for something; that the artillery had not

---

* The brave McCrickett, who was the last man to leave the bloody field of Bull Run, soon after lost his life in the line of duty.

arrived, and they had not sufficient cavalry support; but it is certain that they were demanding transportation by rail which it was impossible to furnish, and if they were ready to move by rail, they were certainly ready to march less than twenty miles.

The General* who declared that he "did not care a ——— for John Pope," and pretended to be so anxious to get to the front that he took military possession of the railroad and undertook to put me in arrest, did not even load his cars when they were furnished to him the next morning in sufficient numbers for his whole command. After waiting for him half a day the cars were withdrawn and used for other service!

General Pope complained in strong terms of the demoralization of the Army of the Potomac, and expressed the opinion that, if Franklin, who had been ordered to march on the 24th, had been at Centreville, or Cox and Sturgis even as far as Bull Run, Jackson's move through Thoroughfare Gap on the 26th would have been impracticable.

During this protracted engagement the President was in a state of extreme anxiety and could have slept but little. Inquiries came from him at all hours of the night, asking for the latest news from the front.

As soon as practicable after the cessation of active operations, I returned to my Headquarters Office in Washington and called upon Secretary of War Stanton. I was received with much cordiality, addressed as General Haupt, and, in the presence of the President and most of the Cabinet, who were in the office at the time, warmly thanked for what he was pleased to consider the important service rendered. The next day I received an appointment as Brigadier-General of Volunteers, "for meritorious services in the recent operations against the enemy near Manassas," dated September 5, 1862.

I returned thanks for the honor conferred and agreed to subscribe to the form of oath and accept the appointment with the single condition that when no public duty required my presence, I should have leave of absence to protect my interests and reputation, which were at stake in Massachusetts, in the Hoosac tunnel contract. The Secretary fully understood the situation, which had become more and more complicated during my absence; but he replied that he was not permitted to include conditions in the commission, and I expressed a willingness to rest upon a simple verbal promise without making a record that might establish a troublesome precedent. No further objections were made, and I continued to perform service, as before, without pay.

---

* General Sturgis.

CHAPTER VI.

AIDING McCLELLAN'S CAMPAIGN.

A FTER the Army of Virginia was merged into the Army of the Potomac under General McClellan, I was occupied for considerable time in the work of reorganization. The Federal Army remained in the defenses around Washington, while the Confederates occupied the Shenandoah Valley and the south side of the Potomac. During this period active operations on the part of the Military Railroads Construction Corps were suspended, and the records furnish no information of special importance.

General Halleck had, on several occasions, spoken to me of the importance of a thorough organization of all the Military Railroads of the United States. He was satisfied that great abuses existed, and had called the attention of the Secretary of War to the fact, but no action had been taken. As a result of another conversation on the subject on the morning of Septemebr 16, I addressed the following communication to General Halleck, accompanied by a plan of organization, for his consideration:

WASHINGTON, September 16, 1862.
Major-General Halleck.

SIR: Since my interview with you this morning I have been giving some thought to the subject of our conversation, and have concluded to venture some suggestions.

As at present informed, the Department of Military Railroads, excepting perhaps for the immediate vicinity of the capital, is without a head.

If you, or the Secretary of War, should desire to be informed as to what roads are in the possession of the United States; how far they are in operation; by whom operated; what their condition; what the amount of rolling stock; what prices are paid for materials and supplies; whether a judicious economy or a lavish expenditure characterizes their operation, it would be impossible to procure any direct information on any of these subjects, and abuses of great magnitude may exist without the power of discovering them.

To procure information, put it in shape to be readily accessible; secure system and uniformity in administration, correct abuses and promote efficiency, the following arrangements appear to be proper.

Yours respectfully,   H. HAUPT.

With this letter a detailed plan of organization and operation was submitted, but no action was at that time taken. However, during the lull in active operations that followed the return of

General McClellan on September 1, my Corps was not idle. It was engaged in repairing cars and engines, providing material and experimenting on devices and expedients for the destruction and reconstruction of roads and bridges.

On Friday, September 19, at Hagerstown, I found Governor Curtin, General John F. Reynolds, John A. Wright, and Edward McPherson, acting aids to the Governor, and several other officers in command of the Pennsylvania Militia.

At night there was quite a scare from a rumor that the enemy was marching to attack Hagerstown. A council was held to consider the expediency of withdrawing the Pennsylvania forces beyond the Pennsylvania line. As they had been called out to defend their own State, the Governor, for political and other reasons, did not wish them to risk an attack beyond their own territory; and General Reynolds and myself were opposed to the movement for reasons stated.

The vote was a tie, but as the Governor was very uneasy, it was decided to order the retirement of the militia. The movement commenced at 1 A. M., but as there were no indications of an attack, it was suspended until daylight. Lee was, in fact, at that time too busy in getting his retreating army safely across the Potomac after the battle of Antietam to attempt an attack on Hagerstown.

The next day I rode over the battlefield, where soldiers were engaged in burying the dead of both armies, and after an interview with General McClellan at his Headquarters, proceeded via Boonsboro to Frederick, and thence, by rail, to Baltimore and Washington.

September 17, a dispatch was received from General Heintzelman desiring an examination of track and bridges as far as Bull Run, stating that a considerable force of the enemy was reported to be at Centreville, and that the 2d Pennsylvania Cavalry had been directed to go as far as Bull Run to cover my reconnoissance. I made this examination personally before starting for Hagerstown, and reported road in good condition.

ARLINGTON, September 17, 1862.

General Haupt:

You will please communicate with General Clough, Military Governor of Alexandria, who has been directed to furnish you with 100 men.

The 2d Pennsylvania Cavalry have been ordered to go beyond Fairfax Court House as far as Bull Run and, if practicable, to cover your reconnoissance on the railroad. They were ordered to start immediately; the order must have reached them about 12 M.

I have information there is a considerable force of the enemy near Centreville.

By command Major-General Heintzelman.

C. McKENER,
Lieutenant-Colonel, A. A. G.

8

On September 19, by request of W. P. Smith, Superintendent of Baltimore & Ohio Railroad, I sent a force of carpenters, under G. W. Nagle, foreman, to assist in repairing damages on that road.

September 23, 1862, the following telegram was sent from Headquarters of General McClellan, and on the same day a request from President Garrett for lumber to assist in the reconstruction of the trestling at Harper's Ferry:

September 23, 1862.

Sir: The Commanding General directs me to inform you that Major-General Heintzelman has been directed to detach two regiments of infantry, with (if possible) a section of artillery, to accompany the construction party you propose sending to Bristoe Station to-morrow.

The troops will meet the construction party at Union Mills. Please acquaint General Heintzelman by telegraph when the former will be at the rendezvous. Very respectfully, your obedient servant,

R. B. IRWIN,
Captain A. D. C., A. A. A. G.

Brigadier-General Haupt.

September 25, 1862, W. W. Wright, one of my assistants, was sent to Harrisburg to take charge of the transportation on the Cumberland Valley Railroad, with instructions as follows:

WASHINGTON, D. C., September 25, 1862.

W. W. Wright, Esq.

Sir: I enclose for your information a copy of "Special Orders, No. 248," from the office of the Adjutant-General; also copies of previous instructions, and an extract from a letter addressed by Captain E. C. Wilson, Assistant Quartermaster, U. S. A., to Quartermaster-General Meigs, complaining of the management on the Cumberland Valley Railroad.

You will, on receipt of this communication, proceed to Harrisburg, see Captain Wilson, ascertain fully the character and magnitude of the evils complained of and, if necessary, assume the direction of train movements on the Cumberland Valley Railroad.

In general, it is desirable that roads used wholly or partially for military purposes should be operated by and through the regular officers in charge of such roads; but when the management is characterized by incompetency, or inefficiency, it becomes necessary to assume military possession and place in charge agents and officers who will promptly forward troops and government supplies. When the amount of rolling stock is insufficient, requisitions must be made upon connecting roads.

I found it necessary last week to take possession of the Franklin Railroad between Chambersburg and Hagerstown, and placed in charge J. D. Potts, with whom you will consult in regard to train arrangements.

My impression was that very little business for the United States Government would be required to be done over the line between Harrisburg and Hagerstown, as troops and supplies can be sent with much greater facility via Sandy Hook or Harper's Ferry; but you can ascertain the facts from Captain Wilson and, if necessary, report to him for additional instructions.

In the management of Military Railroads three points require special attention. They are:

1. Not to allow supplies to be forwarded to the advanced terminus until they are actually required, and only in such quantities as can be promptly removed.

2. To insist on the prompt unloading and return of cars.

3. To permit no delay of trains beyond the time fixed for starting, but when necessary and practicable, to furnish extras, if the proper accommodation of business requires them.

H. HAUPT,

Brigadier-General,

Chief of Construction and Transportation,

United States Military Railroads.

After the enemy re-crossed the Potomac, September 19, no movement was made for some time in pursuit. The enemy re-occupied the Shenandoah Valley and the line of the Rappahannock, and, on October 7, information was received that they had reconstructed the bridge across the Rappahannock on the line of the Orange & Alexandria Railroad, and were running trains to Bristoe, five miles south of Manassas, carrying off the disabled engines, car wheels and axles left at that point after Pope's retreat.

I formed a plan for capturing the rebel train, and sent out a force to proceed beyond Bristoe, secrete themselves in the woods, obstruct the track when the train had passed so that it could not return and capture it. The plan failed by the imprudence of one of our men who exposed himself and was seen by the engineer, who reversed his engine and returned towards the Rappahannock.

The following report embraces the Military Railroad operations from September 18, 1862, to September 27:

WASHINGTON, September 27, 1862.

Major-General Halleck.

SIR: On Thursday, September 18, I was authorized and directed by Special Order No. 248 to do whatever I might deem expedient to facilitate the transportation of troops and supplies to aid the armies in the field in Virginia and Maryland.

I immediately proceeded to Baltimore, where a conference was held with General Wood, Quartermaster Belger, President Garrett and Superintendent Smith of the Baltimore & Ohio Railroad.

This conference resulted in changing the route of several regiments then ordered to the front, and in establishing the following rule for future operations:

RULE. All troops and supplies sent from Baltimore and points south thereof to the army in Maryland shall be forwarded by the Baltimore & Ohio Railroad; and all sent from points north of Baltimore, by the York & Cumberland Railroad.

I was clearly of the opinion that it was expedient in general to operate the railroads used for military purposes by and through the regular officers and employes of such roads, using military authority only when necessary to render assistance to them in procuring rolling stock, or securing regularity in train movements.

The efficiency of the management of the officers of the Baltimore & Ohio Railroad, their readiness to give Government supplies the preference over all other transportation, and the capacity of the road, which is greater than any ordinary, or even extraordinary demands that may be made upon it, left nothing more to be desired except the prompt return of cars from the advanced terminus. Having concluded all necessary arrangements, I proceeded the same night to Harrisburg, arriving in that city on Friday morning, September 19, at 3:30 A. M.

The arrangement of sending supplies from Baltimore and points south thereof over the Baltimore & Ohio Railroad, relieving the Northern Central of its transportation of Government supplies northward, left no question as to the ability of this road to meet any anticipated demands upon it, and I therefore continued my journey at 7:30 A. M. over the York & Cumberland Railroad to Chambersburg where, after many delays caused by passing trains, I arrived at 2:30 P. M.

The amount of business on the York & Cumberland Railroad exceeded its capacity for prompt accommodation. About 18 regiments of Pennsylvania militia had been sent forward, and more were on the way, the Pennsylvania Railroad Company furnishing cars and engines, and assisting, as I understand, in the management of the road. Under the circumstances, the only action at that point which I considered expedient was to order that all private sidings should be vacated, and that all cars belonging to individuals, and all others not required for military purposes, should be either run off the tracks or sent to other stations where the sidings were not required for the use of the Government.

I found a very efficient officer in charge of the depot and station at Chambersburg, J. D. Potts, formerly Assistant Superintendent on the Western Division of the Pennsylvania Railroad, to whom I gave such instructions as appeared to be necessary.

At Hagerstown the main track was blocked with cars; there was no adequate siding or warehouse accommodation, no competent person in charge and much confusion existed. I found it necessary to assume military possession of the Franklin Railroad between Chambersburg and Hagerstown; attended personally to the duty of raising the blockade; cleared the track of five or six trains that had accumulated at Hagerstown; placed Mr. Potts in charge as superintendent; directed him to procure a substitute in the Chambersburg office; left written instructions as to the future management, and also wrote to General Kenly, the officer understood to be in command at Hagerstown, informing him of the existing arrangement for transportation, and giving the names of the officers in charge.

On Saturday, September 20, I rode from Hagerstown to Sharpsburg, where, after a half hour's interview with General McClellan, I repaired to Boonsboro and returned via Frederick City to Baltimore.

At Monocacy I found about 200 loaded cars on the sidings, some of which had been standing nearly a week. General Wool, at my request, sent an efficient officer of his staff to insist upon the unloading and return of cars.

On Monday, September 22, I returned to Washington and made a verbal report to you of my doings.

On Tuesday, September 23, having received information that the Baltimore & Ohio Railroad Company were embarrassed in their operations in consequence of the non-return of cars, I sent two of our most experienced train dispatchers from the O. & A. Railroad over the North-

BENDING RAILS WITH AID OF HORSE.

ern Central, Pennsylvania and connecting roads to search for and return cars of the Baltimore & Ohio Railroad Company and of the United States Military Railroad.

The same evening I started for Baltimore and Harper's Ferry to render such assistance as might be in my power in opening communication with that post.

I arrived at Harper's Ferry about noon on Wednesday, September 24, and remained until Thursday afternoon, September 25. The supply of material being insufficient and the force of mechanics for the railroad bridge very small, I telegraphed for the Construction Corps of the O. & A. Railroad, which was promptly forwarded, together with about 150,000 feet of long square timber, which we fortunately had on hand at Alexandria.

About six days will complete the railroad trestle bridge and secure connection with Harper's Ferry, but a much longer time will be required to replace the permanent structure. The trestle bridge will be in danger of destruction from freshets; the most certain reliance for the supplies, in the event of such a contingency, will be the pontoon bridge, which has been reconstructed. With proper management at Harper's Ferry and Sandy Hook, the supply question presents no difficulty, even in case the trestle bridge should be swept away.

The embarrassments, irregularities and blockades on the United States Military Railroads, which are so frequent and so annoying, result from three causes, which can be and should be avoided. These are:

1. Sending supplies to the advanced terminus before they are required. Such supplies are not unloaded; they block the track, impede retreat, and are in danger of capture or destruction. Nothing should be sent to the extreme front until it is actually needed. A reasonable amount can be kept on some siding a few miles in the rear.

2. Lack of promptness in unloading and returning cars. Sometimes a single car will be unloaded at a time when there should be force sufficient to discharge at once the load of a whole train. Cars are sometimes kept for weeks as storehouses.

3. Detaining trains beyond schedule time. Nothing more certainly throws the business of a line into confusion, especially if there be but single track. Medical directors and officers should conform to the schedule time of trains, or if extras are required for sick, wounded, or for supplies, they should always be furnished when practicable; but when the hour fixed for starting has arrived, the train should be promptly dispatched.

It has been the practice on most roads used for military purposes, under the influence of a pressure of business and the impatience of military officers, to abandon the schedule and resort to the use of the telegraph exclusively for running trains. This practice invariably leads to difficulty, and in case of any derangement to the delicate mechanism of the telegraph, puts an end to all business and blocks everything upon the road. I believe that it is always possible with good management to run the trains by schedule and the telegraph, although valuable as an auxiliary, should not be used as a principal. It is desirable that uniformity should be introduced in the management of all railroads used for military purposes. Very respectfully submitted,

H. HAUPT,
Brigadier-General,
Chief of Construction and Transportation,
United States Military Railroads.

October 9, a communication was sent to Colonel D. C. Mc-Callum in reference to placing bullet-proof cabs upon the engines, which is as follows:

WASHINGTON, D. C., October 9, 1862.

Colonel D. C. McCallum, Director of Military Railroads.

DEAR SIR: I have been thinking over the subject of locomotives. It is one which, at the present time and in view of the future requirements of the service, demands especial attention. Experience has shown that on engines men are targets for the enemy; the cabs where they are usually seated have been riddled by bullets, and they have only escaped by lying on the footboard. It will be necessary to inspire confidence in our men by placing iron cabs (bullet proof) upon all or nearly all our engines, and the necessity will increase as we penetrate further into the enemy's country.

Again, it is desirable that the smaller and more delicate portions of the apparatus should be better protected than at present, and I would be pleased if you could give to the plans, of which I spoke to you recently, a careful consideration. It seems to me that they are peculiarly well adapted to military service. I hope you will investigate the proposed improvements.*

There is also another subject to which I wish to direct your attention. Are you positively sure that the agents you have sent to examine and value rolling stock are perfectly incorruptible? Are you sure that there is no room for jobs or commissions? It seems to me that there is only one way of making sure of it, and that is by direct personal examination and communication with the parties yourself.

Can you not leave for a few days? There is but little to do in the office. Whiton can attend to the business, and if I can assist, I will do it cheerfully.   Yours truly,

H. HAUPT,
Chief of Construction and Transportation.

October 10, 1862, I was requested by General McClellan to take steps to reconstruct the railroad to Winchester. As I considered such reconstruction inexpedient, the following communication was sent to General Halleck, who sustained my position, and the road was not reconstructed:

WASHINGTON, October 11, 1862.

Major-General Halleck.

SIR: I enclose copies of telegrams from General Rufus Ingalls, Chief Quartermaster Army of Potomac, and from W. P. Smith, Esq., Superintendent Baltimore & Ohio Railroad.

On the receipt of the telegram from General Ingalls asking that the Winchester Railroad be reconstructed with T rails, I requested Mr. Smith to report its condition, which was promptly done.

It appears that the road is in very bad order; that even with good ordinary repair and good management, its capacity would not exceed about sixty cars per day. To reconstruct this road under favorable circumstances with T rails will require two months. The ties must be manufactured and the rails purchased.

---

*Protected locomotives and bullet-proof cabs were soon after provided as recommended.

If the object of our military operations should be simply to expel the enemy from Winchester and hold it ourselves without following the enemy further, then the immediate reconstruction of this road might be a military necessity; but I cannot suppose that our armies, if successful in obtaining possession of Winchester, would stop there; and if the pursuit should be continued further, the army supplies will of course be sent via the Manassas Gap Railroad.

Is it expedient, under the circumstances, to reconstruct the Winchester Railroad at present?

A more intimate acquaintance than I now possess with the plans of operations and prospective movements would be required before I could answer this question. I therefore very respectfully refer the subject to you and ask your instructions.

H. HAUPT,
Chief of Construction and Transportation,
United States Military Railroads.

October 12, General Ingalls informed me that General McClellan approved my suggestions; that it would be best to supply the army via the Manassas Gap Railroad and not reconstruct the road to Winchester.

Received orders from the Secretary of War as follows, which were promptly obeyed:

WASHINGTON CITY, D. C., October 17, 1862.
Brigadier-General Haupt, Superintendent and Military Director of Railroads.

GENERAL: You will proceed immediately to inspect the Cumberland Valley Railroad and take such measures as may be necessary to enforce promptness and efficiency in the transportation and delivery of military supplies on that road from Harrisburg to Hagerstown.

It is represented that the service is inefficiently performed by the agents of the Company; that private and express freight is given preference to Government supplies, and that agents are not present to dispatch cars.

If necessary, you will take possession of the road and its stock, and employ the agents needed for running the road as a United States Military Railroad route.

EDWIN M. STANTON,
Secretary of War.

The last battle at Antietam was fought September 17. Lee crossed the Potomac September 19. November 1, General McClellan telegraphed the President that all his Corps had crossed the Potomac.

In reference to complaint that the horses were fatigued and their tongues sore, the President telegraphed to General McClellan: "I have just read your dispatch about sore tongues and fatigued horses. Will you pardon me for asking what the horses of your army have done since the battle of Antietam that fatigues anything?"

October 26, 1862, telegram from General McClellan in cipher:

HEADQUARTERS ARMY OF THE POTOMAC,
October 26, 1862, 10:45 A. M.

General Herman Haupt, Superintendent Railroads:

I have the honor to request you to ascertain how far the Leesburg Railroad is practicable. I have also to request you to be ready to supply this army via Orange & Alexandria and Manassas Gap Railroads, and to take steps at once to reëstablish the wharves, etc., at Acquia, and to be prepared to rebuild the railroad bridge over the Rappahannock at Fredericksburg and to supply that road with rolling stock.

G. B. McCLELLAN,
Major-General Commanding.

The following reply was returned the same day:

WASHINGTON, D. C., October 26, 1862, 2 P. M.

Major-General G. B. McClellan:

Your commands will receive prompt attention. I have the honor to report that from Alexandria to Difficult Creek, a distance of 18 miles, the Leesburg Road is in running order. From Difficult Creek to Leesburg about eighteen miles of track have been destroyed, cross ties burned and iron scattered through the woods. Spans of bridges, most of them 150 feet in length, in six different localities, require to be constructed before the road can be used. The reconstruction of this road beyond Difficult Creek in time for any immediate advance will be impracticable.

Manassas Gap Railroad: General Siegel reports this road in running order to Front Royal. In case of an advance the enemy will no doubt endeavor to destroy the Goose Creek bridges, and I have ordered material to be prepared for their reconstruction. The capacity of this road, with present equipments, is about 700 to 900 tons per day, if cars are promptly returned and no accident occurs. Please report the probable demands upon this line, and how soon.

Acquia Creek & Fredericksburg Railroad: The destruction of this road was an unfortunate piece of vandalism on the part of our troops. I reported to General Halleck that the destruction of this road was unnecessary, and highly censurable. The Potomac Creek bridge was nearly 80 feet high and 400 feet long. Nearly all the available timber within reach was used in its construction. This bridge was blown down, then burned.

The reconstruction of the Rappahannock bridge at this season will be difficult, and the structure, if rebuilt, precarious. Timber at this time is very scarce. Would it not be best to rely on boat and pontoon bridges at Fredericksburg?

The wharf at Acquia Creek was a very complete affair, covering an area of nearly an acre and a half, with double tracks, and commodious buildings. It cannot be reconstructed as it was in four months. The material cannot be procured in any reasonable time.

The cars on this road, some 60 in number, were all destroyed at the time of the evacuation.

If it is absolutely necessary to use this road, extraordinary efforts will be required to reconstruct it in time to be available, and I respectfully request instructions as to the relative military importance of these roads and the order of priority in which they should be prepared for service.

H. HAUPT.

Reference is here made to the destruction of the wharves and property at Acquia Creek on the evacuation by Burnside's Corps. I reported at the time that I considered the destruction of stores, cars and improvements entirely unnecessary. On short notice every pound could have been removed. The landing was at a considerable distance from the shore, the approach by a narrow embankment easily defended, with impassable swamps on both sides.

When the order to burn was given, some of the subordinate officers, it is said, threw up their caps, and expressed much gratification, then adjourned to divide a bottle of whisky.

Why they were pleased is easily explained. The destruction of stores on the evacuation of a post settles accounts for all deficiencies.

I was once present in a company of officers when a young Quartermaster remarked that the sinking of a steamer on the Mississippi had settled more shortages than twenty steamers could have carried.

Upon reporting the fact of the unnecessary destruction of so much valuable property to General Halleck, he promised to investigate the matter, ascertain by whose orders the buildings had been fired and have the party punished; but it was found that General Burnside had given the orders, no doubt on the representations of subordinates, and no action was taken. As Lee's army was away fighting Pope, and no large body of the enemy near, protection during the removal of the property would have presented no difficulty.

At the next evacuation after the battle of Fredericksburg, with Lee's army near at hand on the Rappahannock, the men of my Corps loaded and removed everything of value, even to the sashes of the buildings.

October 27, the following in cipher was received from General McClellan:

HEADQUARTERS ARMY OF THE POTOMAC,
October 27, 11 A. M., 1862.

Brigadier-General Haupt:

Please take immediate steps to enable you to forward supplies via Orange & Alexandria and Manassas Gap Railroads for this army, at rate of seven hundred tons per day. Also, be prepared to repair the Orange & Alexandria Railroad beyond Manassas Junction wherever it may be damaged. Please communicate to the General-in-Chief the information you gave me yesterday in regard to the Fredericksburg Railroad, and consult with him as to the possibility of repairing that road in season to use it for purpose of this campaign.

G. B. McCLELLAN.

The enemy had crossed the Potomac after the battle of Antietam on September 19, but six weeks later the main body of the Army of the Potomac had not yet reached the line of the Manassas Gap Railroad. About this time General Ingalls came to my office and requested transportation to Headquarters, which, he said, had been established at Rectortown.

I expressed my doubts of the fact, but he was positive that General McClellan had reached that point. I then said that if he was determined to go, I would risk it and go with him.

An engine was ordered to which two platform cars were attached to hold a guard which was taken on, I think, at Fairfax Station. We proceeded without interruption to Manassas, and there started on the Gap Road. The road had not been used since spring. It was overgrown with grass, which, when crushed under the wheels, caused the drivers to slip badly, and in a short time the sand became exhausted. It then became necessary to dismount a part of the force and walk ahead of the engine, placing pebbles on the track, the crushing of which would help the adhesion.

Several miles were passed in this way when the water gave out. We had fortunately two buckets, and dipped water from streams and puddles whenever it could be found. It soon became necessary to cut off one of the cars and leave part of the guard; then the other car was soon after left, and a few soldiers were taken on the tender of the engine.

Night overtook us, and Rectortown was not reached until after midnight, but no information could be had of General McClellan, and we were compelled to return in the same manner.

There was a single cavalryman of Gregg's command at Manassas, but none beyond, and at several points we heard of the presence of Mosby's men the day before. How it happened that we were not captured has always been a matter of surprise, for the puffing of steam and the slipping of the wheels made a noise that could have been heard for more than a mile, giving notice to any enemy in the vicinity.

After passing Fairfax on our return, I met a train, the conductor of which informed me that he had just been fired into at the last bridge he crossed. I therefore returned to Fairfax, procured a guard and proceeded to the bridge, which had not been injured. I then sent out the soldiers to search the woods, but no enemy could be found; there were, however, numerous fresh horse tracks, showing that the assailants had been mounted.

HOW TO DESTROY LOCOMOTIVES AND BRIDGES.

I made the following report on how to destroy bridges and locomotive engines expeditiously:

WASHINGTON, D. C., November 1, 1862.

A simple and expeditious mode of destroying bridges, and rendering locomotive engines useless to an enemy, is often a desideratum. Cavalry may penetrate far into an enemy's country, may reach bridges forming viaducts on important lines of communication, which it may be desirable to break effectually; or, in retreat, the destruction of a bridge may be essential to the safety of an army, and yet time may not be sufficient to gather combustibles, or they may not be accessible, or the fire may be extinguished, or the damage may be so slight as to be easily repaired.

What is required is the means of certainly and effectually throwing down a bridge in a period of time not exceeding five minutes, and with apparatus so simple and portable that it can be carried in the pocket or a saddle-bag.

These requirements are fulfilled by a torpedo (see page 101), which consists simply of a short bolt of seven-eighths inch iron, eight inches long, with head and nut—the head to be two inches in diameter, and about one inch thick. A washer of same size as the head must be placed under the nut at the other end, with a fuse-hole in it. Between the washer and the head is a tin cylinder one and three-quarters inches in diameter, open at both ends, which is filled with powder, and, when the washer and nut are put on, forms a case which encloses it.

In using this torpedo, a hole is bored in a timber; the torpedo (head downwards) is driven in by a stone or billet of wood, and the fuse ignited. The explosion blows the timber in pieces, and, if a main support, brings down the whole structure.

The time required is only that which is necessary to bore a hole with an auger. Ordinary cigar lighters, which burn without flame, and cannot be blown out, are best for igniting the fuse, which should be about two feet long.

For portability, the auger should be short, say thirteen inches, and the handle movable and of same length.

The proper place at which to insert the torpedo is of much consequence. Most of the Virginia bridges are Howe trusses without arches. In this kind of bridge, the destruction of the main braces at one end, and on only one side of a span, will be sufficient to bring down the whole structure. There are usually but two main braces in each panel, and two torpedoes will suffice to throw down a span. Two men can bore the two holes at the same time without interfering with each other. (See illustration on page 191.)

Cartridges containing a fulminate would be more portable, but they are not always conveniently procurable, and their use is attended with risk of explosion.

It is only necessary to operate at one side and on one end of a bridge. If one side falls, the other side is pulled down with it.

If the structure contains an arch, two additional torpedoes will be required; but in this case it may be equally advantageous to operate upon the lower chord.

Experiments made at Alexandria proved that a timber placed in the position of a main brace, and similarly loaded, was shattered into many pieces, some of which were projected by the force of explosion more than a hundred feet.

To Render Locomotives Unfit for Service: The most expeditious mode is to fire a cannon ball through the boiler. This damage cannot be repaired without taking out all the flues.

The usual mode of disabling engines consists in burning the flues by letting out the water and making a fire in the fire-box; but this is generally done so imperfectly that the enemy soon gets them in running order.

Cars are Readily Destroyed by Burning: On this subject no instructions are necessary. The destruction of more than four hundred cars by our own troops within the last six months proves that in the work of destroying such property perfection has been attained, and no room left for winning fresh laurels in this field.

The Superintendent of the Orange & Alexandria Military Railroad has instructions to furnish sample torpedoes to officers who may order them.

Address "J. H. DEVEREUX, Superintendent of Orange & Alexandria Railroad, Alexandria, Va."

H. HAUPT,
Brigadier-General,
In Charge of United States Military Railroads.

On November 5, the following telegram was received from Superintendent J. H. Devereux, and also one from General Mc-Clellan, informing me that the Headquarters would that night be near Rectortown:

HEADQUARTERS NEAR RECTORTOWN,
November 5, 1862.

Brigadier-General H. Haupt:

General McClellan directs me to inform you that his Headquarters are to-night at this place. So far as we can learn, railroad is in good condition as far as Piedmont, and arrangements should be made to forward supplies to that and other points as soon as possible. Can you not send an engine to this point at once for the purpose of ascertaining the exact condition of road and to enable the General to communicate with you?

Our troops are on the line of the road from Piedmont to Salem, and we will have troops at White Plains to-morrow. Our cavalry is in the vicinity of Chester Gap. The General is desirous to see you as soon as you can conveniently come up.

A. V. COLBURN,
Assistant Adjutant-General.

ALEXANDRIA, November 5, 1862.

H. Haupt, Brigadier-General:

At 6:40 this morning Moore got back to Manassas from the Gap Road. He reports the road is not guarded at any point, although a large force was at Gainesville and one at Thoroughfare Gap. He did not see a soldier between Gainesville and Manassas, and your outer pickets were at Broad Run. He understood troops were at Rectortown. We have an engine ready to go if you say so. We may get through, and may not.

J. H. D.

On the same day, November 5, 1862, the following General Orders was placed on record:

GENERAL ORDERS,   WAR DEPARTMENT,
No. 182.   November 5, 1862.

By direction of the President it is ordered that Major-General McClellan be relieved from the command of the Army of the Potomac, and that Major-General Burnside take command of that Army.

November 7, 1862, the following were received from General McClellan's Headquarters:

RECTORTOWN, November 6, 1862.

Brigadier-General Haupt:

General McClellan desires me to say that we are in possession of Warrenton. General Sickles has been directed to push troops forward to Warrenton Junction and to cover any working party that you may have on the railroad. The road should be put in running order as soon as possible in order that the movements of the troops need not be delayed.

A. V. COLBURN,
Assistant Adjutant-General.

CAMP RECTORTOWN, November 6, 1862.

General Meigs:

Supplies of subsistence and forage should be forwarded to this army at convenient points. The supplies should be held in readiness in cars on sidings at Manassas so that the trains can be started to any point required at a moment's notice. We require at least one large train of supplies at Salem immediately. It is expected that the amount ordered by General McClellan some days since is now near here. We shall require an equal amount on the 8th at Warrenton or at the Junction.

I request that you will order all the cars that can be obtained shall be loaded with subsistence and grain and be held in readiness at Manassas subject to move on orders from these Headquarters. General Haupt reported to General McClellan that the road can transport seven hundred tons daily. If such is the fact, we will not suffer, but the road must not fail us. Please have the road put in repair from Acquia Creek to Richmond via Fredericksburg.

RUFUS INGALLS,
Lieutenant-Colonel, A. D. C.
Chief Quartermaster Army of Potomac, etc.

November 8, 1862, in consequence of interruption to trains by guards under pretense of examining passes, the following note was sent to the officer in command, which produced the desired effect:

ALEXANDRIA, November 8, 1862.

Colonel Wendell, of New Jersey Volunteers.

SIR: Last night, in returning to Alexandria from General McClellan's Headquarters in special train, I was stopped by guards near Edsall's under command of Captain Plunt, who informed me that he had instructions from you to stop all trains and examine passes of all persons thereon.

As this action is in violation of the orders of the Commander-in-Chief, I suppose it results from ignorance of those orders, and I therefore send you the following, addressed to myself:

"No military officer will give any orders to your subordinates, except through you; nor will any of them attempt to interfere with the running of the trains.

H. W. HALLECK."

It remains for me to say that the stoppage of trains when under full headway on the main track for the purpose of examining passes, or for any other purpose, cannot be permitted. Passes should be examined at stations, and I will afford every facility in my power to enforce proper regulations in this regard.

If, notwithstanding this communication, you intend to persist in stopping trains, please send me copy of the orders under which you are acting, that I may bring the subject to the notice of the General-in-Chief. An immediate answer is requested, which please return by bearer.

Very respectfully yours,

H. HAUPT,

Brigadier-General,

In Charge of United States Military Railroads.

In the attempt to re-establish transportation on the line of the railroad, more trouble was often given by our own soldiers than by the enemy. Camps had been established near the road and near the stations. Soldiers would tear up sidings, break switch-stands, burn the wood provided for the engines, wash clothes and persons with soap in the springs and streams which supplied the water stations, and many engines were stopped on the road by foaming boilers caused by soapy water. In consequence of these annoyances and the delays consequent thereon, a stringent special order was issued by the Secretary of War.

ALEXANDRIA, November 9, 1862, 9:15 P. M.

General Haupt:

The sidings at Camp Upton, on Loudon & Hampshire Railroad, have been destroyed by our own soldiers so as to render them unfit for use until repaired. Other acts of vandalism occur daily along the line of Orange & Alexandria Railroad, such as wasting water and burning all the wood distributed at stations. I sent to Manassas yesterday wood sufficient to last until Tuesday; it was all consumed this evening.

Broad Run bridge was finished this evening and trains will leave Manassas to-morrow morning at 6 o'clock to run through to Warrenton Junction, repairing track, etc., on the way up. I go to Manassas to-night.

J. J. MOORE.

WASHINGTON, November 4, 1862.

Major-General Heintzelman.

SIR: I reported to Major-General McClellan, in reply to a call for information, that the capacity of the Orange & Alexandria Railroad, with the equipments at our command, without accident or detention, was from 700 to 900 tons per day. The demands, I find, will exceed 1,500 tons per day. We have taken 200 cars from other roads and must procure 350 cars in addition. We have lost 402 cars captured, or destroyed, and we have now less than 300, only part of which are available. Demands are made daily for troop transportation which I have directed the Superintendent to refuse if it will interfere with the transportation of supplies. As the road is in bad order and detention and blockades may occur, I recommend the establishment of a depot at Manassas sufficient for three days, if we occupy it in such strength that we cannot be driven out.

I learn that there is not a guard on the road between Fairfax Station and Union Mills, although we have five bridges in that interval. I do not know that the line of the Occoquan is watched, and you may consider it officious if I inquire, but I have heretofore considered it my duty to look after everything which affected the safe and efficient operation of the railroads under my charge.

General McDowell, when in command, directed the officers in command of guards to confer with me in regard to details. If you will inform me whose duty it is to attend to these details, I will communicate directly with that officer and relieve you of any further annoyance.

Efforts should be made to prevent, if possible, the destruction of the bridges between Manassas and the Rappahannock; also the bridges between Rectortown and Markham on the Manassas Gap Railroad.

I may, perhaps, appear to you officious in making so many inquiries and suggestions in regard to the protection of the road and bridges, but, as the successor of General Banks, I consider it my duty to consult with you as I did and was directed to do with him.

Our railroad men, although unarmed and defenseless, do not shirk any duty, however hazardous, if I direct them to proceed. They have occupied the most exposed positions; some of them have been killed and some captured, but we cannot afford to risk them unnecessarily. Their places cannot readily be supplied, and I have therefore presumed to inquire as to the arrangements for guarding the roads and the numbers, positions and instructions of the forces detailed for this duty, in order that I might be able to give directions and assurances to our men based on a personal knowledge of the facts.

Before ordering our men to exposed positions, I wished to feel satisfied that such reasonable and proper arrangements had been planned for their protection as circumstances would permit, and that instructions had been actually carried out, guards and outposts in position, before commencing railroad transportation or construction.

At our last interview you remarked that the officers sent to guard the roads would no doubt attend to their business, and that you could not go yourself, from which I inferred that my frequent calls upon you were becoming annoying; but excuse me for saying that from past experience I have but little confidence that the lines will be guarded properly, unless specific instructions are given as to the positions to be occupied in advance, the forces required, and manner in which the duty is to be performed. It is also desirable, even if not absolutely necessary, that the officer in charge of the construction and operation of the roads should know what the arrangements are. If you think it not improper that I should have this information, and will suggest any way of obtaining it, other than by calling upon yourself, I will refrain from trespassing upon your time. Very respectfully submitted,

H. HAUPT,
In Charge of Construction and Operation
United States Military Railroads.

November 6, 1862.

P. H. Watson, Assistant Secretary of War.

Dear Sir: Mr. Moore, engineer of tracks, telegraphs that he has been over the road beyond Piedmont, over the Goose Creek bridges, and found everything all right.

I go to Rectortown to see General McClellan to-morrow.

We will have tough times on the railroad. You recollect the difficulty of supplying General McDowell's army and the confusion that reigned for some time. That was in June, when grass could be obtained; now 60,000 animals must be fed exclusively by rail, and General McClellan's requirements for transportation are four or five times as great as McDowell's. Never before, perhaps, has a single-track railroad, of such limited capacity, been so severely taxed, and if we can succeed in forwarding necessary supplies, it will only be by most extraordinary good management and good luck combined. Expect plenty of grumbling, but I shall go ahead. Yours truly, H. HAUPT.

ALEXANDRIA, November 8, 1862.

P. H. Watson, Assistant Secretary of War.

SIR: I have just returned from Headquarters of General McClellan, and report as follows:

Of the cars sent over the Manassas Gap Railroad but few had been unloaded and returned. Even the places for depots had not been determined upon. Of course, the movements of the line were blocked. No more cars could be sent until those in advance were unloaded and returned.

At a conference with General McClellan and Colonels Ingalls and Clark last night, the whole subject of transportation was discussed, explained and, I think, understood; and if arrangements then and there made and ordered to be carried out are conformed to, there will be no trouble about supplies in future. I was gratified to receive the assurance from both the Chief Quartermaster and the Chief Commissary that there had been no suffering or inconvenience from deficiency of supplies up to the present time. The details of arrangements it is unnecessary to trouble you with. It is sufficient to say that they were satisfactory to all parties.

The propriety of reconstructing the Fredericksburg Railroad was considered, and a reconnoissance ordered to ascertain the exact present condition of the bridges. I will go personally to see what can be done towards reconstructing the wharf, or providing a substitute.

By obstructing temporarily the passage for vessels, we have been able to run cars and engines over the Long Bridge without much interruption. Yesterday, in consequence of the high wind, but little progress could be made in driving piles, but I am informed that the work will be advanced so far as to permit the passage of boats to-night.

A construction party was sent to Broad Run, and the bridges will be reconstructed to-day.

Trains are daily stopped by guards about five miles from Alexandria under the pretense of examining passes; this must not be permitted. I cannot ascertain what general officer, if any, ordered it. I have sent a communication to the officer in command, and if the practice is not discontinued, I will take such further action as may appear to be necessary. Yours very respectfully, H. HAUPT.

The last telegram that I find among my records from General McClellan is dated November 7, on which day he probably received notice that he had been relieved. I had been confidentially advised of the change of commanders by Assistant Secretary Watson, and had brought out the bearer of dispatches, General Wadsworth, I think, in a special train.

I took supper with McClellan that evening in his tent, and he seemed to be entirely ignorant at the time of the fact that, within one hour, he would be relieved. He was speaking to me of proposed operations, which I knew he would have no opportunity to carry into effect.

General McClellan always treated me with kindness and consideration, and my suggestions in regard to the lines of communication, by which his army could be best supplied, were approved and acted upon. I felt a warm sympathy for the pain he must experience when the intelligence of his removal should reach him. Personally, I esteemed General McClellan highly, but as a commander he was too slow and his caution excessive. He did not wish to move until he could strike with positive certainty. When all the reinforcements and supplies he invariably asked for had been furnished, he would continue to ask for something more, something else, until the patience of the President, following that of Secretary Stanton, became completely exhausted.

General McClellan has been severely criticised for allowing Lee to cross the Potomac and escape after the battle of Antietam, but I am not prepared to say that, under the conditions then existing, it could have been prevented.

If General McClellan had been aware of Lee's intended movements; if he had himself been free from any apprehension of attack and could have detached safely a considerable portion of his force to occupy the south bank of the Potomac with artillery and destroy the bridges, then Lee might have been captured; but the retreat was made so promptly that the enemy had crossed before McClellan was aware of the fact.

Of course, it was natural to suppose that, after his defeat at Antietam, when Lee had moved south to the Potomac, he would recross the river. It is possible, therefore, that if McClellan had immediately placed the main body of his army in a defensible position on the river below Lee, and thrown a part of his force on the south side, he might have prevented the escape; but there were few Generals who were capable of moving with the celerity that this would have required, for in two days after the battle Lee's extraordinary activity had landed him safely on the soil of Virginia, while McClellan was actually expecting a renewal of the battle on the north side!

CHAPTER VII.

OPERATIONS UNDER MAJOR-GENERAL
A. E. BURNSIDE.

I ACCOMPANIED General Halleck, at his request, to the Headquarters of General Burnside, and after he had been placed in command no time was lost by me in informing him of the condition of the railroads, upon which he was dependent for supplies, and the absolute necessity of proper order and system in their operation. He assented to the propriety of the positions taken, and gave assurances that he would coöperate in all measures to promote safety and efficiency, yet there was no other commander of any of the armies with which I was connected, who so frequently forgot his promises and caused so much delay and embarrassment by giving orders to subordinates in conflict with instructions from the head of the Department.

On the next day the following communication was sent to General Burnside:

WASHINGTON, November 9, 1862.

Major-General Burnside:

Arrangements in regard to transportation were fully discussed, explanations made, and a program determined upon between General McClellan, his chief Quartermaster and Commissary, and myself previous to his removal. As you are now in chief command, I think it proper to report to you and ask instructions in regard to certain points.

The road by which your army is to be supplied is a single track, without sidings sufficient for long trains, without wood and with insufficient supply of water, a road which has heretofore failed to supply an army of one-fourth the size of that which you command, a road, the ordinary working capacity of which is not equal to the half of your requirements, but which, by a combination of good management and good fortune, may be able to furnish your supplies. To do this, it is absolutely necessary that at each and every depot a force should be in readiness to unload a train as soon as it arrives; the contents of cars must be unloaded on the ground and afterwards moved, if necessary, to more convenient points. The force should be sufficient to unload all the cars of a train at once.

Railway employes are required to be civil and accommodating, and if they are not, they will be promptly dismissed; but the convenience of local quartermasters and commissaries must give way before the requirements of a service far more imperative than it has ever been before. Trains have been frequently detained for hours to move supplies for very short distances to save handling. I desire respectfully but most urgently to impress upon you the importance of making your orders so imperative that they dare not be disobeyed, and that cars shall, on their arrival at each and every depot, be immediately unloaded and returned. I say again, that without this the supply of your army is impossible. No man living can accomplish it.

A second point to which I wish to direct your attention is the importance of establishing a depot of reserve supplies at Manassas to draw upon in case of any break in the road between Manassas and Alexandria, and as the army advances, depots at intervals of 30 or 40 miles should be made to guard against the consequences of breaks in the connection. If you advance far, the operation of the road will present greater difficulty; its protection against raids will be almost impossible, and the breaks of connection will become frequent from various causes not dependent on the movement of the enemy.

The difficulty of operating a long line of railroad, with an exposed flank, satisfies me that the reconstruction of the Fredericksburg Railroad, so uselessly destroyed, is a military necessity. If this is your opinion, please advise me of the fact, that no time may be lost in preparation. The last time I spoke to General Halleck on this subject, he said that the question of reconstructing this road was not settled; when it was, he would advise me. Since then I have not heard from him, but I am sure that when you advance the Orange & Alexandria Railroad alone will be a very insecure reliance.

The subject of guarding the railroad is a very important one, but no detention of trains by guards on any pretense should be permitted. The proper protection of the road between Alexandria and Manassas requires that the line of the Occoquan should be well watched.

As other duties will prevent me from seeing you for some days, I hope you will not consider these suggestions and statements as out of place.

H. HAUPT,
Brigadier-General,
In Charge of Construction and Operation of
United States Military Railroads.

November 10, 8 A. M.

General Haupt:

Your dispatch received and suggestions approved, for which I am much obliged. I send to General Halleck special messenger to-day with plan of operations. Please get from General Cullum a copy of my suggestions as to the Acquia Creek Road, sent some days ago from Pleasant Valley, and get ready for the work on that road. Don't fail to send me at any time your views.

A. E. BURNSIDE,
Major-General Commanding.

In order to make my plans as nearly absolutely effective as possible, Secretary Stanton issued the following:

WAR DEPARTMENT,
WASHINGTON, November 10, 1862.

SPECIAL ORDER.

I. Commanding officers of troops along the Orange & Alexandria Railroad will give all facilities to the officers of the road and the Quartermaster for loading and unloading cars, so as to prevent any delay. On arrival at depots, whether in the day or night, the cars will be instantly unloaded, and working parties will always be in readiness for that duty, and sufficient to unload the whole train at once. Commanding officers will be charged with guarding the track, sidings, wood, water tanks, etc., within their several commands, and will be held responsible for the result. Any military officer who shall neglect his duty in this respect will be reported by the Quartermasters and officers of the railroad, and his name will be stricken from the rolls of the army.

II. Depots will be established at suitable points under the direction of the Commanding General of the Army of the Potomac, and properly guarded.

III. No officer, whatever may be his rank, will interfere with the running of the cars, as directed by the Superintendent of the road. Any one who so interferes will be dismissed from the service for disobedience of orders.

By order of the Secretary of War.

J. C. KELTON.

Instructions were given to W. W. Wright to prepare for the reconstruction of the wharves at Acquia Creek and the road to Fredericksburg. It was recommended that several regiments of infantry, some cavalry, and a couple of gunboats be sent to protect the working parties, and that canal barges be collected upon which to remove loaded cars from Alexandria as soon as General Halleck gave authority for the commencement of the work.

On November 11, requisition was made upon the Quartermaster for a large number of Schuylkill barges, pile-drivers, piles, scows, boats and anchors.

On the same day General Halleck notified General Burnside to arrange for a meeting with him the next day, and that General Meigs and General Haupt would accompany him, asking General Burnside also to carefully consider the views of the President as expressed in a letter of September 13, of which he inclosed a copy, that it might be talked over understandingly when they met.

At this interview, at which I was present by request of General Halleck, General Burnside expressed a strong disinclination to take the command. He said: "I am not fit for it. There are many more in the army better fitted than I am; but if you and the President insist, I will take it and do the best I can."

After other matters were settled, I endeavored to impress upon the General the absolute necessity of preventing military interference with the trains, and the importance of prompt unloading and returning of cars.

On November 12, 1862, an order was received from the Secretary of War to give receipt for property delivered to railroads for transportation.

CONFEDERATE MODE OF DESTROYING RAILROAD TRACK.

WASHINGTON, November 12, 1862.

Brigadier-General H. Haupt, United States Volunteers.

SIR: The Secretary of War directs that you instruct your agents to give receipts for all supplies heretofore turned over to them for transportation to the staff officers accountable for such supplies.

I am, sir, very respectfully, your obedient servant,

E. D. TOWNSEND,
Assistant Adjutant-General.

Attempts had been made previously by officers, both of the Quartermaster and Commissary Department, to induce our agents to give receipts for Government property. Such requests were simply absurd and unreasonable. The Railway Department was charged simply with the construction and operation of roads, not with the custody of property.

Had the Secretary gone outside of his interested army officers, as he finally did, for advice on this point he would not have committed the error of issuing such an order. On receipt of it, I immediately sent the following reply:

WASHINGTON, November 13, 1862.

Hon. E. M. Stanton, Secretary of War.

SIR: A communication this day received, signed E. D. Townsend, Assistant Adjutant-General, informs me that by your direction I am instructed to require my agents to receipt for all supplies heretofore turned over to them for transportation to the staff officer accountable for such supplies.

It affords me pleasure at all times to comply with your wishes and carry out your instructions, but if impediments exist, or if I am cognizant of material facts which I have reason to believe you are unacquainted with, I consider it my duty to suspend action, report the facts, and ask instructions.

The object of the receipt is, of course, to relieve the officers of the Commissary and Quartermaster Department of all responsibility after the cars are loaded, and it is perfectly right and proper that they should have such relief, but it does not appear to be right to throw the responsibility upon a railway superintendent, who has nothing to do with loading or unloading the cars, no opportunity of examining their contents, and no power to protect them when on the road.

Even guards themselves, I am informed, have broken into cars containing hospital stores and appropriated stimulants.

The responsibilities and labors of the superintendents are very great, and I could not find really competent men who would be willing to accept the position if they were increased, as proposed.

Very respectfully submitted,

H. HAUPT,
In Charge of United States Military Railroads.

This communication was followed by a personal interview with the Secretary, in which he declined to recede from his position, and insisted that the order should be complied with. I therefore sent the following next morning:

WASHINGTON, November 15, 1862.

Hon. E. M. Stanton, Secretary of War.

SIR: Since my conversation with you last evening, I have given the subject of freight receipts further consideration, and the more I reflect upon it, the greater do the difficulties appear.

The cars are loaded and unloaded by the Quartermaster, and the custody of the contents does not, as I have understood it, pass out of that Department. The cars can be locked by the Quartermaster; he can seal them as cars of through freights are sealed in the West; he can send his own special agent with each train to deliver to and secure receipts from the consignee and to report any loss by robbery or otherwise that may occur upon the route.

The duties of railway employes are, or ought to be, confined simply to the movements of the trains, not to the custody of the contents of the cars, and the transfer of responsibility to them, instead of increasing the security of the Government, would, on the contrary, impair it greatly.

Suppose the present representatives of the Quartermaster's Department should be succeeded by gentlemen whose integrity was less unquestionable, and they should ask for and receive receipts from the railway managers for a greater quantity of stores than had been loaded in the cars, the doors would be open to fraud to an unlimited extent, and the temptation might, in some cases, be too strong for human weakness.

Suppose the transfer of custody should take place and a deficiency be discovered upon delivery, the value of that deficiency could not be recovered from the railway employes or agents, and if you should proceed a step farther and require them to give bonds, they could not comply, for no responsible party with a knowledge of the facts would ever enter into bonds.

If security is required of railway agents, they could only protect themselves by placing a careful and incorruptible representative at each and every car that is loaded by day or night, but even this would not be sufficient; it would afford a check only on the number of packages, none whatever upon the contents and weights. It would be further necessary to weigh every package and examine contents before the check could be complete. Such an arrangement would require a large addition to the force of employes, would be expensive, would cause great inconvenience and delay, and there would still be an opening for fraud by collusion between the two classes of employes.

I think the enclosed order would simply, effectually, and economically dispose of the whole difficulty.

One remark more appears to be proper. If the railroad were managed by the Quartermaster's Department, as was at one time proposed, it would have been necessary, either to send supplies over the road without receipts, or send an officer in charge to give and receive them. This is precisely what I now propose, and have several times previously proposed should be done, and which the consignors have had the privilege of doing at any and all times. The mere fact that the trains are moved by a set of employes, trained and skilled in that particular service, should not affect in any way the responsibilities of the shippers and receivers. The movement of a car does not necessarily involve responsibility for its contents.

The above remarks and suggestions are very respectfully submitted.

H. HAUPT,
In Charge of United States Military Railroads.

"Ordered: That the agents and employes of the United States Military Railroads shall have no control or responsibility for the contents of cars containing supplies, such supplies shall not pass out of the custody of the consignor until delivered to and receipted for by the consignee.

"The consignor shall be permitted, at his discretion, to seal or lock any cars containing stores that might be stolen, and to send a special agent with each train, who will report any robbery to the proper officer."

Mr. Stanton sent for Assistant Secretary Watson to come and read my communication and give his opinion. Watson said I was right. This did not seem to satisfy the Secretary, who replied: "Take it to Meigs and see what he thinks of it." This was done and, after a perusal of the papers, they were returned with the remark: "I think General Haupt is entirely correct."

When this was repeated to the Secretary he jumped from his seat, as Watson told me, paced the room for some time, and then stopping in front of him said: "To rescind this order will make me ridiculous. I issued a peremptory order, and will not take it back; but if you and Meigs say that it cannot be enforced, go to Haupt and tell him to consider it a dead letter."

The scheme was a nice one for those who had charge of Government property to throw the responsibility upon the Railroad Bureau, and hold its officers accountable for shortages. It would have been easier to settle accounts in this way than by burning depots, a plan resorted to occasionally.

No further efforts were made to extort receipts from the Military Railroad Department.

The reconstruction of the wharves and track from Acquia Creek to Fredericksburg was prosecuted with unprecedented expedition. It was on November 10 that I directed W. W. Wright to hold himself in readiness to commence work so soon as General Halleck should decide upon its necessity. It was November 11 when a telegram was sent to Colonel Belger at Baltimore to provide canal boats, and five days later, November 17, considerable progress had already been made in the work of reconstruction. The Superintendent reported that, in five days after commencement, a section of the wharf 1,000 feet long was completed, and a locomotive and cars landed and trains commenced running to Potomac Creek. In five days more trains were running to the Rappahannock.

The Schuylkill barges answered admirably, and thus was formed a new era in Military Railroad transportation. Two of these barges were placed parallel to each other and long timbers bolted transversely. The length of the barges was sufficient for eight tracks carrying eight cars, and two such floats would carry the sixteen cars which constituted a train.

In this way hundreds of loaded cars were transferred from the advanced position of the Army, on the Orange & Alexandria Railroad, loaded on the floats, towed sixty miles to Acquia Creek, transferred from river to rail, and sent to Falmouth without break of bulk, in about the same time required to march the army across the country by land. Supplies were at Falmouth as soon as there were forces there for their protection.

WASHINGTON, D. C., November 17, 1862.

Major-General Burnside:

I have just returned from Acquia Creek. Some stores were on transports yesterday afternoon ready to be landed at Belle Plain. Several companies of the Engineer brigade on transports are probably now ashore. The wharf at Acquia is not entirely burned, but is worst where the track was located. I have ordered the track to be moved over and reconstructed on the side least damaged. Cars and engines will be loaded immediately and sent to Acquia to be unloaded as soon as the track will bear their weight.

Eight small cars will be sent to-day, landed by lighters, loaded with tents, tools and rations, pushed by hand to the broken bridges, and accompanied by carpenters with escort of Engineer troops to have bridges repaired, if possible, by the time cars and engines are landed and put on track. As soon as bridges are repaired and even five or six cars landed, we will begin to run in supplies to Falmouth to relieve wagons to that extent, and increase daily.

The construction of a floating wharf or new pile wharf at Acquia is not a question for present consideration while time is so much of an object. New construction could not be made in double the time required for repairs of former structure. A machine shop will be extemporized at Acquia by sending lathe, planer, portable engine, small tools and shafting. Army forges will be furnished to smithshops.

H. HAUPT.

A very costly irregularity in military detail is treated in the following communication:

WASHINGTON, November 18, 1862.

Hon. E. M. Stanton, Secretary of War.

SIR: The Superintendent of the Orange & Alexandria Railroad, in his daily report of operations, states that 142 cars were yesterday and last night returned loaded from Warrenton and other stations.

I call your attention to this fact as indicating the probable existence of an evil which requires a corrective. While the Railway Department has been making the most extraordinary efforts, day and night, to forward supplies represented as necessary, to enable the army to move forward, requisitions have been made and filled for articles which appear to be entirely unnecessary, and which, when the army moves, must be reloaded and sent back, or, as has been frequently the case in exposed positions, destroyed by the application of the torch. The 142 cars returned loaded in the recent movement have a capacity of 2,800,000 pounds—equivalent to six days' rations of three pounds each of 150,000 men, or its equal in weight in other supplies.

The fact of returning so large an amount unused, would seem to indicate an excessive supply for the army at a time when it was only awaiting a sufficient supply to enable it to advance, but owing to inequalities of distribution, this excess had probably not been general, and has not been a consequence of necessary depot requirements. Some regiments or brigades may have had, and I understand have had, an excess, and others a deficiency.

The irregularity of distribution appears to be an evil vitally affecting the efficiency of the army, and results apparently from the fact that the authority to make requisitions is not sufficiently centralized. Each Quartermaster acts independently, and with the approval of his immediate superior; sends orders which are filled, without regard to any rules of priority. Hence, it may follow that Quartermasters who are most frequent and most importunate in their applications may receive an excess beyond their power properly and economically to use, while others may not procure that which is absolutely necessary for the troops which it is their duty to supply.

The avoidance of these very serious evils may be difficult, and I may not comprehend all that is in the way; but with my present information the remedy would appear to be both simple and practical. It consists in requiring all Quartermasters and Commissaries in an Army Corps to make their requisitions through one staff officer, who should keep a record of such requisitions and be able to ascertain at a glance the supplies that have been delivered to each regiment and their comparative necessities.

At the principal depots the requisitions of the different Army Corps could in like manner be equalized, and the deliveries proportioned to the numerical strength and actual requirements of each Corps.

As the armies in the field are mainly supplied by rail, and as the responsibilities of rail transportation devolve chiefly upon myself, these suggestions, designed to promote the efficiency of the service in this Department, will not, I trust, be deemed officious or impertinent.

Yours very respectfully,

H. HAUPT,
In Charge of Construction and Operation
United States Military Railroads.

WASHINGTON, November 17, 1862.
Wm. W. Wright, Esq., Superintendent R. F. & P. R. R.:

In resuming operations on the Richmond, Fredericksburg & Potomac Railroad you will conform to the following instructions:

Your position will be that of Superintendent of the Richmond, Fredericksburg & Potomac Railroad, and, until otherwise ordered, you will also perform the duties of engineer.

You will nominate and, with my approval, appoint, assistants and employes, and fix their compensations, which shall not exceed the rates heretofore paid on other Military Railroads.

Employes now in service of Military Railway Department, who can be transferred, to have preference over new appointees.

Requisitions for material or supplies to be made through the Quartermaster, unless the amount is small or the necessities urgent. Such requisitions should be submitted to Colonel D. C. McCallum for approval.

Time of employes, certified by you, to be returned to the paymaster.

Trains to be run on former schedule and in convoys in preference to extras. Force to be sufficient to unload a whole train at once; if not, the fact and names of officers to be reported. See Special Order 337 and circular, the instructions in which are to be conformed to.

Transportation to be commenced as soon as an engine and a few cars can be landed. The train, so long as there is but a single one, will run without regard to schedule, as rapidly as cars can be loaded and unloaded. There must be no intermission day or night. When a second engine is landed, one can run by day and one at night. Until fifty or sixty cars are delivered, you will not require a third engine.

The details of construction and the order of priority have been discussed, and you have my views. I will only say, work all the force upon the wharf that is possible. If boats cannot be procured, make floats. Put up no buildings until the wharf is finished. Let the forwarding of supplies be the first consideration, and personal convenience the last.

Yours respectfully,

H. HAUPT,
In Charge of United States Military Railroads.

November 18, 1862.

Major-General Burnside:

In resuming transportation southward from Acquia Creek, certain matters will require your attention, which I think should be regulated by orders from Headquarters.

Passes—I forbid the Superintendent of the Military Railroads to give any passes except to employes. All other passes must be given by the military authorities. The ordinary practice has been for the Provost Marshal of Washington or Alexandria to give passes to Acquia Creek. The commandant at the post gives passes to Fredericksburg, which are examined by a guard at the depot. This system is perhaps as good as any, if officers acting as aides to Provost Marshals will cease to scatter these passes broadcast, as has been too often the case.

Newspapers—Newspaper boys traveling daily on trains are an unnecessary nuisance. The proper plan is for the Superintendent to forward the bundles of papers properly directed to a local agent, by whom they can be distributed.

Smuggling—Large quantities of contraband goods have no doubt been sent over the road by Jews, sutlers and others, marked with the names of officers. Just before General Pope's retreat I procured the issuing of an order that all such packages should be delivered by the railway agents to the Provost Marshal, who would deliver to the party named thereon only upon a written declaration that the package contained the private property of the individual, and nothing else, such declaration not to interfere with the right of examination, and when the amounts were excessive, the facts were to be reported to the General in command.

These are some of the abuses which only stringent orders, faithfully executed by Provost Marshals, can prevent. I respectfully report them for your consideration and action.

H. HAUPT,
In Charge of United States Military Railroads.

On November 17, a telegram from General Burnside expressed gratification at progress at Acquia Creek, and informed me that General Sumner would occupy Falmouth that night.

At this time the advanced positions on the line of the Orange & Alexandria Railroad had been abandoned, and the officer in command of the rear guard applied for a train to remove his men and material. General Burnside, having decided that the road was no longer safe, the officer was directed to use his wagons, horses and legs.

On November 22, I sent a telegram in cipher to General Burnside, making certain suggestions which I thought worthy of consideration: To cross the river and occupy Fredericksburg and the strong position on the height before the enemy could concentrate.

There may have been good reasons for not taking this course, and General Burnside was in a far better position to know the whole situation than myself. The movement may have been impracticable or inexpedient at that time, and I knew that General Burnside would not act on any suggestion from me, unless his own judgment approved, and if there might be assurance, there would at least be no harm in making suggestions.

If this movement could have been made at the time indicated instead of waiting until the enemy had concentrated and occupied a position which the natural topography made almost impregnable, the result of the battle of Fredericksburg, if fought at all, might have been very different.

November 22, 1862.

Major-General Burnside:

Several days must elapse before the railroad to Fredericksburg can be reconstructed, several days more before, in addition to daily supplies, ten or twelve days' rations can be accumulated in advance. Cars and engines must be transported from Alexandria and unloaded singly. This takes time.

Suppose your whole army should be thrown on the south side of the Rappahannock, communicating by boat and pontoon bridges, would it not cover and protect the navigation of the stream? Could not supplies of all kinds be sent by water to Fredericksburg in greater quantities and in shorter time than in any other way?

Could you not be prepared to advance much sooner than if dependent upon supplies exclusively by rail? If unsuccessful, could you not retire behind the Rappahannock, by which time a full depot would be formed at Falmouth? If successful, could you not draw supplies from White House or James River while we reconstruct the road to Richmond for the purpose of daily communication with Washington?

I make these suggestions reluctantly. You have no doubt considered them already. If you have or have not, they can do no harm.

H. HAUPT.

November 29, 1862, a communication was sent to Quartermaster-General Meigs giving an estimate of the saving to be effected by the plan of transportation adopted by the Military Railroad Department in the substitution of barges for steamboats at the price then paid, which saving was at the rate of $1,352,000 per annum, between Alexandria and Acquia Creek.

On December 2, an officer sent to inquire into the condition of the Army Corps as regards supplies, reported to General Burnside that all the Corps were supplied liberally, and one of them had rations for seventeen days in advance.

Telegram to General Burnside:

December 5, 1862.

Major-General Burnside:

General Ingalls telegraphs this morning in regard to railroad iron, and says it is your wish to have some afloat to be taken up the Rappahannock.

Is this the best practical arrangement? If rails are taken by water to Fredericksburg, they cannot be loaded and transported on the railroad without cars and engines, and cars and engines cannot be procured until the bridge is finished. If we wait for the bridge, we can send the iron ready loaded to where we may wish to use it, without a transhipment at Fredericksburg, which would be very troublesome. If the idea is to haul by wagons from Fredericksburg, in case the track is torn up near that place, it will be almost as convenient to haul from Falmouth over the wagon bridge, which must necessarily be built in the event of our getting possession of the city. In any event, I do not perceive that the sending of rails by water to Fredericksburg is necessary, but it shall be done if you desire it.

My latest information is that the rebels were still running trains to Fredericksburg; if so, the track is not yet torn up, and if you turn their position, the retreat of the enemy will probably be too precipitate to permit them to do much damage.

Although we have probably iron enough, I will order ten miles more immediately to make sure. Please show this telegram to General Ingalls to avoid the necessity of repeating it to him.

H. HAUPT.

WASHINGTON, December 19, 1862.

To Agents and other Employes of the United States Military Railroad Department:

Complaints have been made that employes of the United States Military Railroads do not treat officers with respect; that they are uncivil, offensive in their language, and unaccommodating.

While I appreciate the difficult position in which officers of the Military Railroad Department are placed during a period of active operations, their incessant labors night and day, and the innumerable sources of difficulty and annoyance from which ordinary railroads are exempt, I wish it distinctly to be understood, that no profanity, incivility, or indisposition to accommodate will be permitted; but if complaints are made by officers, which, on investigation, shall be proven to be well founded, the offender will be removed as soon as a properly qualified substitute can be found to perform his duties.

While conscious of no disposition to shield the employes or agents of the Military Railroads from any censure or punishment that is really merited, justice to them requires me to state that, so far, examination has shown that complaints against them have been generally without proper foundation; and when demands were not promptly complied with, the cause has been inability, arising from want of proper notice, and not indisposition.

STRAIGHTENING SLIGHT BENDS IN RAILS BY USE OF JACK-SCREW.

Officers at posts entrusted with the performance of certain local duties, and anxious, as they generally are, to discharge them efficiently, are not always able, or disposed, to look beyond their own particular spheres; they expect demands on railway agents to be promptly complied with, without considering that similar demands at the same time, in addition to the regular train service and routine duties, may come from Quartermasters, Commissaries, Medical Directors, Surgeons, Ordnance Officers, the Commanding General, the War Department, and from other sources. The Military Railroads have utterly failed to furnish transportation to even one-fifth of their capacity, when managed without a strict conformity to schedule and established rules. Punctuality and discipline are even more important to the operation of a railroad, than to the movements of an army, and they are vital in both.

If all cars, on their arrival at a depot, are immediately loaded or unloaded and returned, and trains are run to schedule, a single track road, in good order and properly equipped, may supply an army of 200,-000 men, when, if these conditions are not complied with, the same road will not supply 30,000.

Let it be understood that requisitions for cars should always be made with sufficient notice *through* the Quartermaster, and *to* the Superintendent or his representatives, the agents at stations. In time of action, it is sometimes necessary to suspend the use of the road for supply trains, and hold it for the exclusive use of ammunition. Orders to this effect must come from the Chief Quartermaster of the Army, or the Commanding General, to the Superintendent; no other orders will be respected by him which conflict with the regular operation of the road.

Attention is directed to the following extracts from orders of Major-General Halleck, addressed to myself:

"No military officer will give any orders to your subordinates except through you, nor will any of them attempt to interfere with the running of the trains.

"In case of an attack upon the road, you will consult the commander of the nearest forces.

"The railroad is entirely under your control. No military officer has any right to interfere with it. Your orders are supreme."

While no officer has any right to interfere with or interrupt the regular business of the road, by detaining trains or otherwise, employes will be expected to comply with every reasonable request of officers, when not incompatible with prescribed duty, and answer questions with civility.

To avoid unnecessary interruption to answer questions in regard to the time of starting trains, a clock should be conspicuously placed at each station, and several notices posted giving the necessary information.

The aides of the Commanding General and the train dispatcher can be admitted to the telegraph offices; all others must be excluded. As messages are read by sound, no loud conversation can be permitted. Officers and soldiers crowding into telegraph offices have been a source of serious annoyance. In all such cases, operators will seek the protection of the Provost Marshal and ask for a guard.

H. HAUPT,
Brigadier-General,
Chief of Construction and Transportation,
United States Military Railroads.

A few days before the battle of Fredericksburg a gentleman called at my office and announced his name as Rev. Alexander Reed, General Agent of the Christian Commission. He stated that some carloads of hospital supplies had been sent to the front, and that it was a matter of the greatest importance that he should attend to the distribution, or all would be lost; that he had applied for a pass to the President, the Secretary of War, to General Halleck and to the Military Governor of Washington, but he had been refused, as all passes had been prohibited, and no exception would be made, however urgent the necessity. He wished to know if I could not give him a pass.

I asked him how he expected to get a pass from me when my superiors had positively refused him. He did not know, but hoped that some way could be discovered, as the stores were very valuable, and if lost, the Christian Commission would be discouraged from future efforts. I appreciated the situation, and turning to my desk wrote a few lines:

"Alexander Reed is hereby appointed brakeman in the service of the Military Railroad Department, and will enter upon his duties forthwith. He is directed to report without delay at Falmouth. He will be furnished transportation by boat and rail, and this order will be recognized as a pass by all guards."

I handed the note to the reverend gentleman, who seemed puzzled, and asked what it meant, saying that he did not understand the duties of brakeman. I replied: "It means that in no other capacity can I send you to the front. When you get to Falmouth, if you do not like the service you can resign."

Some years after the war I attended evening service at the First Presbyterian Church at Pittsburg. The pastor, Rev. William Paxton, D.D., was an old acquaintance. The pulpit was filled that evening by Rev. Alexander Reed. After service I remained to have some conversation with the pastor, who introduced his friend, Dr. Reed.

I remarked that I had met the gentleman before. Dr. Reed looked at me with some surprise and said that he was not aware that he had ever had the pleasure of meeting me previously.

I replied: "Perhaps you are ashamed to acknowledge that you once held the position of brakeman on a Military Railroad." This recalled the incident, which was related, much to the amusement of my friend.

This recalls another incident, which illustrates the annoyances caused by ladies who would sometimes get passes to meet their husbands before an expected engagement. During McDowell's forced march to Front Royal, I had ordered several trains of supplies, expected to arrive during the night at Rectortown, to move forward four miles to Piedmont by daylight. I was waiting at Piedmont for them, but as they did not arrive, I walked towards Rectortown to meet them. I did not find them until that station was reached, where they were still standing on the track.

I asked the conductor why he had not obeyed orders, and was told that the wife of a prominent officer had been a passenger on the train and had gone to a farmhouse to seek accommodations for the night. I ordered him to start at once, but just then an elegantly dressed lady came tripping across the field to take her place in one of the cars. I did not display extra gallantry on the occasion, nor even offer the lady assistance. She had detained four trains for three hours during a period of urgency, and I was not in an amiable mood.

CHAPTER VIII.

BATTLE OF FREDERICKSBURG.

ON December 11, I received a telegram at Washington from General J. G. Parke, Chief of Staff: "Our troops now occupy Fredericksburg. The bridge material can now be forwarded as rapidly as possible." I sent the following at once:

WASHINGTON, December 11, 1862.
W. W. Wright, Acquia Creek:
    I leave here to-morrow morning for Acquia Creek. Make all possible preparations for the immediate construction of the bridge on the Rappahannock.
                                                            H. HAUPT.

Wright was also instructed to load the cars and send them up that night and have E. C. Smeed in readiness to commence the bridge at daylight.

I reached Falmouth on the 12th, and secured from General Burnside a detail of 200 men to assist in building the railroad bridge across the Rappahannock on the morning of December 13, but as soon as the fight commenced the soldiers all deserted and went to a neighboring hill overlooking the city, from which they could make observations.

Leaving Smeed and his civilians at work, I repaired to the Headquarters of General Burnside to report the situation and ask for more men to replace the deserters, but he replied that no more could be spared.

I then returned to the bridge and found it deserted. Not a human being was in sight in that vicinity.

I walked out to the end of the bridge, but could see no one. I returned to the cut at the end of the embankment, where I found my foreman behind a tree watching the fight across the river.

He explained that the ropes had been cut and the pulleys broken by the shells and that, as no work could be done, he and his men had followed the example of the soldiers, and skedaddled to the woods.

I told him it was all right; that civilians should not be expected to work under fire when nothing could be accomplished by it, and I then returned to Burnside's Headquarters, where I remained in the room with him all day, looking from a window over the battlefield and listening to reports as they came in.

The next day I returned to Washington, where I met Hon. John Covode, of Pennsylvania, and he went with me to see the President at about 9 P. M. The President was much interested in the report, and asked me to walk with him to General Halleck's quarters, then on I street, between 15th and 16th streets. When we arrived he requested Covode and others present to step into the next room, as he desired a private conference, and then asked me to repeat the substance of my report to him, which I did.

On its conclusion, the President asked General Halleck to telegraph orders to General Burnside to withdraw his army to the north side of the river. General Halleck rose and paced the room for some time, and then stopped, facing the President, and said decidedly: "I will do no such thing. If we were personally present and knew the exact situation, we might assume such responsibility. If such orders are issued, you must issue them yourself. I hold that a General in command of an army in the field is the best judge of existing conditions."

The President made no reply, but seemed much troubled. I then remarked that I did not consider the situation as critical as the President imagined it to be, and proceeded to describe more in detail the topographical configuration. There was a low flat, or plateau, near the river on which our troops were massed. Above this was a second more extensive plateau, on which the city was built, which completely masked the position of our army. Beyond this the ground rose gradually to Marye's Heights, where the enemy's batteries were posted. Our bridges could not be enfiladed by the batteries, and no attempt could be made to fire upon our troops without destroying the town, filled as it was with citizens, which the enemy would not attempt to do. I expressed a confident opinion that Burnside would withdraw his forces during the night, and that he could do it without loss or interference, and he did.

When I finished, the President sighed and said: "What you say gives me a great many grains of comfort."

The position General Halleck took on this occasion is one which, so far as my knowledge extends, he always maintained. He has been charged repeatedly with interference. It is an error. He would indicate to the commander of an army the objects to be accomplished, but would leave him untrammelled as far as details were concerned.

After the interview with the President and General Halleck, I made arrangements to return to Burnside's Headquarters. It was expected that another forward movement would soon be attempted, and, if successful, that a very rapid advance towards

Richmond would be made, requiring an expeditious reconstruction of the railroad and bridges, if the enemy in their retreat should destroy them.   I had a profile of the line and knew the dimensions of all the bridges, so that I had a clear idea of the work to be accomplished.   On the 14th the following dispatch was sent to General Burnside:

WASHINGTON, December 14, 1862.

Major-General Burnside:

I am using my best exertions to procure civilians to work on wharves and bridges, but they are gathered slowly.

General Halleck does not much favor my idea of forming a Construction and Transportation Corps of, say 500 civilians, for our work. He thinks that the Engineer troops, who have been enlisted and receive double pay for this particular duty, should attend to it.

If one of the Engineer regiments were placed under my orders, as a permanent detail, I could get them in time organized, drilled, and made efficient for bridge purposes, provided I could pick them and get rid of the drones; but civilians would be preferable.

If we get possession of the line beyond Fredericksburg, all the bridges should be started at once.   They should be reconstructed of sticks cut in the woods and hauled by oxen.   No dependence should be placed in the railroad for the transportation of material for them.   I have ordered 200 oxen with yokes to be in readiness.   Colonel Ingalls should provide ox chains and wheels, say 30 pairs, and 2,000 men can be employed and should be ready.   The Engineer brigades can alone furnish this force in time.   I leave to return to-night.   H. HAUPT.

Notwithstanding the assurances of General Burnside that the regular transportation should not be interfered with, he would frequently telegraph the Superintendent to hold a train for his accommodation, and then compel it to wait for several hours until he made his appearance.   This caused an abandonment of the schedule, and threw all the trains into confusion.

As a remedy I ordered that an engine, under steam, should be kept constantly at Falmouth subject to the General's orders.   On one occasion a train had become derailed, and the special engine had been sent to render assistance.   While absent on this service and, impatient of delay, General Burnside walked down the road to meet it.   As it was night, the engineer did not recognize him and passed him on the way, then returned, took him up and carried him to Acquia Creek.

Upon entering the office in an irate mood, he demanded of the Superintendent why he had disobeyed his orders.   Wright handed him my telegram, saying: "Here are my instructions," upon reading which the General turned on his heel with the remark: "This is a nice condition of things if the General in command of an army can be snubbed by a brigadier."   The General knew that the action was proper, and did not allude to it in any of our subsequent interviews.

On receiving the report of the Superintendent concerning this incident, the following answer was returned:

WASHINGTON, D. C., January 24, 1863.

Wm. W. Wright, Superintendent R., F. & P. R. R.

DEAR SIR: Your communication of yesterday, enclosing fourteen telegrams on the subject of the delay of a special train ordered for the accommodation of General Burnside, was received by messenger to-day. You report the fact that when a special train is required at a particular hour, the party is not always, and not even generally, ready to use it at that hour; that in the case referred to the train was ordered at 9:30 P. M., and the General did not arrive until 11:10 P. M. at the Falmouth depot; that an accident having occurred which blocked the road at Stoneman's, the engine of the special train was sent to clear it, and being away when General Burnside arrived, was the cause of much dissatisfaction.

You ask for instructions to govern your action in future cases that may occur, and desire to be informed whether the track is to be kept clear for a special train and all other business suspended until it has passed.

I answer unhesitatingly, no. The regular and most important duty of the railroads is to forward supplies to the army. To accomplish this, the most indispensable requisite is exact punctuality in running schedule trains. Every Superintendent knows this, but no one but the Superintendent of a Military Railroad can appreciate it to its full extent, or realize the difficulties which do not exist elsewhere.

General Burnside is one of the most reasonable and practical men I have ever met, and he will not expect impossibilities. He does not, with the multiplicity of his own duties, understand yours. All you have to do is to conform to the established rules, furnish extras whenever General Burnside orders them, if it is in your power to do so, but extras must keep out of the way of schedule trains, unless the Commanding General expressly orders all other business which conflicts with the special to be stopped. If this is done, obey the order and straighten out the confusion which will ensue as soon as you can. The responsibility of failure elsewhere in consequence of it will not rest with you; you will have your record straight.

Your action, as exhibited by the communication forwarded and accompanying telegrams, is approved.

Yours respectfully,   H. HAUPT,

Chief of Construction and Transportation.

The forward movement of the Army of the Potomac under General Burnside was not made. Nothing more of importance occurred in connection with Military Railroad operations while he continued in command. The army had been at all times well supplied, and the plan of transferring loaded cars from Alexandria to Acquia Creek by water had been a great success. It required but about an hour to transfer trains of cars from the track to floats, and the same from floats to track, and no accident ever occurred in the transfer.

The time for towage between landings was about six hours. To have transported the contents of a train from the Alexandria

Railroad to Falmouth would have required nearly 200 wagons from four to six days, dependent upon the condition of the roads, and the saving in expense as compared with water transportation by means of transports was nearly $3,000 per day on the supplies transferred.

The plans of General Burnside did not meet the cordial approval of the President and General Halleck, and their assent was given with reluctance. In the letter of the President to General McClellan, of October 13, 1862, a copy of which was sent to General Burnside with request for careful consideration preparatory to the visit of Generals Halleck, Meigs and myself, on November 12, the program that was considered most satisfactory was clearly defined.

It was stated that the army could march on interior lines covering Washington and the line of communication, while the enemy must take a more circuitous and longer route to reach either Fredericksburg or Richmond; that, of the several routes presented, he was recommended to take that which was *nearest* to the enemy, so as to operate on his communications, keep fully advised of his movements, and strike whenever opportunity offered.

This plan, if followed, would have taken the army to Fredericksburg on the south side of the Rappahannock instead of to Falmouth on the north side, and, with a few bridges, the communication with Acquia Creek would have been the same.

Had the movement been made, Lee could not have occupied Fredericksburg, and the battle would have been fought at some point between Fredericksburg and Richmond.

What General Burnside's reasons were for departing from this plan of operation, I never knew. Perhaps he thought it safer to move with the river between his forces and those of the enemy; but even then, if he had moved quickly and occupied Fredericksburg before Lee, the reverses at that point would not have been experienced.

The assault upon Marye's Heights in the center was a mistake, and inexcusable on the supposition that General Burnside had any idea of the strength of the position.

I had an opportunity of examining the ground afterwards, and never saw a stronger natural position. It was almost as impregnable as a permanent fortification on the most approved plans of Vaubon. A road ran in front of Marye's house, parallel to the river. On the river side was a stone wall, the top of which was level with the ground in front of it, which sloped gently towards the town and river like the glacis of a permanent fortification. Immediately in rear were high hills, with projecting salients

STRAIGHTENING BENDS IN RAILS BY LETTING THEM FALL ACROSS A TIE.

like bastions, on which batteries were placed commanding the whole plain in front, with cross fire in all directions. The road was filled with rebel troops perfectly protected; they could stoop to load, then rise and fire without exposure. An assaulting column had no chance. It was as hopeless as the Balaklava charge in the Crimea.

From the window in Burnside's room I could, with a field glass, see our columns move to the attack, then the smoke of battle would obscure everything. When it cleared away, our forces were found driven back and the ground strewn with dead and wounded.

CHAPTER IX.

OPENING OPERATIONS UNDER GENERAL HOOKER.

THE following characteristic letter from the President to General Joseph Hooker was sent on the day upon which he was placed in command to succeed General Burnside:

WASHINGTON, D. C., January 26, 1863.

Major-General Hooker.

GENERAL: I have placed you at the head of the Army of the Potomac. Of course, I have done this upon what appears to me to be sufficient reasons, and yet I think it best for you to know that there are some things in regard to which I am not quite satisfied with you. I believe you to be a brave and skilful soldier, which, of course, I like. I also believe you do not mix politics with your profession, in which you are right. You have confidence in yourself, which is a valuable, if not an indispensable quality. You are ambitious, which, with reasonable bounds, does good rather than harm; but I think that during General Burnside's command of the army you have taken counsel of your ambition and thwarted him as much as you could, in which you did a great wrong to the country and to a most meritorious and honorable brother officer.

I have heard in such a way as I believe it, of your recently saying that both the army and the Government needed a dictator. Of course, it was not for this, but in spite of it, that I have given you the command. Only those Generals who gain success can set up dictators. What I now ask of you is military success, and I will risk the dictatorship.

The Government will support you to the extent of its ability, which is neither more nor less than it has done and will do to all commanders.

I much fear that the spirit which you have aided to infuse into the army, of criticising their commanders and withholding confidence from them, will now turn upon you. I shall assist you, as far as I can, to put it down. Neither you, nor Napoleon, if he was alive again, could get any good out of an army while such a spirit prevails in it. And now beware of rashness. Beware of rashness, but with energy and sleepless vigilance go forward and give us victories.

Yours very truly,   A. LINCOLN.

On his assuming command of the army, I addressed the following letter to General Hooker:

WASHINGTON, D. C., January 27, 1863.

Major-General Hooker, Commander of the Army of Potomac.

GENERAL: Allow me to offer my sincere congratulations on your elevation to the command of the Army of the Potomac, and to express the hope that your administration of affairs will secure for our arms the success to which the justice of the cause entitles them.

It will be my effort, so far as the Department of Military Railroads is concerned, to coöperate efficiently in your movements, and I am well aware that the success or failure of a movement is often a question of prompt supply.

In assuming the duties of Commander-in-Chief, it is proper that you should know the conditions essential to the efficient operation of the Military Railroads.

The difficulties connected with the operation of Military Railroads are innumerable; yet with the cordial support which I have always received from General Halleck and from McDowell, McClellan, Pope and Burnside, the army, since my connection with it, I believe, never suffered from a deficiency of any supplies dependent upon the transportation which they could furnish.

To insure regularity in supplies, regularity in running trains and prompt loading and unloading of cars are indispensable. As far as practicable, all business should be done by regular schedule trains, and no regular schedule train should, from any cause, be detained a minute, unless from accident. The Superintendent has orders to furnish an extra to the Commanding General whenever it is in his power to do so, but extras must keep out of the way of schedule trains, and extras should only be called for when an urgent necessity requires them.

The existing organization and arrangements work very satisfactorily. J. H. Devereux is Superintendent of the Orange & Alexandria Railroad; William W. Wright, Superintendent of the Fredericksburg Railroad; Adna Anderson, engineer of construction on both roads. I have directed Mr. Anderson, who is a very efficient and experienced civil engineer, to report to you and keep you advised of his whereabouts, so that, in the event of any movement, you can communicate with him. Colonel McCallum attends to the routine and red-tape business of the Department.

For myself, I am generally present when active operations are in progress, organizing and directing where my presence seems essential.

I may be absent for some weeks during the present session of the Massachusetts Legislature, but my arrangements are such that nothing will suffer in my absence. In everything pertaining to railroad transportation consult with or direct Mr. Wright, and in all that pertains to construction, Mr. Anderson.

Assured that in all my efforts to continue or increase the efficiency of the Railway Department I will receive your cordial coöperation, I remain,   Yours very respectfully,

H. HAUPT,
Chief of Construction and Transportation.

The long interval from January 26, 1863, when General Hooker took command, until May, 1863, was a period of comparative inactivity in military operations. The Army of the Potomac was encamped on the north side of the Rappahannock opposite Fredericksburg, and supplies were forwarded by river and rail via Acquia Creek. We were not troubled by guerrilla raids or military interference. The trains were run with regularity by schedule, and the telegraph was left for the almost exclusive use of the military authorities.

The Construction Corps, during this period, was not idle, but performed services of great value in perfecting organization, procuring material, and preparing for rapid advance movements whenever they should be ordered.

A large number of bridge trusses were prepared in spans of 60 feet to be transported on flat cars, hauled by oxen to the sites of the bridges, and hoisted bodily into position by suitable portable machinery. These trusses were called "shadbellies" by the workmen from their peculiar shape.

A plan was also designed for a military truss bridge, the parts of which were interchangeable, and which could be put together without previous fitting, and with so much rapidity that, as my foreman, E. C. Smeed, expressed it, he could put the bridge together about as fast as a dog could trot.

Torpedoes were also prepared for blowing down bridges in operating on the communications of the enemy. These torpedoes consisted simply of an iron bolt with a head and washer of such diameter that they could be driven easily into a two-inch auger-hole. Between the head and the washer was a tin case 8 inches long, open at both ends, filled with powder. Experiments were made in blowing up trunks of trees which proved their efficiency, and by means of them any ordinary wooden bridge could be thrown down in five minutes.

Other experiments were made on old sidings near Alexandria to determine the best mode of rapidly destroying tracks. The usual mode adopted by the enemy had been to tear up the rails, pile the cross ties, place the rails upon them, set the pile on fire, and bend the rails when heated. I found this mode entirely too slow, as several hours were required to heat the rails sufficiently and, when bent, we could generally straighten them for use in a few minutes, in fact, in less than one-tenth of the time required to heat and bend them.

We had been experimenting for some time with no results that I considered satisfactory, when one day Smeed came into my office with a couple of U-shaped irons in his hands (see illustration on page 111) and exclaimed: "I've got it!" "Got what?" I asked. "Got the thing that will tear up track as quickly as you can say 'Jack Robinson,' and spoil the rails so that nothing but a rolling mill can ever repair them."

"That is just what I want," was my reply; "but how are you to do it with that pair of horseshoes?"

He explained his plan. The irons were turned up and over at the ends so as firmly to embrace the base of the rail. Into the cavity of the U a stout lever of wood was to be inserted. A rope at the end of the lever would allow half a dozen men to pull upon it and twist the rail. When the lever was pulled down to the ground and held there, another iron was to be placed beside it, and another twist given, then the first iron removed and the process repeated four or five times until a corkscrew twist was given to the rail. After hearing the explanation, I said: "I think it will do; let us go at once and try it." Smeed's plan was found to answer perfectly, and the problem of the simplest and quickest mode of destroying track was satisfactorily solved.

The photographic department in connection with the operations of the Construction Corps was of great value. All the more important operations in connection with the construction of bridges, the expedients for rapidly crossing streams, the destruction of track, etc., were photographed and with printed explanations were sent to heads of departments and to Corps commanders wherever our armies were in the field. Many hundreds of torpedoes and instruments for destroying track were ordered and prepared at the Alexandria shops, but we had more work to do to protect and restore our own communications than in operating on those of the enemy.

General Burnside told me that he once paid $3,000 to have a bridge destroyed, and that the work had not been done effectually. A couple of the bridge torpedoes would have saved that expenditure.

On February 7, 1863, I sent a letter to General Hooker with explanation of a system of ferriage by means of blanket boats, accompanied by a diagram showing mode of operation. These boats are fairly illustrated by the photographs reproduced in this volume.

CHAPTER X.

IRREGULARITIES IN THE WEST.

DURING the late winter and spring lull I spent some time in Massachusetts attending to private affairs.

On March 20, at Cambridge, I received a message from the Secretary of War stating that he wished to see me at my earliest convenience. I returned to Washington, and on the 24th called upon the Secretary, who wished to know the condition of the railroads used for Government transportation in the West and Southwest.

I replied that I knew nothing about them, although nominally in charge of the Military Railroads of the United States.

He remarked that he had reason to believe that these roads were used for the benefit of Jew peddlers, speculators, contractors and sutlers; in fact, for anything and everything except the legitimate business of Government transportation, and directed me to go at once and straighten things out.

I answered: "I will do so cheerfully if I have the requisite authority, but I must go to Headquarters, see General Hooker and leave things in proper shape in case his forward movement should be made before my return."

On returning to my office, I drew up a form of orders defining the duties to be performed and giving the necessary authority.

The Secretary read the paper, and remarked that I had made it pretty strong. I replied that it was necessary; there was no use in going without full authority to act. He then said: "Leave it with me; I will think it over for a day or two."

I then went to Falmouth to see General Hooker, and informed him that the Secretary of War proposed to send me to the West to straighten out the Military Railroads. The General was decidedly opposed to any such movement; said that when he made his advance my personal presence was indispensable; he would move rapidly and trust to me to reconstruct the railroads and bridges and keep his army in supplies, and my absence would possibly render his campaign a failure.

On my return to Washington, the Secretary said that General Hooker had telegraphed that it would not do for me to leave, and that some other plan must be adopted. Then the following order was issued:

WASHINGTON CITY, March 25, 1863.

Ordered: That Brigadier-General H. Haupt, Superintendent of Railroads, cause an inspection to be made of the condition of the railroad transportation service where the armies of the United States are operating in the Western States, and make a report to this Department upon all points relating thereto, material to the service, with such recommendations as may be necessary to promote the efficiency and economy of the transporting service. He may designate to this Department, for approval, the names of the persons to whom he proposes to commit this inspection.

EDWIN M. STANTON,
Secretary of War.

In compliance with these instructions, I appointed F. H. Forbes, of Massachusetts, a gentleman whose long training as a newspaper reporter admirably fitted him to act as a detective and find out things, and I knew that his personal relations to me were such that I could depend upon him.

I wrote out full detailed instructions for the Special Agent, had them approved by the Secretary of War, and orders given to all officers to furnish any information called for.

An order was also issued by Quartermaster-General M. C. Meigs, as follows:

WASHINGTON CITY, April 23, 1863.

Officers and agents of the Quartermaster's Department will furnish information called for by F. H. Forbes, Special Agent in the Department of United States Military Railroads, under the instructions of Brigadier-General Haupt of 21st April, 1863, approved by the Secretary of War.

Necessary transportation will be furnished to enable Mr. Forbes to visit the several roads in charge of the War Department, and every facility will be afforded to him for accomplishing the object of his mission—a general inspection of the Military Railroads.

M. C. MEIGS,
Quartermaster General.

Reports were made by the Special Agent, as directed, at short intervals. These reports indicated the existence of as widespread corruption as the Secretary had intimated. Steamboats were detained at landings under pretense that they were required for Government use, and then released upon payment of a liberal sum of money. Property was sold and the proceeds appropriated by the sutlers; forage and hardtack were exposed to the weather without protection, and, when condemned, new supplies ordered for the benefit of contractors.

Some large game was hit in these reports, and I had letters of remonstrance from parties who wished me to suppress the reports. I replied that the reports must go to the Secretary of War, but if they wished to make any denials or explanations I would forward them. Some weeks thereafter the Secretary took a trip West, and on his return removed the Special Agent and sent him home. I never heard in what manner the abuses were corrected.

It was a frequent remark of Confederates that our army wasted more than their army consumed, and there appeared to be some reason for the assertion.

On one occasion two contractors were captured by General Stuart. Upon interrogating them he learned that they had made and delivered a large number of wagons for the Government. He offered to release them if they would pledge their honor to do honest work, saying that the United States Government contractors were relied upon to supply the Confederate army, but that most of the wagons were so badly constructed that they were constantly breaking down and making trouble.

The exposed condition of the depot grounds at Alexandria induced me to ask and obtain permission from General Halleck to construct a substantial stockade, enclosing sixteen squares.

A raid by two or three hundred cavalry could have made an attack at night and destroyed the buildings, shops, cars, engines and stores, and retired without damage to themselves.

The forts were so distant that before notice could be given and a force collected the damage could be done, and the enemy escape.

Our men took much pride in building this stockade as a model to show the engineer troops, as they said, how such work should be done. Straight trees were selected, nicely pointed on top, set three or four feet in the ground, with loop-holes provided at short intervals. In the middle of the sides and at the corners were projecting bastions, so as to afford a flanking fire along the sides; and at the south end, commanding the road by which the enemy would approach, were placed pieces of artillery. The men were provided with repeating rifles, and so divided and organized as to be capable of very efficient defense.

These arrangements did not appear satisfactory to the Government engineers, who made complaint to the Secretary of War that General Haupt had constructed a line of interior defenses that was an interference with their general plans for the defense of the capital. (See illustration, page 299.)

When this complaint reached me through the circumlocution office with a number of indorsements, I added one more indorsement to the effect that I was not able to comprehend how the construction of a fence around the depot-grounds of Alex-

POCKET AUGER FOR MAKING MORTICES AND TENONS FOR BLANKET BOATS.

andria could interfere with the defenses of Washington. No action was taken by the Secretary of War.

As the time was approaching for the resumption of active operations, I gave directions to Chief Engineer Anderson to have everything in readiness for rapid reconstruction of roads and bridges.

One day I received a telegram from General Hooker, who wished to see me immediately. I started at once in a little steamer, reached Acquia at daylight, breakfasted with Wright and then ran to Falmouth on an engine, reporting to General Hooker as he was going to breakfast. He asked me to accompany him, which I declined, as I had already taken my morning meal.

He then handed me a paper to read over, saying that it contained his plan of operations, but I must not on any consideration open my lips to any living soul; that even the members of his staff did not know what his plans were, and would not know until the time arrived for putting them in execution; he had left them under the impression that a very different movement was contemplated. He added that when he did move he expected to advance very rapidly, and as he would depend upon me for his supplies I had a very important duty to perform; that upon its performance success or failure might depend, and he had concluded to advise me fully so that I might make the necessary preparations.

When the General returned from breakfast I had read the papers, and told him we would be ready.

After leaving General Hooker I determined at once to build a new bridge across the Potomac run. One of the Corps commanders had, very unwisely, as I thought, cut down all the timber in the valley above the bridge, which, in case of a freshet, would be carried against the bridge and sweep away the trestle-work. I therefore gave orders to E. C. Smeed to proceed at once to erect a new military truss-bridge in spans of 120 feet resting on the stone piers, and remove the old bridge.

As soon as the work was commenced I was summoned again by General Hooker, who wished to see me immediately.

I reported at Headquarters, when he said rather excitedly: "I understand you are going to take down that large bridge at Potomac Creek and build another."

"Yes, sir."

"Well! I cannot permit it. I am now loading my wagons, and cannot allow any interruption to the trains."

I rejoined: "I do not propose to interrupt the trains."

"Why, how can you take down that bridge and build another without stopping transportation for some days at least?"

I said: "General, it is your place to indicate to me what you wish to have done, and mine to carry out your wishes in such manner as will best secure the results desired. If you wish a detailed explanation, I will make it; but I say to you now that the bridge will, before you are ready to move, be replaced by a more safe and substantial structure, and not a single train will be detained for a single hour."

"Well!" replied the General, "if you say so, go ahead; but I don't see how you can do it." His chief of staff, General Butterfield, echoed: "And I don't see how you can do it, either."

The new bridge was erected and was in use for some weeks before the forward movement commenced, and no train was delayed during its construction. I cannot find the report of the time required in its erection, but my impression is that it did not exceed three or four days.

On April 11, 1863, General Hooker informed the President that he proposed to turn the enemy's position to his (Hooker's) right, and sever his connections with Richmond by a dragoon force.

On May 1, 1862, General Butterfield telegraphed to Hooker: "Sedgwick's troops are now advancing. Haupt is ready to spring with the bridge."

Lowe reports, from balloon observations, "Long trains of enemy's wagons moving to the right."

On May 2, Sedgwick was directed to cross the river as soon as indications would permit, capture Fredericksburg, and pursue the enemy.

On May 3, Hooker engaged the enemy at Chancellorsville and was wounded.

Butterfield telegraphed to Hooker regrets that he is wounded, also, "Haupt is at Falmouth with his force ready to spring with the railroad bridge when ordered. Affairs seem to justify it now here."

On May 3, 12:30 P. M., Sedgwick had carried the heights; 5 P. M., Sedgwick's advance was three and one-half miles from Fredericksburg, near Guest's house.

On the morning of the 4th, while waiting for orders to commence the bridge, I walked over the battle-ground, and examined the heights beyond Marye's house. I then realized the great strength of the position and the impossibility of taking it, if properly defended, by a direct assault in front, as had been attempted by Burnside with disastrous results. My photographic artist, Captain Russell, was with me and secured several large photographic negatives—one very good one of the stone wall, with the rebel dead lying behind it. The position seemed to have been taken by a flank movement. (See illustration, page 307.)

During the afternoon of the 4th the enemy, 15,000 strong, re-entered the earthworks south of Fredericksburg, Gibbon still holding the city.

About the same time, in ignorance of the fact that the enemy had resumed possession of the heights, I walked out with Superintendent Wright to examine a pile of lumber some distance beyond the depot, to see if it could be utilized in building the bridge. A short distance beyond was a fence and ditch, lined with trees, behind which some riflemen were firing at short intervals, but I could not imagine what they were firing at, as I supposed they were our own men, and I could see no enemy beyond. On returning leisurely to the depot, looking at the dead bodies along the track and wondering why they had not been buried, I asked one of the soldiers, sheltered behind a building, what those men were firing at.

"Popping at us when we shows ourselves. Them's the rebs."

Wright and I had walked into a trap without knowing it, but the apparent boldness of the move no doubt saved us. As we were not in uniform it was probably supposed that none but loyal citizens of Fredericksburg would approach so near the Confederate lines.

On the morning of May 5 the President was notified that Hooker considered it expedient to retire across the river, so that I was not called upon to build the bridge, and all my extensive preparations for a forward movement were rendered useless.

On the evening of May 4 I was notified from Hooker's Headquarters not to send any more supplies until further orders and to ask protection at Acquia in case of necessity, "though we trust to fight it out in excellent style yet."

May 4 I received a communication from the depot Quartermaster at Acquia, notifying me that the first-class steamer John Brooks had been specially assigned to the use of the Railroad and Construction Department for the purpose of removing employes, etc.

I was much surprised at this courtesy, as I had just indulged in a little amusement at that officer's expense. Like many others who had been appointed from civil life, he seemed to have a high idea of the importance of his position and was inclined to make others recognize it by issuing orders. He had made complaint to the Department at Washington that, although he had issued orders that all *steamers* landing at Acquia should come to his office to report, yet in defiance of such orders and in violation of the courtesy due to his position, the steamers detailed in the service of the Military Railroad Department had neglected or refused to obey such orders.

In reply I stated that I had not seen the orders referred to; that no want of courtesy to the distinguished representative of the Quartermaster's Department was intended; that without raising any question as to his rights, or my duties, I would cheerfully comply with any reasonable and proper regulations; but that, inasmuch as we had no marine railway or other equivalent facilities; as the office was at a considerable distance from the landing, and steamboats were not furnished with organs of speech, I could not comprehend how it was possible for said steamers to go to the office to report. The captains might do it, and if it was the wish of the Quartermaster, I would give orders accordingly.

As there was considerable merriment at the gentleman's expense, I was not prepared to expect so much consideration for our safety and comfort as was exhibited in placing one of the largest steamers at my disposal. I did not, however, consider that there was the slightest danger. The landing, as previously stated, was a long distance from the shore, connected by a straight and narrow railroad track, on each side of which were marshes impassable by horse or foot. There were two gunboats anchored in the stream, and the track could easily have been barricaded if any attack had been apprehended. The tender of the steamer was respectfully declined, and the Quartermaster requested to use it for other more necessary purposes. I remained on shore with all my force, and our sleep that night was not disturbed by apprehensions of capture. All the rest, officers and men, of the other departments, took refuge on steamers.

We retained the position at Acquia Creek without any annoyance from an enemy until June 14, when orders were received to abandon the post.

In three days from the receipt of these orders all the stores and other property left by the army, together with all railroad property and about ten or twelve thousand sick and wounded men from the hospitals, amounting in all to over 500 car-loads, were moved to the landing and safely loaded on vessels. No railroad property was left behind or destroyed. Even the window sashes were taken from the houses and brought away.

An equally successful removal of supplies could have been effected on the occasion of the former evacuation under Burnside, if an opportunity had been given us, but there seemed to be no desire at that time to save property.

CHAPTER XI.

PORTABLE TRACK-WRECKING APPARATUS.

IN order that the entire Union army might have the benefit during the summer and future campaigns of my investigations, I submitted the following report on experiments made to determine the most expeditious mode of destroying track by portable apparatus, with a view to operations against the communications of the enemy:

WASHINGTON, May 16, 1863.

Major-General H. W. Halleck, General-in-Chief of the Army of the United States.

GENERAL: The attempts made by the forces of the United States to break the communications of the enemy, and destroy his roads and bridges, have not been as numerous as the interests of the service would seem to require; and, when made, they have rarely resulted satisfactorily. The communications ineffectually broken have been restored in a few hours, and no serious or permanent damage has been inflicted.

To tear up the track of a railroad is a very difficult operation with any implements heretofore known or used which cavalry can carry with them in an expedition. The claw and clevis bars, used by track repairers for drawing spikes, are very heavy; they could not be carried with an expedition, except in wagons, and no portable substitutes have ever yet been proposed.

Even when track is torn up, if the cross-ties are not burned and the rails destroyed, the time required to repair is less than is necessary to inflict the damage.

The enemy have been more successful in the destruction of track than our own troops, but their success has been the work of time, operating on their own territory, without fear of interruption. On the Loudoun & Hampshire Railroad the ties were burned, the rails heated and bent around trees, forming sometimes complete circles; rails so damaged have never been again used.

On the Richmond, Fredericksburg & Potomac Railroad three miles of track were torn up in April, 1862, near Acquia Creek. The rails were carried south of the Rappahannock, and the ties burned; yet it required but three days for the Construction Corps of the Army of the Rappahannock to cut new ties and reconstruct the track with new iron brought from Alexandria.

The writer has been engaged during the last week in prosecuting a series of experiments, with a view to determine the most expeditious and effectual mode of destroying a railway communication by the use of means and appliances which fulfill the essentially important condition of portability.

Rails which are simply bent can, with the use of levers and sledges, or, still better, with jack screws, be straightened so as to permit their use. If the rails are twisted spirally, like a corkscrew or auger, the difficulty of straightening is greatly enhanced, and if bent, in addition to the spiral twist, it is not probable that any attempt would ever be made to repair or use them.

The experiments have been completely successful, and have resulted in the construction of apparatus which is simple, portable, and efficacious; which tears up track in one-sixth of the time required to construct it; twists and bends the rails so as to render them entirely unfit for use, and does it all in a cold state, without the delay caused by heating.

The accompanying series of photographs will illustrate the experiments.

The illustrations on pages 111 and 121 represent various small instruments for loosening rails. They consist of steel hooks, provided with sockets, into which wooden handles are inserted; the handles may be pieces of round poles, four feet long and three inches in diameter at the larger end. These hooks are designed simply to force back the heads of the spikes without extracting them. They perform the work very expeditiously; about four spikes in a minute can be bent back, so as to unclasp the rail and permit its removal.

The chair presents the greatest difficulty to the removal of the rail: the spikes which pass through the chairs can neither be forced back nor drawn out with implements which are effectual when applied to the intermediate spikes.

After repeated trials, the only portable contrivance which gave satisfactory results in the removal of the chair, consisted of two socket wedges of iron, with wood inserted in the back: These wedges should be 2¾ inches broad; they are driven under the chair, and between it and the tie, by means of axes. The time required to remove a chair from a hard, firm tie, if the intermediate spikes have been forced back, is only three minutes. As the intermediate spikes can be unclasped in the same time by other hands, four men can remove a rail in three minutes, and the implements required for the purpose are two steel hooks, two wedges and two axes.

This mode of removing rails, although far superior to any known previous to the commencement of the experiments, is completely eclipsed by a simple and portable contrivance, suggested by E. C. Smeed, one of the most efficient officers of the Construction Corps. The contrivance consists of two pieces of iron, of the form represented in illustration on page 111. They are placed under the two ends of the rail, as in illustration on page 121; levers, 11 or 12 feet long and 4½ or 5 inches diameter at the larger end, are inserted in the irons, when, by pulling on the levers, the whole rail is ripped from its fastening in less than half a minute, and the chair is broken.

These irons weigh about 6½ pounds; in using them fence rails will answer for levers. They not only furnish the most expeditious mode yet devised of tearing up track, but they can be used to twist the rails spirally in a cold state. To accomplish this object the levers should be applied at one end of the rail, the other end remaining in the chair; one lever having been applied and bent down to the ground, the second should be attached and a further twist given as far as the lever can be moved; then a fresh hold can be taken with the first, and the operation continued until the twist is sufficient. The rail can then be bent by pulling on a rope attached to the loose end, and afterwards thrown out by applying one of the levers to the end which had remained fastened.

If the rail is loose, it can be twisted in the manner represented in illustration on page 131. Illustration on page 121 shows a short piece of T rail that has been twisted cold by the levers, and illustration on page 131 a short U rail, which is more difficult to twist than the T pattern.*

Experiments were made to determine the time required to destroy rails in the manner which has usually been adopted by the enemy, which consists in heating and bending. Two piles of ties were made, one of thirty-two ties, across which eight rails were placed, and another of sixteen ties, with four rails laid thereon. The fire was started by splitting two of the ties into kindling wood, and pouring half a gallon of coal oil on each of the piles. (See illustration on page 161.)

Although the ties were not wet, the fires burned so slowly that in three hours the rails had not become heated to any considerable extent. The piles were then left until the next morning, when they were found to be entirely consumed, but the rails were lying on the ground uninjured; the weight of the projecting ends had not bent the rails.

This experiment proves that burning is too slow a process to be relied upon for destroying rails, where time is any object; and that in any expedition to operate on the communications of an enemy, such plans must be adopted as will permit the rails to be destroyed without heating.

A successful attempt to bend and break rails was made by placing a rail parallel to, and in contact with, one of the rails of the track; three spikes were then driven about three feet from the end to serve as a fulcrum; ten men carried the rail around, bending it at the place where it is spiked, and finally breaking it at that point.

A similar experiment is represented in illustration on page 141. In this case, instead of the spikes, a chain was passed around the rails at about three feet from the end of the loose rail experimented upon. A horse was attached to the other end, who doubled the rail into the shape of the letter U without difficulty.

On the opposite side of the track (see illustration on page 141), a joint is shown, raised from the tie by driving wedges under the chair.

Another plan, which was used successfully for bending and breaking rails cold, is represented in illustration on page 151. It consisted in boring a hole in a tree, inserting a stout iron pin nearly two inches diameter, passing a log chain over the pin, placing the end of the rail in a loop of the chain, and pulling on the other end. In this case the rail was of the U pattern, short and stiff, and required two horses to break it.

A rail was also bent readily by the plan which follows: A hole was bored in a tie, in which was inserted a two-inch pin for a fulcrum; the short end of the rail to be bent rested against the end of a rail in the track that had not yet been taken up. The horse, hitched to the long end of the rail, walked around and doubled it without difficulty.

The results given by these experiments are all of much practical value, and prove that there is no serious difficulty in bending rails without heating them, so as to render them useless. But the most satisfactory results are secured by the U-shaped iron represented in illustra-

---

* NOTE.—Wiggins and other writers have given the credit of this invention to Colonel Poe, of General Sheridan's staff. This is a mistake. E. C. Smeed is entitled to the credit of the invention, the knowledge of which was communicated to the commanders of armies by the photograph and accompanying descriptions which were sent to them.

tion on page 121. With them a rail can be torn from its fastenings in less than a minute, without previously drawing the spikes; and with the same apparatus rails can be twisted and afterwards bent.

A thousand cavalry marching two abreast, and following each other closely, will occup a space of one mile. At least one-half should be reserved for protection, leaving the other half for work. Suppose the working parties to be divided into squads of ten men, and that to each squad be assigned the duty of removing and destroying twelve rails, supposed to be each 20 feet long. The number of squads in one mile will be 44, requiring 440 men, and leaving 560 for defense out of the thousand. Each squad should be supplied with the following implements: 2 U-shaped irons; 2 stout wooden levers, 12 feet long and 4½ inches diameter; 2 pieces of rope, each 6 yards long, to tie to the levers; 2 axes and 2 wooden wedges to place between levers and rails.

The levers can be cut from the woods, or stout fence rails can be used; the axes, ropes, and U irons must be carried. The whole weight to be carried for a squad of ten men would be but twenty-five pounds; one pack-horse or one mule would carry the implements for six or eight squads.

Five minutes is sufficient time to twist, bend, and remove a rail; in one hour the twelve rails, which form the task of a squad, could be destroyed. 440 men in the same time (one hour) will destroy a mile. 2,200 men in the same time can destroy five miles. 5,000 cavalry sent on an expedition to break communications, could detail 2,200 men for the work, 2,800 for protection, and in one hour could effectually destroy five miles of track; they could then ride for two hours and destroy five miles more.

In destroying track it is best to pile and burn the cross ties. Each squad will have forty-eight ties to burn. To pile these ties, split two of them for kindling, pour over two canteens of coal oil, and set fire to the heap, will consume but fifteen minutes. A small detachment may be left to prevent residents in the vicinity from extinguishing the fires.

Heretofore it has been possible to operate effectually against the communications of an enemy only where there were important bridges that could be destroyed. The plans herein described for destroying track will permit communications to be broken wherever they can be reached, and in so effectual a manner that repairs will be impossible without new material, which, without tearing up some other road, it may be impossible for the enemy to procure.

A cavalry expedition, led by intelligent and dashing officers, provided with the appliances herein described, and with the bridge torpedoes for the destruction of bridges, could traverse the whole South and inflict irreparable damage upon the communications of the enemy. If a working force of 2,200 men can destroy five miles of track in one hour, and two or three men to a span, with the use of the torpedoes, throw down the largest bridges in five minutes, the movement of the forces can be too rapid to admit of pursuit, except by cavalry, to prevent which the numerical strength should be great enough to oppose any possible force of cavalry that the enemy can bring against it. Fresh horses should be seized, wherever practicable, and abandoned ones shot.

The telegraph should be cut frequently; but instead of leaving the ends loose, the break should be at a pole, and the ends connected by small pieces of insulated wire, concealed by the insulators, so that the point of break would not be discernible.

DRILL—CONSTRUCTING BLANKET BOATS.

On an expedition of this kind a few men, expert in repairs of track, bridges, and telegraph lines, would prove of great value. Still more important is it that the officers, and at least a portion of the force, say one or two men in each squad, should be actually drilled in laying track and in tearing it up, and in bending and twisting old and useless rails, if any can be found.

In the hope that the results of these experiments will prove beneficial for the service, they are respectfully submitted by

H. HAUPT,
Brigadier-General,
In Charge of United States Military Railroads.

CHAPTER XII.

HOOKER FLUNKS AND IS RELIEVED.

AFTER the battle of Chancellorsville, General Hooker marched towards the line of the Orange & Alexandria Railroad, which once more became a base of supplies, and we were again subjected to the usual annoyances inflicted by guerrilla parties, such as burning bridges, obstructing track, and firing upon trains. It became necessary to run all trains with 30 to 50 men as a guard. On one occasion a bridge was found burning in the middle and at both ends, and five men made their escape on horseback when the train approached.

General Hooker to the President, June 10, 1863, refers to contemplated raid by Lee into Maryland, and remarks:

> If it should be the intention to send a heavy column of infantry to accompany the cavalry on the proposed raid, he can leave nothing behind to interpose any serious obstacle to my rapid advance on Richmond. If it should be found to be the case, would it not promote the true interests of the cause for me to march to Richmond at once?
>
> If left to operate from my own judgment, with my present information, I do not hesitate to say that I should adopt this course as being the most speedy and certain mode of giving the rebellion a mortal blow.
>
> From information which I deem reliable, the only troops remaining in Richmond is the provost guard, 1,500, and all the troops between here and there are brought well to the front.

To this the President replied:

June 10, 1863, 6:40 P. M.

Major-General Hooker:
Your long dispatch of to-day is just received. If left to me I would not go south of Rappahannock upon Lee's moving north of it. If you had Richmond invested to-day, you would not be able to take it in twenty days; while your communications, and with them your army, would be ruined. I think Lee's army and not Richmond is your objective point. If he comes toward the upper Potomac, follow in his flank and on his inside track, shortening your lines while he lengthens his. Fight him, too, when opportunity offers. If he stays where he is, fret him and fret him.

A. LINCOLN.

June 11 General Halleck telegraphs that he fully agrees with the President.

204

On June 14, 1863, Mr. Lincoln telegraphed to General Hooker:

If the head of Lee's army is at Martinsburg and the tail of it on the plank road between Fredericksburg and Chancellorsville, the animal must be slim somewhere. Could you not break him?

On June 15, 10:20 A. M., General Hooker's Headquarters were at Dumfries. On same day, 6:30 P. M., he had moved to Fairfax Station. At 8:30 he received a telegram from the President, to which he replied: "It seems to disclose the intention of the enemy to make an invasion, and if so, it is not in my power to prevent it."

On June 16 General Hooker had established his Headquarters near Fairfax Station. The Blue Ridge divided the opposing forces. Lee was moving towards the Potomac with the evident design of another invasion of Maryland. I supposed, of course, that Hooker would oppose this movement and throw his forces forward to the Potomac, in which case our railroad operations would be transferred to the line of the Baltimore & Ohio Railroad.

It was important for me to know what moves General Hooker designed to make, so that I could prepare for them. I went to see him at Fairfax to make inquiries, and found him in a decidedly bad humor. He said that he did not intend to move at all until he got orders, and would then obey them literally and let the responsibility rest where it belonged; that he had made various suggestions which had not been approved by the powers that be in Washington, and if he could not carry out his own plans, others must give orders, and if disaster ensued his skirts would be clear, or words to that effect.

I was greatly surprised at the spirit exhibited, and at the close of the interview returned as rapidly as possible to Washington and reported the situation to General Halleck, stating that General Hooker would not move until he got orders, and that action ought to be taken immediately.

General Halleck replied that some of the statements of General Hooker were not in accordance with the facts, and then, opening his desk, took out a bundle of papers and read to me, from copies in his possession, part of the correspondence between General Hooker and the President, from which it appeared that Hooker's plan was to take advantage of the absence of Lee's army to capture Richmond.

To this the President had replied in his characteristic style, as nearly as I can recollect it: "General, you may be right, but I think you are wrong. It seems to me that it would be a very poor exchange to give Washington for Richmond. If the enemy is scattered, as you report, in a long thin line, with one flank at Fredericksburg and the other on the Potomac, why can you not keep your shoulder well up to him, break through somewhere in the middle and beat him in detail ?"

This is the substance of the letter, as I recollect it, and it made a decided impression upon my memory. I do not find a letter in these exact words amongst the records; but there are others expressive of the same ideas.

After reading the letters to me, General Halleck put on his cap and left the office. I remained in conversation with his chief of staff, General Cullom, for more than half an hour, when General Halleck returned, threw his cap on the table and remarked: "Hooker will get his orders."

On June 16, at 11 A. M., General Hooker telegraphed to the President from Fairfax Station:

You have long been aware, Mr. President, that I have not enjoyed the confidence of the Major-General commanding the army, and I can assure you so long as this continues we may look in vain for success, especially as future operations will require our relations to be more dependent upon each other than heretofore.

At 11:30 A. M. of the same day, General Halleck telegraphed General Hooker that there was no reliable information that the enemy had crossed the Potomac in any force, and advised him to keep his army near enough to the enemy to ascertain his movements.

Several other telegrams about the same time indicate a desire on the part of General Hooker to avoid the exercise of any discretion in regard to the movements of his army and secure explicit and detailed instruction from the Commander-in-Chief. At 7:30 P. M. he telegraphed General Halleck: "In compliance with your instructions, I shall march to the relief of Harper's Ferry," to which General Halleck replied, 10:15 P. M.:

I have given no directions for your army to move to Harper's Ferry; I have advised the movement of a force sufficiently strong to ascertain where the enemy is, and then move to the relief of Harper's Ferry, or elsewhere, as circumstances may require. You are in command of the Army of the Potomac and will make the particular dispositions as you deem proper. I shall only indicate the objects to be arrived at. We have no positive information of any large force against Harper's Ferry, and it cannot be known whether it will be necessary to go there until you can feel the enemy and ascertain his whereabouts.

At 10 P. M. the President telegraphed General Hooker:

To remove all misunderstanding, I now place you in the strict military relation to General Halleck of a commander of one of the armies to the General-in-Chief of all the armies. I have not intended differently, but it seems to be differently understood. I shall direct him to give you orders and you to obey them.

On June 27, 1 P. M., General Hooker telegraphed from Sandy Hook, a station of the Baltimore & Ohio Railroad, on the Potomac near Harper's Ferry:

My original instructions require me to cover Harper's Ferry and Washington. I have now imposed upon me, in addition, an enemy in my front of more than my number. I beg to be understood, respectfully but firmly, that I am unable to comply with this condition with the means at my disposal, and earnestly request that I may at once be relieved from the position I occupy.

The request of General Hooker to be relieved from the command was immediately complied with, and on the same afternoon the President issued orders placing General Meade in command of the army.

The report of General-in-Chief Henry W. Halleck is characteristic:

WASHINGTON, D. C., November 15, 1863.

SIR: In compliance with your orders I submit the following summary of military operations since my last annual report:

General Hooker relieved General Burnside from his command on January 26, but no advance movement was attempted until near the end of April, when a large cavalry force, under General Stoneman, was sent across the upper Rappahannock towards Richmond to destroy the enemy's communications, while General Hooker, with his main army, crossed the Rappahannock and the Rapidan above their junction and took position at Chancellorsville. At the same time General Sedgwick crossed near Fredericksburg and stormed and carried the heights.

A severe battle took place on May 2 and 3; and on May 5 our army was again withdrawn to the south side of the river.

From want of official data, I am unable to give any detailed accounts of their operations, or of our losses.

It is also proper to remark in this place, that from the time he was placed in command of the Army of the Potomac, till he reached Fairfax Station, on June 16, a few days before he was relieved from the command, General Hooker reported directly to the President, and received instructions directly from him. I received no official information of his plans, or of their execution.   *   *   *

Very respectfully your obedient servant,

H. W. HALLECK,
General-in-Chief.

Hon. E. M. Stanton, Secretary of War.

CHAPTER XIII.

BATTLE OF GETTYSBURG.

WHEN the order was issued relieving General Hooker and placing General Meade in command, the army of General Lee occupied the Cumberland Valley in Maryland and Pennsylvania, and the Army of the Potomac was on or near the line of the Baltimore & Ohio Railroad.

I proposed, as soon as practicable, to join General Meade in the field and ascertain his requirements, acting under the following special order:

WASHINGTON, June 27, 1863.

SPECIAL ORDER
No. 286.

Brigadier-General H. Haupt, U. S. Volunteers, is hereby authorized and directed to do whatever he may deem expedient to facilitate the transportation of troops and supplies to aid the armies in the field in Virginia, Maryland, and Pennsylvania.

By command of Major-General Halleck.

E. D. TOWNSEND,
Assistant Adjutant General.

On June 28, 1863, General Meade telegraphed General Halleck, acknowledging receipt of order placing him in command of the army, and stated that he was in ignorance of the exact condition of the troops and position of the enemy.

Having called upon the Secretary of War and communicated my intentions, he directed me to remain in Washington, as he had some other service for me to perform.

After waiting two or three days very impatiently, during which time I had no orders from the Secretary, I reported the situation to General Halleck, who agreed with me that I should be in the field, and advised me to go again to the Secretary and say to him that, unless he had more important duties for me to attend to elsewhere, General Halleck desired me to leave at once. The Secretary replied, "I do not know that I have anything for you to attend to; you had better go."

By this time General Meade had moved northward. The Baltimore & Ohio Railroad had been cut by the enemy, and I concluded that the most efficient service that I could render would be to go to Harrisburg, ascertain the condition of affairs in Pennsyl-

DRILL—BLANKET BOATS PARTLY CONSTRUCTED.

vania—especially the numbers and position of the forces that had been raised—and then make my way across the country on foot, or horseback, and give General Meade all the information I could gather.

With this object in view, I started for Harrisburg, but as the Northern Central Railroad had been badly injured, I was compelled to travel via Philadelphia and Reading. I reached Harrisburg late in the evening of June 30, and repaired at once to the capitol, where I found Governor Curtin and his staff. The room was filled with aides and other officers. Much confusion and excitement prevailed. I could get very little information, and asked where I could find Colonel Thomas A. Scott.

Having been informed that he was at the station engaged in dispatching troops to protect the bridges on the Pennsylvania Railroad that had been threatened by a cavalry raid, I repaired to the station, and, when the trains had been started, requested him, after showing my instructions, to give me a full and detailed report of the situation.

The request was complied with, from which I learned that, until the morning of that day, the enemy had occupied the opposite side of the river in large force; that at an early hour they had commenced to retreat, and with so much precipitancy that in some cases provisions had been left uncooked; that the artillery had gone through Mechanicsburg at a fast trot. Numerous other details were also given.

I then asked what explanation could be given as to the cause of these movements, and the answer was, that the enemy had been deceived by the representation that we had 60,000 men on the east side of the river, when, in fact, there were but 15,000 raw recruits, and that, unwilling to risk the passage of the river in the face of so large a force, Lee had concluded to retreat.

I replied to Colonel Scott: "You are entirely in error. These movements do not mean retreat; they mean concentration. Retreat would not be made hastily with no enemy pushing; it would be done deliberately, foraging on the country on the route. My explanation is this: Lee has just received the intelligence that Hooker has been relieved and Meade put in command. He knows that our Army Corps are scattered, and that Meade cannot get the reins in hand for some days at least, and he has formed the design to concentrate with all possible expedition and fall, with a largely superior force, upon our isolated Army Corps and overwhelm them successively. We are in the most critical condition we have been in since the war commenced, and nothing but the interposition of Providence can save us. If the army is destroyed, no new force can be collected in time to make effectual resistance. Washington,

Baltimore, Philadelphia and New York will fall, and the enemy can then, as masters of the situation, dictate their own terms."*

Scott replied, "I think you are right." I answered, "I am sure I am," and immediately wrote and forwarded this telegram at 10:30 P. M. :

HARRISBURG, PA., June 30, 1863.

Major-General Halleck, General-in-Chief:

Lee is falling back suddenly from the vicinity of Harrisburg, and concentrating all his forces. York has been evacuated. Carlisle is being evacuated. The concentration appears to be at or near Chambersburg. The object, apparently, a sudden movement against Meade, of which he should be advised by courier immediately. A courier might reach Frederick by way of Western Maryland Railroad to Westminster. This information comes from T. A. Scott, and I think it reliable.

H. HAUPT,
Brigadier-General.

Further information continued to be received, and at 12:45 A. M. I sent a second telegram, stating that information just received indicated that the point of concentration of Lee's forces was at Gettysburg, and not at Chambersburg. General Meade received this information at 3 A. M. by special courier from Westminster, as he subsequently informed me.

HARRISBURG, July 1, 1863, 6 A. M.

Major-General Halleck, General-in-Chief U. S. Army.

GENERAL: I sent two telegrams last night and sent the same to General Schenck.

Finding the communications cut with Meade's army, I concluded to run to Harrisburg, ascertain the position of affairs, then return to Baltimore, and try to work my way through to Frederick.

I found that there had been some skirmishing near Harrisburg yesterday; that the forces gathered for the protection of the place amounted to 16,000 men, and that the information in regard to the movements, position, and numbers of the enemy and arrangements for keeping advised of the same, were apparently reliable.

It appears to have been the intention of the enemy to attack Harrisburg yesterday. Our forces, supposed to be Pleasanton's, were resisting their movements and T. A. Scott said, had actually succeeded in retarding their advance upon Harrisburg and compelled a retreat. I thought I saw a much more decisive and important move on the tapis. Lee had received information of the removal of Hooker and the situation of Meade. He knew, also, that Meade's communications had been cut off by Stuart; that some confusion must exist from the change of commanders; that Meade could not at once get his forces in hand, and that, by suddenly concentrating and falling upon Meade, he could be crushed, when Washington, Baltimore, and Philadelphia would all be at the mercy of the enemy. I mentioned to Scott my opinion, in which he at once

---

* NOTE.—After the war I happened to travel in the same car with General Longstreet between New Orleans and Richmond, and he fully confirmed the opinion here expressed as to the design of Lee in the movement towards Gettysburg.

concurred, and I immediately sent the telegram to you and to General Schenck last night.

The most reliable information as to the number of the enemy, as given by Scott, is as follows:

Ewell 23,000 men, 48 pieces; Longstreet 30,000 men, 122 pieces; Hill 24,000 men, pieces not known; Early 15,000 men, 26 pieces; total 92,000 men and 236 pieces, exclusive of Hill's. Forces of Ewell were counted in Carlisle Friday P. M., June 26, as they passed. They left Carlisle by the Balitmore pike, Tuesday, June 30, 5 A. M.

Longstreet's Corps passed through Chambersburg on Friday and Saturday (27th) in the direction of Carlisle. In Carlisle Sunday evening; left on Monday afternoon; went through Newville with artillery in full trot, in the direction of Shippensburg, probably to take the Gettysburg road from this point.

Lee was in the square at Chambersburg at 9 A. M., Saturday, with 8,000 men and 40 pieces (part of Hill's). Left after conference with Hill in the direction of Gettysburg. Hill's Corps commenced leaving Chambersburg at 12 M. Saturday, three hours after Lee, in the same direction.

Early left Gettysburg for York Saturday, entered York Sunday; left York 2 P. M. Tuesday.

Firing Tuesday for several hours about Dillsburg and Petersburg, on the line between York and Gettysburg.

I am leaving for Baltimore.

Respectfully submitted,

H. HAUPT.

I left Harrisburg on the morning of July 1, reached Baltimore in the evening, and at once proceeded to organize transportation on the Western Maryland Railroad. On reaching Westminster, I found everything in great confusion, hundreds of wagons waiting, and the officers clamoring for supplies.

I asked them to give me a few minutes to think, and to escape the crowd I crept into a covered wagon and hid myself. In a short time I emerged, having organized a plan of operations, and, as soon as I could reach the wires, commenced to put it in operation.

J. N. Du Barry, the Superintendent of the Northern Central Railroad, was relieved at his own request. Adna Anderson was ordered from Alexandria, with a force of 400 railroad men, a train of split wood, lanterns, buckets, etc., and under his efficient management thirty trains per day were passed over the Westminster Railroad, 29 miles, on which there were no sidings sufficient to pass trains, and which had previously accommodated only three or four per day. Water was dipped in buckets from the streams, and the wood was brought from Alexandria, ready cut and split. The operation of this road, under the circumstances, was a very creditable performance, and was so successful that, as General Ingalls stated, the army at no time had less than three days' rations ahead.

The following telegrams will furnish further information in regard to the Military Railroad operations during the battle on the second, third and fourth days of July:

HARRISBURG, PA., July 1, 1863, 12:45 A. M.

*Major-General H. W. Halleck. General-in-Chief:**

Information just received, 12:45 A. M., leads to the belief that the concentration of the forces of the enemy will be at Gettysburg rather than at Chambersburg. The movement on their part is very rapid and hurried. They returned from Carlisle in the direction of Gettysburg by way of the Petersburg pike. Firing about Petersburg and Dillstown this P. M. continued some hours. Meade should, by all means, be informed, and be prepared for a sudden attack from Lee's whole army.

H. HAUPT,
Brigadier-General.

General Meade subsequently informed me that he received both of my former dispatches by courier in his tent at 3 A. M.

At Harrisburg I received a copy of General Jubal A. Early's proclamation to the citizens of York, Pa., as follows:

YORK, PA., June 30, 1863.

To the Citizens of York:

I have abstained from burning the railroad buildings and car shops in your town because, after examination, I am satisfied the safety of the town would be endangered, and acting in the spirit of humanity, which has ever characterized my government and its military authorities, I do not desire to involve the innocent in the same punishment with the guilty. Had I applied the torch, without regard to consequences, I would have pursued a course that would have been fully vindicated as an act of just retaliation for the authorized acts of barbarity perpetrated by your own army on our soil; but we do not war upon women and children, and I trust that the treatment you have met with at the hands of my soldiers will open your eyes to the monstrous iniquity of the war waged by your Government upon the people of the Confederate States, and that you will make an effort to shake off the revolting tyranny under which it is apparent to all you are yourselves groaning.

J. A. EARLY,
Major-General C. S. Army.

EUTAW HOUSE,
BALTIMORE, July 1, 1863.

General R. Ingalls:

The Western Maryland Railroad is in running order, but there are numerous small bridges in danger of destruction from rebel sympathizers. As guards cannot be provided, it will be necessary to run trains with escorts. The road is not in good condition; it has but a single track, no adequate sidings, and the time consumed in running the ordinary trains has been five hours for twenty-nine miles. There is no telegraph line on the road.

---

* NOTE.—And to General Meade and General Schenck.

To forward supplies by this line, the following arrangements will be required:

1. Trains must be run in convoys of five or six with guards sufficient for protection.

2. Half a dozen men should be placed at each bridge to keep off individuals mischievously inclined.

3. No schedule can be used, but when a convoy is dispatched from Junction no others can be sent until they have returned, so long as there are no telegraph lines.

4. It will be all-important, on the arrival of a convey, to unload each and every car on the main track and send back immediately. This duty will require the most efficient officer of your staff. The rapidity with which cars can be unloaded will measure the capacity of this road to supply the army.

5. No extras or specials should be run over the road until a telegraph line is established, as great risk and delay will result from it.

I have ordered iron, cars and engines from Alexandria, and will increase the business facilities at the depot as rapidly as possible.

Please communicate with me at the Eutaw House and let me know your wishes. It is not necessary to say that no time will be lost in carrying them into effect.

H. HAUPT,
Brigadier-General,
In Charge of United States Military Railroads.

July 1, 1863.

General M. C. Meigs, Quartermaster General:

I find that the communication with the Army of the Potomac by rail to Westminster will be very slow and uncertain, besides interfering most seriously with the supply trains. It has, therefore, been arranged to start immediately horse expresses at intervals of three hours, with relays every seven miles, to run day and night. The distance from Baltimore to Westminster is only twenty-eight miles, the road a good turnpike. The distance by rail is much longer. The time usually required by rail has been five hours from junction. The time by express from Baltimore will be three hours.

I send copy of note to General Ingalls to be forwarded by first express. Please communicate contents to General Halleck and Secretary of War, that the arrangement may be understood.

Adams' Express Company will run the horse express. S. M. Shoemaker, Esq., has made the necessary arangements with aid of General Schenck.

H. HAUPT,
Brigadier-General,
In Charge of United States Military Railroads.

WASHINGTON, July 1, 1863.

For Brigadier-General H. Haupt, U. S. A.:

General Meade desires that you be prepared to push on the repairs of the Northern Central Road to open connection with him from Baltimore as soon as he reaches the line of the road. I have ordered Construction Corps and train to Western Maryland Road, now open, to prepare siding and turnouts and be ready to transfer to the Northern Central. As soon as that is safe, you will proceed via Baltimore to these two lines to take charge of operations. These roads have sent away much of their equipments. Some of the military stock will be sent forward; it is lighter than the B. & O. R. R. engines.

M. C. MEIGS,
Quartermaster General.

July 2, 1863.

General Haupt:

Anderson and Construction Corps of 400 men left here yesterday P. M. The force has undoubtedly gone up the Northern Central to Westminster Branch to build turnouts. I requested Mr. Anderson to find you if he could; if not, to proceed up the line. Four car-loads of iron have been forwarded; more will be sent to-day. Have telegraphed you fully, addressed to Eutaw House, Baltimore.

D. C. McCALLUM.

July 2, 1863, 3 o'clock.

Hon. E. M. Stanton, Secretary of War:

I have, after careful inspection of condition and estimate of capacity of the Western Maryland Road, arranged for fifteen trains per day each way, in convoys of five trains each, at intervals of eight hours. Trains cannot pass at any point on this road from want of sidings, and there is no telegraph line. Still, if cars are promptly unloaded, and no accident occurs, I hope to pass 150 cars per day each way, capable of carrying from 2,000 to 4,000 wounded in return cars. The rapidity of loading and unloading will measure the capacity of the road. My men have passed over the Northern Central Railroad to Hanover Junction, and over Hanover and Gettysburg. A branch is marked on the map from Hanover to Littlestown, but my information is that the track is actually laid only a few hundred yards from Hanover. I have informed General Ingalls by courier of all these facts, and it rests with him to designate the route. I have no very recent information from Gettysburg, but at last account, the position of the enemy would not permit the reconstruction and operation of the Gettysburg Branch of that line. I can soon open the branch road to Gettysburg after we have full and undisturbed possession.

H. HAUPT,
Brigadier-General,
In Charge of United States Military Railroads.

RELAY STATION, N. C. R. R., July 2, 1863.

Brigadier-General Haupt, Eutaw House:

Just returned from New Oxford and Hanover Junction. There are nineteen bridges destroyed. Between York Haven and Hanover Junction and Gettysburg there are two small ones gone and one partly. I think these three bridges can be put up in from one to two days.

J. B. CLOUGH,
12 midnight.   *Engineer of Construction.*

July 2, 1863.

Colonel D. C. McCallum, Washington:

Trainmen have reported. I expect to see Du Barry to-day and make arrangements. The Western Maryland Railroad to Westminster, the Baltimore & Ohio Railroad to Frederick, and the Northern Central to Hanover Junction are in order.

H. HAUPT.

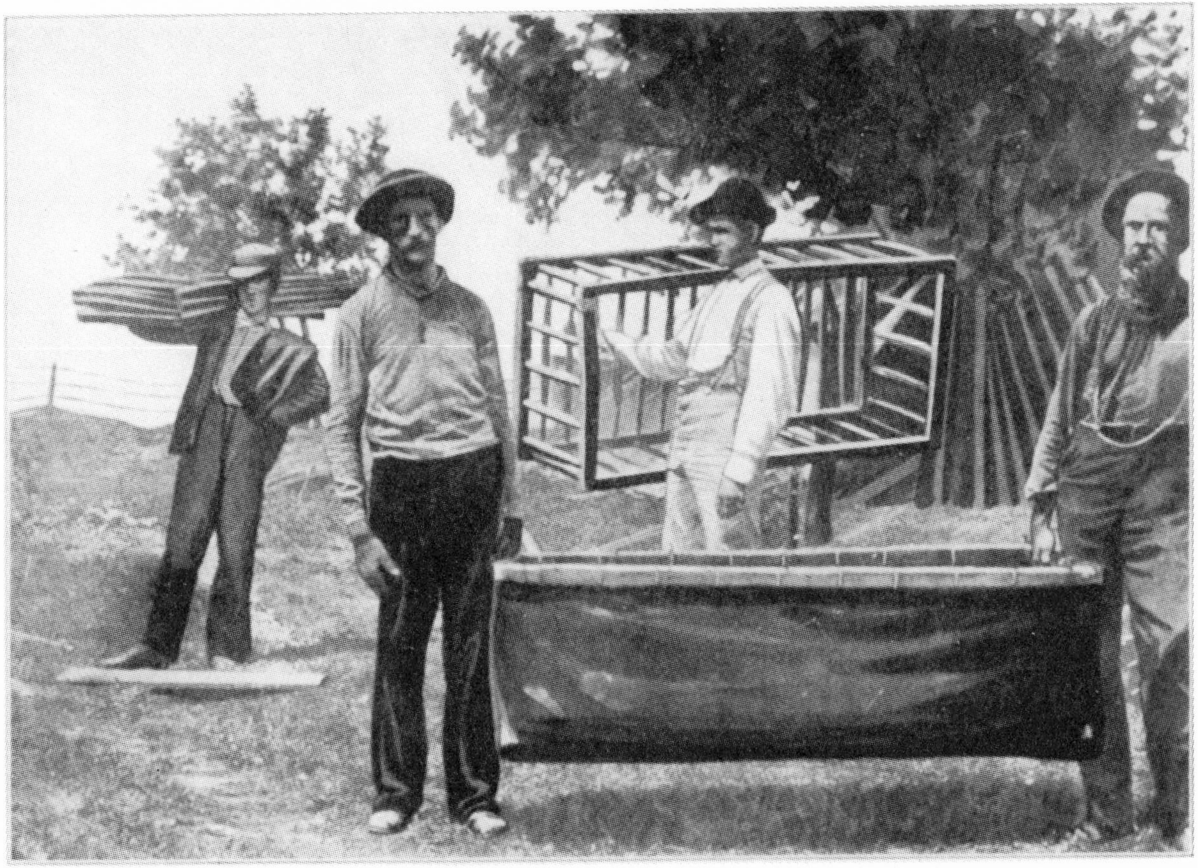

Blanket Boat Finished and Boat Frame Ready for Cover.

BUEHLER HOUSE,
HARRISBURG, July 2, 1863.

General:

Your telegram directing me to report to Mr. Du Barry is received, but before it arrived General Couch, in consequence of some trouble with railroads here, had issued an order appointing me "Superintendent of Railroad Transportation" in his Department, and in accordance with permit "To make myself useful in any way" I had accepted the position subject to your orders, and have taken measures to remove the difficulties complained of. I think this a much better arrangement than taking military possession of the railroad, as suggested by Colonel Thomson.

Below please find copy of General Couch's Special Order No. 22:

2. Colonel W. W. Wright, Superintendent U. S. Military Railroads, is hereby appointed Superintendent of Railroad Transportation in this Department.

I have seen Mr. Cameron, President Northern Central Railroad, and have consulted with General Couch, and he does not think it advisable to commence the reconstruction of the Northern Central at this end at present. Mr. Cameron informs me that Mr. Anderson's Construction Corps are at work on the Baltimore end of the road, and that Mr. Du Barry is at Baltimore.

I will, therefore, hold on until I can hear from you as to whether you wish me to remain here or not.

W. W. WRIGHT,
Superintendent of United States Military Railroads.

Brigadier-General H. Haupt,
Chief Construction and Transportation.

July 2, 1863.

Colonel Ambrose Thomson, Assistant Quartermaster:

If Mr. Wright's services to you are invaluable, I will allow him to remain with you. I cannot, however, delegate to any one the power, at his discretion, to take military possession of any or all railroads. It is best to operate roads by and through the regular officers and agents. If a necessity should arise for taking possession of the Chambersburg and of the Hanover branch roads for a short time, the proper orders will issue when the necessity arises, but I would not consent to any seizure of, or interference with, the Pennsylvania or the Northern Central Railroads.

There should be no confusion. No orders should be given except by or through you as Quartermaster, and your orders should be given only to the Superintendent of each road, or some one designated by him.

The Pennsylvania Central, Northern Central and Lebanon Valley Railroads are managed by experienced officers, and preference will always be given by them to Government transportation. To assert or exercise authority will not be necessary or proper.

H. HAUPT,
Brigadier-General,
In Charge of United States Military Railroads.

July 2, 1863.

We drove the rebels on our left this afternoon some distance. Our line formed an arc, but our left is now tangent.

Prospect of heavy work to-morrow. Rebels having been foiled in four attempts to carry our right and left wings, I think will next try to get in our rear.

URIAH H. PAINTER.

BALTIMORE, July 3, 1863.

General D. H. Rucker, Washington:

I am just informed that supplies have been ordered by you to Union Bridge. They have heretofore been manifested to Westminster. The arrangements for running the road have been completed under the impression that Westminster was to be the depot. The amount of supplies that can be forwarded to Union Bridge will be much less than can be handled at Westminster, and will involve an entire change of our arrangements.

The distance of Union Bridge from the headquarters of the army is about the same as from Westminster and the road from Westminster much better. Can you not telegraph orders immediately to have the supplies unloaded at Westminster instead of Union Bridge?

H. HAUPT.

WASHINGTON, July 3, 1863.

General Haupt:

Your dispatch received. You have full authority to do whatever you think proper in respect to transportation. You will please give to J. N. Du Barry, Superintendent Northern Central Road, the thanks of the Department for his energetic coöperation.

EDWIN M. STANTON,
Secretary of War.

WAR DEPARTMENT,
July 3, 1863, 12 M.

General H. Haupt, Baltimore:

Spare no efforts to send trains to bring in the wounded. It is said that the road from Baltimore to Littlestown, only seven (7) miles from the field, is in working order and protected. If transportation by rail cannot be had, provide it in any other practicable mode.

EDWIN M. STANTON,
Secretary of War.

HANOVER JUNCTION, July 4, 1863.

Major-General Halleck, General-in-Chief:

All the supplies offered for transportation on Westminster branch have been sent forward, and sidings at Relay are clear. Our arrangements work well. Transportation of the wounded should be via Westminster, to fill return cars. I have so requested.

Our men rebuilt entirely the bridge at this junction, three spans about forty feet, this morning. They expect to reach York to-morrow night. The reconstruction of the Northern Central entire at this time may not be an imperative military necessity, but as my Corps would not be otherwise employed, it is best to do it. I will endeavor to secure for you, when I reach Hanover, more rapid communication by telegraph with Gettysburg.

H. HAUPT.

HANOVER, PA., July 4, 1863.

Major-General Halleck, General-in-Chief:

I am now at Hanover Station. A bridge is broken between this place and Littlestown. I will proceed at once to repair it, and commence to send off wounded; then return and take the Gettysburg Railroad and commence repairing it. It will be well to make a good hospital in York, with which place I expect in two days to be in communication by rail. Until then, temporary arrangements can be made for wounded. I learn that the wire is intact for nine miles towards Gettysburg. I will have it repaired, and communicate any information of importance that I can obtain.

H. HAUPT,
Brigadier-General.

HANOVER, PA., July 4, 1863, 4 P. M.

Major-General Halleck, General-in-Chief:

I have just returned from Littlestown. Bridge repaired; trains with wounded following. Saw Captain Fry, of General Sickles' staff. Have arranged to bring General Sickles by special train to Washington. General Meade's Headquarters said to be nine miles from Littlestown, on Taneytown road. I am now starting towards Gettysburg to repair road and telegraph. Captain Fry reports that Pleasanton sent a note to General Sickles last evening, saying he had routed and driven the enemy; reported that Longstreet and Hill are both wounded and prisoners; that 3,000 prisoners passed through Littlestown this morning; that we are in possession of Gettysburg, and that Lee is retreating by Chambersburg road. I give these reports as I get them from Captain Fry. They may not be correct. No firing heard to-day. Telegram from General Meade received by courier says enemy retreated from Gettysburg at 3 A. M. He will follow when rations are received for men and horses.

H. HAUPT,
Brigadier-General.

OXFORD, PA., July 4, 1863, 11 P. M.

Major-General Halleck, General-in-Chief:

Night has overtaken me at Oxford, seven miles east of Gettysburg. We have been at work on a large bridge near this town, which is considerably damaged. It will require two hours to-morrow to finish it, when we will proceed to Gettysburg. A portion of track is torn up. I have found the foreman of repairs, and he will commence to repair the track at daylight. About a mile of the telegraph wire is down and wire carried off. I have sent my engine to junction for men and material to repair it. When an office is ready and line in order to Gettysburg, the operator will report to General Meade's Headquarters.

Persons just in from Gettysburg report the position of affairs. I fear that while Meade rests to refresh his men and collect supplies, Lee will be off so far that he cannot intercept him. A good force on the line of the Potomac to prevent Lee from crossing would, I think, insure his destruction.

By 11 o'clock to-night about two thousand tons of supplies should have been forwarded since yesterday morning to Meade's army if so much has been offered for transportation. I had arranged for 1,500 tons per day on Western Maryland Railroad. The reopening of the Northern Central Railroad from Hanover Junction to York will permit the rapid and convenient removal of wounded to that city, which is an excellent location for hospitals. I expect to have this completed by to-morrow (Sunday) night.

H. HAUPT.

Saturday night, July 4, the Construction Corps reached the last bridge on the road to Gettysburg. It was dark and rainy, and the men were required to do their work by the aid of lanterns, but at such a time personal convenience was not consulted. After getting the work properly started, I walked to Oxford, 10 miles from Gettysburg, and passed the night at the house of a friend.

CHAPTER XIV.

MEADE URGED IN VAIN TO FIGHT.

THE next morning, Sunday, July 5, and the day after Lee's retreat, my friend drove me in his buggy to Gettysburg. I found General Patrick in the square, and was directed by him to Meade's Headquarters on the Baltimore pike, near Rock Creek, two and a half miles from town. Here I found Generals Meade and Pleasanton. I informed them that by noon that day they would be in communication with Washington, both by rail and telegraph, at which much surprise and gratification were expressed, as it had been understood that the destruction of the bridges had been so complete that two or three weeks would be required for their renewal.

As this interview was an important one, I propose to describe it as accurately as possible. General Meade was seated at a small table in a farm house; General Pleasanton on his left. I was facing them on the opposite side. They gave me a brief history of the engagement, during which General Pleasanton made the remark that if Longstreet had concentrated his fire more in the center instead of scattering it over the whole of our left flank and held on a little longer, we would have been beaten. General Meade made no reply. He did not dissent, and I concluded from this fact that he acquiesced to this opinion.

During the conversation General Barksdales' sword was brought, and a number of relics of the battlefield, some of which were given to me.

After an hour or more spent in general conversation, I asked General Meade in reference to his future movements, so that I could arrange for his supplies, and observed that I supposed he would march at once to the Potomac and cut off Lee's retreat. He replied that he could not start immediately. The men required rest.

I ventured to remark that the men had been well supplied with rations; that they had been stationary behind the stone walls during the battle; that they could not be footsore; that the enemy before and after the battle had been in motion more than our army; that it was but little more than a day's march to the river, and that if advantage were not taken of Lee's present condition, he would escape.

To this General Meade answered that Lee had no pontoon train and that the river was swollen by rains and was not fordable.

I replied: "Do not place confidence in that. I have men in my Construction Corps who could construct bridges in forty-eight hours sufficient to pass that army, if they have no other material than such as they could gather from old buildings or from the woods, and it is not safe to assume that the enemy cannot do what we can."

There was more conversation on the subject. As a class-mate of General Meade at West Point, I did not hesitate to express my opinions freely without fear of offense. I could not, however, remove the idea from General Meade that a period of rest was necessary.

I left much discouraged, and as soon as practicable, communicated the situation to General Halleck at Washington, in hopes that something could be done to urge General Meade to more prompt action than he appeared to contemplate. I took an engine the same night after the interview with General Meade and went to Washington to make a report to General Halleck in person early on Monday morning, July 6.

General Meade informed me that he proposed to move his Headquarters towards Creagerstown, but there was nothing to indicate any disposition to move rapidly with any considerable portion of his force to cut off Lee's retreat, and I left him with the impression upon my mind that there would be no advance of any considerable portion of the army for some days, and that Lee would be sure to escape and the fruits of the victory be lost. These fears were realized, although Lee did not cross the river until July 14.

At the opening of the Northern Pacific Railroad in 1884, of which I was General Manager, President Arthur and Secretary of War Robert T. Lincoln were invited guests. Lincoln sent word that he wished to see me, and when I presented myself he inquired about information given by me immediately after the battle of Gettysburg. He said that upon entering his father's room one day he found him in great trouble, and upon inquiring the cause the President said that information had been received from General Haupt which led to the belief that Meade did not intend immediately to follow up his victory and that Lee would escape. He asked for my exact recollection of the facts, which I gave him as here stated.

My telegram to General Halleck of Sunday, July 5, after the interview with General Meade, shows very clearly that I had little

General Haupt on Float Made of Two Small Rubber Cylinders, Used for Scouting Purposes.

hope that Lee would be intercepted and prevented from crossing the river, and my hope then was, by a very prompt movement to head him off, intercept his supplies and reinforcements and starve him out, or compel him to fight again under unfavorable conditions.

BALTIMORE, MD., July 5, 1863.
Major-General Halleck, General-in-Chief:

I have just returned from Headquarters of General Meade. I left him about 1 P. M., about moving for Creagerstown. The main body of the enemy appears to have taken the Hagerstown road. They will reach the Potomac before Meade can possibly overtake them. Would it not be well to send immediately forces to occupy all the gaps on the side of Shenandoah Valley; ascertain condition of Manassas Gap Railroad, and, by a very prompt movement, throw a large force on Front Royal to intercept them? I will see you to-morrow.

H. HAUPT.

On Monday morning I had a personal interview with General Halleck, and explained verbally the situation, then I called upon the Secretary of War and the President separately. After the interview with General Halleck I returned to my office and wrote the following letter, in which I assumed, from the position taken by General Meade, that he would certainly permit Lee to escape, and suggested the course that should be pursued to minimize to some extent the evil effects:

WASHINGTON, D. C., July 6, 1863.
Major-General Halleck, General-in-Chief U. S. Army.

GENERAL: I fear that in my brief statement this morning I did not express clearly the idea I intended to convey. I did not mean to suggest that the principle of concentration should be violated, for in this I am well aware, has heretofore consisted the enemy's strength and our weakness. My idea is this:

Lee left Gettysburg Saturday morning in retreat, Meade more than one day behind.

Lee would nearly have reached Hagerstown when Meade started from Gettysburg.

From Hagerstown to South Mountain Gap or from Frederick to same point the distance is about thirteen miles. Lee could reach the Gap of South Mountain one day ahead of Meade, unless the Gap was occupied by French, and I was not aware of the fact until to-day that he had such orders.

By holding Meade in check at the Gap of South Mountain for a few days, the fords would become passable and Lee could cross the Potomac.

Once across, he could move more rapidly than we could follow and instead of attempting it, Meade would probably move on the inside track east of the Blue Ridge.

In this condition of affairs, the railroad would be indispensable, and as the country must now be nearly clear of the enemy, a very small force could occupy the Gaps of the Blue Ridge, make descents into the valley to cut off any trains of supplies sent to relieve Lee and put the Manassas Gap and Orange & Alexandria Railroads in condition for use, if sudden demand should be made upon them.

Even if Lee's army should be captured or dispersed north of the Potomac, I suppose the railroad will be required for a movement south to strike rapidly and follow up our advantages until every strong place has fallen and the rebellion be completely crushed.

If the enemy succeeded in crossing the Potomac, then a large number of troops could be sent by rail to Front Royal or Gordonsville, instead of following the enemy by marches.

McDowell used to say that I was always seeking to anticipate positions for a year ahead and provide for them, but if this be a fault, I think it is on the safe side; better look too far ahead than not be ready.

Excuse my suggestions; they may be and probably are of no value whatever. I have neither your judgment, experience, nor sources of information, but anxious to do something to finish up the war. I feel better satisfied with myself if I make them than if I do nothing.

I am again off for Frederick to-day.

Very respectfully submitted,

H. HAUPT.

The foregoing letter, which I find in my old letter-book, is important as throwing light upon a point on which I had some doubts.

I had been with Meade until noon Sunday, July 5. I then spent two or three hours in walking over the battlefield, and on Monday, July 6, I was in Washington and wrote the above letter. It shows that at that early date (Monday, July 6), I anticipated the escape of Lee, which was not accomplished until July 14, and that I sought to repair the error in part by rapid movements to intercept his supplies and embarrass his retreat.

It is ungenerous to criticise faults, and it is always easy, after an event, to say what might have been; but so far as my opinions are concerned, they were matters of record before, and not after the event. I clearly predicted what would probably occur, and what did actually occur, and I am probably largely responsible for what has been denounced as an act of great injustice to General Meade in the correspondence between himself and the President and General Halleck, which caused him to ask to be relieved from the command.

My ideas of the situation then, and I have seen no reason to change them since, can be briefly stated.

Lee's army had been badly beaten; it was fatigued, much more than ours, from forced marches and charges; it had suffered great losses; it must have been, to a great extent, dispirited and demoralized, and, it was reasonable to suppose, very short of artillery ammunition which could not be supplied north of the Potomac.

In this condition retreat was interrupted by an impassable river. The army was in a trap. It must either find means to get across that river, fight another battle, or surrender.

Meade's army could have reached the Potomac certainly in less than two days; it was less fatigued than its enemy; it would be marching towards its base of supplies via the Baltimore & Ohio Railroad; no large supply of rations was required and, as General Ingalls reported, they had an abundance; they had, I understood, two pontoon trains for bridges, and there was no large, if any, force of the enemy on the south side of the Potomac, for Lee had carried with him into Pennsylvania all his available forces.

Now, it is possible that if Meade had attacked Lee in a strong defensive position, the enemy would. have fought desperately so long as their scant supply of ammunition lasted, and our losses might have been heavy, although I cannot believe that the result would have been disastrous even then.

But this was not necessary. Meade could have taken position below Lee on the river, covering Washington and his base of supplies at the same time. He could have chosen a spot readily defensible against attack, and thrown a part of his force, by means of his bridges, across the river, keeping them within supporting distance. This force could safely have been spared and, if necessary in case of attack, could have been recalled. A force on the south side with a small amount of artillery would have effectually cut off all reinforcements and supplies, and the construction of bridges under fire would never have been attempted. Lee would never have renewed the attack if Meade had occupied a defensible position; he would have sent in a flag of truce and capitulated then and there.

This result I anticipated until after the conference with Meade on Sunday morning. After that, I had but little doubt that Lee would escape, and directed my attention to the best means of repairing the damage that would be caused by such disaster.

To build a bridge across the Potomac I knew to be a very simple matter, if unmolested by the fire of the enemy. The photographs and accompanying printed explanations that had been sent to nearly all the Corps commanders would have enabled any intelligent engineer officer to construct bridges from timbers cut in the woods and from material from old buildings; and the fact is that the enemy did build their bridges precisely as I had predicted that they would.

Assuming that the enemy would succeed in crossing the Potomac, and continue their retreat up the Shenandoah Valley towards Front Royal and Staunton, the question then was, what movements should be made by the Federal army?

To follow after the enemy would be folly. It would be like a tortoise attempting to catch a greyhound. Lee would be moving towards his base and growing stronger daily, while Meade would be leaving his base behind with an increasing line of communication, subject to constant interruption by guerrillas and cavalry raids.

The Shenandoah Valley is bounded on the east by the high range of the Blue Ridge Mountains, extending through the State; and near the base of the Blue Ridge runs the line of the Orange & Alexandria Railroad from Alexandria through Fairfax, Manassas, Charlottesville and Lynchburg.

Two railroads crossed the Blue Ridge—the Chesapeake & Ohio through Charlottesville, crossing at Rockfish Gap; and the road from Norfolk to Bristol through Lynchburg, crossing at Blue Ridge Station. These two railroads would be the main sources of supply for Lee's army.

With the bridge torpedoes and the implements for destroying track, described elsewhere, a force of cavalry could quickly wreck these roads and bridges, and, by occupying the gaps of the mountain through which the common roads passed and obstructing them with fallen trees, could prevent wagons from the east from reaching the rebel army.

This would have cut off communication with Richmond and the ammunition supplies of which they were in need, and compelled them to scatter to subsist upon the country.

Then would have been the time to watch the movements from the mountains and strike blows when opportunity offered, risking a general engagement only when the conditions were favorable for success.

My letter to General Halleck outlined such a plan as this. In fact, after the escape of Lee, the line of the Orange & Alexandria Railroad was reoccupied after some weeks of delay, and became once more the base of supplies; but the movements of the military were too slow, and the advantages they might have gained by celerity were lost.

With 30,000 men, the great Napoleon could beat 100,000. He manœuvred until his enemy was separated, then struck like a thunderbolt, and repeated the blows until his enemy was vanquished. After victory he did not stop to rest and let his enemy recuperate.

We had no Napoleons in the armies of the East on either side. Stonewall Jackson was the nearest approach to one, and if he had lived possibly the fate of the rebellion might have been different.

A feather's weight would have turned the scale at Gettysburg!

The opinion has been expressed by some that if Meade had moved as I have indicated and occupied a defensive position on the Potomac below Lee's army, the enemy could have reoccupied the Cumberland Valley and drawn supplies of forage and rations from this rich country. Lee certainly, in the condition of his army, would not have attempted a retrograde movement, and as the Corps of General Couch, which had not been in action, occupied the Valley, any foraging parties would have been cut off.

Subsistence could have been obtained only for a very short time, and ammunition, of which he was greatly in need, could not have been secured north of the Potomac. While he might have successfully resisted an attack from Meade, a renewal of the offensive in the condition of his army would have been a desperate movement with no prospect of success, and there is no reason to believe that it would have been attempted. Lee was in a trap, and if he had been prevented from crossing the river, he must have surrendered.

General Hunt, in the *Century* of January, 1887, gives the relative strength of the contending armies—Federal 77,208 infantry, Confederates 59,484; but remarks that "neither return is worth much except as a basis for guessing."

At my last interview with General Hooker just before he was relieved, he informed me that the total of his effective men did not exceed 60,000. My report to General Halleck of July 1, from information obtained from Colonel Thomas A. Scott, from actual count of the Confederate forces in Chambersburg and Carlisle, gave 92,000 men and 236 pieces of artillery, exclusive of Hill's.

I have never doubted that the Confederate forces in the battle of Gettysburg were largely in excess of our own.

In an article in the *Century*, General Longstreet states that he objected to the attack on the Cemetery Ridge on the second day, and advisd Lee to turn Meade's position by the right flank, which would have compelled a precipitate evacuation by Meade of his strong position and compelled him to give battle when the advantage of position would have been on the side of the enemy.

I can see no reason why such a movement would not have been successful. The movement could readily have been concealed for some time by the character of the country, and before Meade could have discovered it the bulk of the Confederate army could have been interposed between him and Washington.

Another critic defends Lee and lays the blame on Longstreet, charging him with dilatory movements. It is stated that Longstreet was ordered to make an attack early in the day, and that, had he done so, the Union forces holding Cemetery Ridge would have been overwhelmed before the arrival of reinforcements. This may be true also, and shows how little would have turned the scale and how narrowly the Union army escaped a disastrous defeat and gained a glorious victory. That the fruits of victory were not harvested when the opportunity was presented must ever remain a source of profound regret.

CHAPTER XV.

OFFICIAL RECORDS OF GETTYSBURG.

HARRISBURG, July 6, 1863.

General Haupt:

Message received. No U. S. M. cars on our line. Your construction cars, eight in number, are on Northern Central, but cannot be spared from your operating force. The roads centering at Philadelphia can give you only number of cars that may be needed if your own and B. & O. and Feltons are not sufficient. Please advise fully. Lee's army is flying for Potomac; the Cumberland Valley from Greenvillage south is full of them. General Conch is harassing them. Captured 500 prisoners, 100 wagons and three pieces artillery near Greencastle last night.

If good forces are thrown forward from Frederick to Boonsboro and Hagerstown, most of Lee's army will be captured.

THOMAS A. SCOTT.

July 6, 1863, the President telegraphed to General Halleck:

I left the telegraph office a good deal dissatisfied. I see a dispatch from General French saying the enemy is crossing his wounded over the river in flats; still later, another dispatch from General Pleasanton, by direction of General Meade, to General French, stating that the main army is halted, because it is believed the rebels are concentrating, and is not to move until it is ascertained that the rebels intend to evacuate Cumberland Valley.

These things all appear to me to be connected with a purpose to cover Baltimore and Washington and get the enemy across the river again without a further collision, and they do not appear to be connected with a purpose to prevent his crossing and to destroy him. I do fear the former purpose is acted upon, and the latter rejected.

Although, perhaps, it was more the concern of some other officer to do so, I addressed to the presidents of the Boston & Worcester; New Haven, Hartford & Springfield; Camden & Amboy; Philadelphia, Wilmington & Baltimore; Cleveland & Toledo; Pittsburg, Columbus & Cincinnati; Pennsylvania Central; Indiana Central; Cleveland & Pittsburg; New Jersey Railroad & Transportation Co.; New York & New Haven; and Michigan Southern Railroads this telegram:

WASHINGTON CITY, July 6, 1863.

I am informed by the Quartermaster General that, in order to reap the fruits of victory, a large number of fresh horses are most urgently required. They are needed to recruit the cavalry and restore the batteries to a condition of efficiency. Extraordinary efforts should

SMALL RAFT OF BLANKET BOATS CROSSING THE POTOMAC RIVER.

be made by the officers of all railroads over which horses are transported to push them forward without delay, day and night.

Please give this subject prompt personal attention. In no other way can more efficient service be rendered at this time to the country. The enemy must not escape if in our own power to prevent it.

H. HAUPT,

Brigadier-General,

Chief of Construction and Transportation

United States Military Railroads.

General Halleck to General Meade July 7, 1863:

You have given the enemy a stunning blow at Gettysburg. Follow it up and give him another before he can reach the Potomac. When he crosses, circumstances will determine whether it will not be best to pursue him by the Shenandoah Valley, or on this side of the Blue Ridge. There is strong evidence that he is short of artillery ammunition, and if vigorously pressed, he must suffer.

My operations during the week of the battle of Gettysburg are summarized in the following report to the Secretary of War:

WASHINGTON, D. C., July 7, 1863.

SIR: I herewith submit a brief report of operations in the Military Railway Department for the last week.

On Monday, June 29, acting under Special Orders 286, a copy of which is inclosed, I repaired to Baltimore intending to join General Meade at Frederick and ascertain the condition and requirements of the Army of the Potomac.

Finding the communications broken both by rail and telegraph, and the road near Sykesville in the possession of the enemy, I concluded to proceed to Harrisburg, ascertain the precise condition of affairs, then work my way by some means to General Meade and inform him what degree of assistance and coöperation he might expect from the Pennsylvania forces.

Owing to the interruptions of travel, I proceeded to Harrisburg via Reading, arrived in that city Tuesday morning, spent several hours with Governor Curtin and Thomas A. Scott, and learned the position of affairs.

I had written to the Governor from Falmouth soon after the battle of Chancellorsville, informing him that the enemy would soon be in Pennsylvania, and made suggestions of means proper to be resorted to to impede his progress and protect the Pennsylvania Railroad.

I found that Colonel Scott had been very active and efficient, and that the Pennsylvania Railroad had been as well protected as the short time would permit.

Very extensive arrangements had been made to procure information from scouts, and I saw clearly that instead of attacking Harrisburg, an exceedingly rapid concentration of the enemy's forces had been going on that day tending towards Gettysburg, evidently designed to fall upon and crush in detail the Army of the Potomac before it could fully concentrate or its new commander get it well in hand.

I at once telegraphed to General Halleck and to General Schenck and suggested that an engine be run from Baltimore to Westminster with express, and a mounted courier be dispatched to General Meade.

The dispatch was received and it helped to confirm the correctness of information derived from other sources. It came from the rear of the enemy, while other information could only be derived from the front.

Wednesday I returned to Baltimore and proceeded to the Relay House on the Northern Central Railroad. I found the Western Maryland Railroad entirely without equipment or facilities for the business to be thrown immediately upon it. It had no experienced officers, no water stations, sidings or turntables, or wood for a business exceeding three or four trains per day, while the necessities of the service required thirty trains per day to be passed over it. I had engines and cars sent from Alexandria with full sets of hands. A train of sawed and split wood and a supply of buckets was also forwarded. Tanks were filled by dipping water from the streams, and with other arrangements required by the circumstances of the case we were enabled to provide for a transportation of 1,500 tons per day each way. In two days the army was supplied not only with everything required, but with an excess which has been left for the use of the hospitals.

The Chief Quartermaster of the Army of the Potomac informed me that their supplies had at no time become so low that they could not have been stretched over three days, and on Sunday, when the pursuit of the enemy commenced, they had more than they wished to carry with them.

After organizing the transportation on the Western Maryland Railroad and leaving it in charge of Adna Anderson, Esq., the efficient Chief Engineer of Construction, I proceeded to Hanover with a construction train, passed over the Littlestown branch; reconstructed a bridge that had been broken down; found General Sickles [who was wounded] without means of transportation; arranged to have him sent immediately to Washington; returned to Hanover and switched off on Gettysburg Branch; proceeded to Oxford, where a large bridge across the Conewago had been burned; decided on mode of repair; set the gangs at work, returned to Oxford and dispatched train to junction for more men and materials.

The next morning I left instructions with foreman after finishing the Conewago bridge, to proceed to next bridge, repair it, and work on to Gettysburg, unless he received word from me that the enemy, who were on the road near Gettysburg the previous afternoon, were still there. I then procured a buggy and proceeded over the turnpike to Gettysburg, finding no enemy except wounded at the farmhouses, the last having retreated the previous evening.

After about three hours with General Meade and other officers at Headquarters, I returned to Oxford, and after completing the railroad to Gettysburg, returned to Baltimore Sunday night after a very active week, in which my Corps, both in construction and transportation, performed services of very great importance. I am particularly indebted to A. Anderson, Esq., Chief Engineer, for his sound judgment and efficiency; also to J. N. Du Barry, Superintendent of Northern Central Railroad, for his active coöperation. I have presented to him, as you directed, the thanks of your Department.

The Construction Corps is still at work on the bridges of the Northern Central Railroad, of which nineteen were destroyed, and in two days more I expect that communication with Harrisburg will be reestablished.

I cannot speak in terms of too strong commendation of the Corps for Reconstruction and Transportation. No department of the military service is of more importance than that which is charged with constructing, reopening and maintaining communications and forwarding supplies. Volunteers have always been ready for any service, however dangerous. At the second battle of Manassas General Kearney desired me to run a pilot engine over the road, in advance of his troop trains, after a train had been fired upon by a large force of the enemy, and men were found to perform the service without hesitation.

Employes of the Transportation Department have remained at stations long after they had been evacuated by the military in retreat, and have brought away stores to save them from the enemy. At the battle of Fredericksburg a small force of carpenters, under E. C. Smeed and G. W. Nagle, superintendents of bridge construction, worked for nearly half a day under fire, until their ropes were cut, the pulleys smashed, and the timbers knocked about with shells. A military force of 200 men, which had been detailed to assist, straggled off soon after the action commenced, not leaving a single man.

These men are not in a position to acquire military distinction or rewards, but I would fail in my duty if I omitted to signify to you my high appreciation of the labors, services, courage and fidelity of the Corps for Construction and Transportation in the Department of U. S. Military Railroads, and suggest that some recognition of their services would be a great encouragement to men who so richly deserve it.

Very respectfully submitted,

H. HAUPT,
In Charge of United States Military Railroads.

Hon. E. M. Stanton,
Secretary of War.

July 7, 1863, General Halleck to General Meade:

I have seen your dispatch to General Couch of 4:40 P. M. You are perfectly right. Push forward and fight Lee before he can cross the Potomac.

July 8, 1863, General Halleck to General Meade:

There is reliable information that the enemy is crossing at Williamsport. The opportunity to attack his divided forces should not be lost. The President is urgent and anxious that your army should move against him by forced marches.

July 8, 1863, General Meade to General Halleck, 3 P. M.:

My army is and has been making forced marches short of rations and barefooted. One Corps marched yesterday and last night over thirty miles.

July 8, 1863, General Halleck to General Meade:

You will have sufficient forces to render your victory certain. My only fear now is that the enemy may escape by crossing the river.

WASHINGTON CITY, July 7, 1863.
Brigadier-General Haupt, in Charge of Railroads.

GENERAL: The following is a copy of telegram sent you on the 4th inst., viz.:

Adams Express, by Mr. Shoemaker, Superintendent, proposes to organize and send forward a hospital corps to assist in caring for and removing the wounded with stores, supplies, men, vehicles and spring wagons. They ask transportation to Westminster by Summit Railway for men and material. The Secretary of War has consented, and referred them to you for such transportation as can be furnished by rail without interfering with forwarding of supplies which the army needs to enable it to pursue the enemy—advising them at the same time that probably the best and speediest route will be with their spring wagons over the turnpike roads from Baltimore to Westminster. Also, that latest reports show eleven hundred (1100) ambulances with the Army of the Potomac.

Let nothing interfere with the supply of rations to the men and grain for the horses.
By order of the Secretary of War.

(Signed)   M. C. MEIGS,
Quartermaster General.

By order of Quartermaster General.

Very respectfully,
Your obedient servant,
CHAS. THOMAS,
Colonel and Assistant Quartermaster General.

PLANE No. 4, MD., July 8, 1863.

Hon. E. M. Stanton:
The blockade at Frederick is raised. Everything now works smoothly. I am on my way to Harrisburg to open the Cumberland Valley Railroad, which is now very necessary for army operations.

H. HAUPT.

A telegram to M. C. Meigs, Quartermaster-General, dated Frederick, July 8, 1863, announced that a train blockade at that point had been relieved; that fifteen trains had been returned, "and I am needed here no longer." Also this:

I will return immediately to Harrisburg and pass through the line to Hagerstown as fast as we can get possession. We should be able to capture many prisoners and take wagons and ambulances and perhaps artillery before the enemy can cross the river. The late rains and bad roads will help us, but I do not believe we can prevent Lee's army from crossing. I could build trestle-bridges of round sticks and floor with fence rails. It is too much to assume the rebels cannot do the same.*

Other suggestions were made with the request that if General Meigs concurred in their expediency, he should talk the matter over with General Halleck. I did not wish to appear officious by too frequent suggestions to my superior officers.

Under date July 8, 1863, 3 P. M., General Meade telegraphed General Halleck:

My information as to the crossing of the enemy does not agree with that just received in your dispatch. His whole force is in position between Funkstown and Williamsport.

My army is and has been making forced marches, short of rations and barefooted. One Corps marched yesterday and last night thirty miles.

This statement that the army was short of rations and barefoot is in direct conflict with the report of the Chief Quartermaster that their supplies had at no time become so low that they could not have been stretched over three days, and, on Sunday, July 5,

---

* NOTE.—This refers to a remark made to me by General Meade on Sunday morning, July 5, that the enemy had no pontoon trains, that the river was up and he could not cross. He did not cross until the 14th, during which time he had ample time to construct bridges, in fact, double the time required.

when the pursuit of the enemy commenced, they had more than they wished to carry with them.

As the Chief Quartermaster was the officer whose duty it was to know the condition of the supplies, and as the amount was so large on the 5th that it was necessary to leave a surplus for the use of the hospitals, and as the reconstruction of the railroad to Gettysburg was completed by noon Sunday, July 5, and trains running constantly to Baltimore and Washington, it is difficult to understand how the army could be barefoot and out of rations on the 8th.

If some Corps or Brigade happened to be short, it must have resulted from inequalities of distribution, which could have been remedied quickly and easily. Besides, in moving towards the line of the Baltimore & Ohio Railroad, Meade would have been moving *towards* and not *from* his proper base of supplies.

HANOVER, July 9, 1863, 1:20 P. M.

General M. C. Meigs:

I am on my way to Gettysburg again. Find things in great confusion. Road blocked; cars not unloaded; stores ordered to Gettysburg, where they stand for a long time, completely preventing all movement there; ordered back without unloading; wounded lying for hours without ability to carry them off; all because the simple rule of promptly unloading and returning cars is violated.

I have ordered my track gangs from Alexandria to Gettysburg, to be sent to Chambersburg by wagon, to repair Hagerstown road.

H. HAUPT,
Brigadier-General.

SOUTH MOUNTAIN, July 10, 1863.

General Haupt:

The enemy is in force at Hagerstown. We move towards that place to-day. General Meade wishes you to refer to General Couch for information as to affairs north of that place; we only know that the enemy is there. I hope Generals Couch and Smith will push up rapidly and vigorously; now is the time.

RUFUS INGALLS,
Brigadier-General.

CHAMBERSBURG, 8 P. M., July 11, 1863.

General Haupt:

It is now reasonably certain that the railroad must be put in order to Hagerstown as quickly as possible. Send your best forces. The enemy evacuated Hagerstown last night and our forces will certainly move to Hagerstown or beyond.

THOS. A. SCOTT.

WASHINGTON, D. C., July 11, 1863.

General R. Ingalls, Headquarters Army of the Potomac:

The Northern Central Railroad through to Harrisburg will not be opened before Tuesday. With great exertion I have impressed four teams, and my force of 180 trackmen is now started to march to Chambersburg. The report of damages leads me to expect great difficulty

13

in procuring materials to reconstruct the Hagerstown road. I go to Chambersburg to-morrow, and will spare no efforts to open the communication.

H. HAUPT.

July 13, 1863, General Halleck to General Meade, 9: 30 P. M.:

Yours of 5 P. M. received. You are strong enough to attack and defeat the enemy before he can effect a crossing. Act upon your own judgment and make your Generals execute your orders. Call no council of war. It is proverbial that councils of war never fight. Reinforcements are pushed on as rapidly as possible. Do not let the enemy escape.

CHAMBERSBURG, July 13, 1863.

General M. C. Meigs, Quartermaster-General, Washington:
     I am engaged with a part of my Construction Corps in reconstructing the Hagerstown Railroad. Ten miles have been destroyed and ties burned. While engaged on Northern Central, Western Maryland and Gettysburg roads, I requested T. A. Scott to send forces from Pennsylvania Railroad to reconstruct road to Hagerstown, and get iron wherever he could find it. We could not send it from Alexandria in time. 400 tons of rails have been procured from Cambria. An account will be kept of work and materials on each road, to be charged against transportation bills. Any iron not used can be returned.

H. HAUPT.

CHAMBERSBURG, July 13, 1863.

D. J. Morrell, Johnstown, Pa.:
     The Government must have the iron. Please send it on without delay. The reopening of the Hagerstown Railroad in the shortest time possible is an imperative military necessity.

H. HAUPT,
Brigadier-General.

July 13, 1863.

A. Anderson, Hanover; J. H. Devereux, Alexandria:
     Send immediately twenty-five yoke of our oxen with yokes, chains, drivers, and attendants. Put them in cars on receipt of this and forward them by special train to Chambersburg, by most expeditious route. Ten miles of track on Hagerstown road have been destroyed. We must cut and haul ties, and no transportation to be had in the country. Show this telegram to railroad superintendents, and ask them to hurry the oxen along.

H. HAUPT,
Brigadier-General.

CHAMBERSBURG, July 14, 1863.

General R. Ingalls, Headquarters Army of the Potomac:
     We have a sweet time reconstructing Hagerstown road. Rain or drizzle all the time; men work but accomplish little; several bridges on Northern Central Railroad twice carried away since we commenced to reconstruct them. We started a steam saw-mill yesterday; run it day and night; make cross-ties of slabs, planks—anything we can get. Telegraph poles between this place and Hagerstown cut down and burned; no poles or teams to be had. Line must be reconstructed from Hagerstown end. To-day I suppose the Northern Central Railroad will

SMALL RAFT OF BLANKET BOATS.

be finished, when the balance of my force, with tools and material, will be able to get here; the work will then progress very rapidly. I marched my track force of 180 men across mountain; they are doing good service, but want tools and transportation. Send me a telegram every afternoon giving position of affairs.

H. HAUPT,
Brigadier-General.

On July 14, 1863, General Meade reported to General Halleck that upon advancing his lines he found the enemy's position evacuated.

On July 14, 1863, General Halleck to General Meade, 1 P. M.:

The enemy should be pursued and cut up wherever he may have gone. This pursuit may or may not be upon the rear or flank, as circumstances may require. The inner flank towards Washington presents the greatest advantages. Supply yourself from the country as far as possible. I cannot advise details, as I do not know where Lee's army is, nor where your pontoon bridges are. I need hardly say to you that the escape of Lee's army without another battle has created great dissatisfaction in the mind of the President, and it will require an active and energetic pursuit on your part to remove the impression that it has not been sufficiently active heretofore.*

[Translated cipher.]

WASHINGTON, July 14, 1863, 3 P. M.

Brigadier-General Haupt:
Withdraw all your Construction Corps from Northern Central Railroad and bring them as quickly as possible to Alexandria. Lee has crossed the Potomac.

M. C. MEIGS,
Quartermaster General.

July 14, 1863.

General M. C. Meigs, Quartermaster-General, Washington:
Construction Corps will be ordered immediately back to Alexandria. This movement is precisely as I expected and predicted. I did not see how we could prevent the enemy from crossing. It is now of the greatest importance to occupy the gaps of the Blue Ridge and push forces ahead to secure any bridges on the Orange & Alexandria Railroad that may still remain from destruction.

H. HAUPT,
Brigadier-General.

CHAMBERSBURG, July 14, 1863.

D. J. Morrell, Johnstown:
No iron will be required; the movement of the army renders the reconstruction of Hagerstown road unnecessary. I have requested T. A. Scott to return all that you have delivered.

H. HAUPT,
Brigadier-General,
In Charge of United States Military Railroads.

---

* NOTE.—This was the dispatch that induced Meade to ask to be relieved. The word "disappointment" was substituted for "dissatisfaction" in subsequent correspondence.

CHAMBERSBURG, July 14, 1863.

General R. Ingalls:

The Winchester Road cannot be relied upon for any transportation whatever. The rail is strap iron, the supports rotten. The lighter engines run off the track continually. I am moving my whole force to Alexandria. You cannot catch Lee by following in his rear. The bridges on the Orange & Alexandria Railroad which are not burned should be saved if possible; also on Manassas Gap Railroad.

H. HAUPT,
Brigadier-General.

CHAMBERSBURG, July 14, 1863.

J. N. Bu Barry, Harrisburg:

Send the construction forces, tools and material, back to Alexandria with all possible expedition.

H. HAUPT,
Brigadier-General.

CHAMBERSBURG, July 14, 1863.

A. Anderson, Esq., Hanover:

Turn over your charge to W. W. Wright and return to Alexandria with your whole force with all possible expedition.

H. HAUPT,
Brigadier-General.

CHAMBERSBURG, July 14, 1863.

E. C. Smeed, G. W. Nevin, Bridgeport:

Return to Alexandria with all your men, tools and material without delay. Apply for transportation immediately.

H. HAUPT,
Brigadier-General.

CHAMBERSBURG, July 14, 1863.

Colonel D. C. McCallum, Washington, D. C.:

Construction Corps, tools and material ordered to repair to Alexandria. Assist in providing transportation by special trains. Order back oxen if they have been forwarded.

H. HAUPT,
Brigadier-General.

CHAMBERSBURG, July 14, 1863.

A. Anderson, Hanover:

I would like to leave Gettysburg to-morrow about noon and run through to Baltimore the same evening. Can it be arranged without inconvenience?

H. HAUPT,
Brigadier-General.

On July 14, 1863, General O. O. Howard reports that the rebels crossed, infantry and cavalry, at a ford just above Williamsport. The ford was reported to be from four to four and a half feet; also that they constructed pontoons at a point where there was lumber and floated the bridge to Falling Waters, where the greatest portion of the army crossed over.

On July 14, General Ingalls, Chief Quartermaster, tele-graphed General Meigs to ask me to put the Orange & Alexandria Railroad in order, adding: "It will be utterly fruitless to move this army down the Winchester Valley." A similar telegram was sent direct to me.

CHAPTER XVI.

LEE'S ESCAPE UNINTERRUPTED.

ON July 15, 1863, 9 A. M., President Lincoln, in reply to a telegram from General Simon Cameron, said:

Your dispatch of yesterday received. Lee was already across the river when you sent it.

I would give much to be relieved of the impression that Meade, Couch, Smith and all, since the battle of Gettysburg, have striven only to get Lee over the river without another fight. Please tell me if you know who was the one Corps commander who was for fighting in the council of war.

On July 14, 1863, General Meade to General Halleck, 2:30 P. M.:

Having performed my duty conscientiously and to the best of my ability, the censure of the President, conveyed in your dispatch of 1 P. M. this day is, in my judgment, so undeserved that I feel compelled most respectfully to ask to be immediately relieved from the command of this army.

July 16, 1863.

General H. Haupt, Superintendent Military Railroads:
Your dispatch to General Ingalls received. General Meade says that as soon as this army crosses the Potomac his cavalry will be sent to guard the gaps in the Blue Ridge. General Ingalls has gone to Washington to-day.

C. G. SAWTELLE,
Chief Quartermaster.

HEADQUARTERS ARMY OF THE POTOMAC,
July 16, 1863.
Brigadier-General H. Haupt, Superintendent Military Railroads:
Your dispatch is received. I am directed by the Major-General Commanding to say that his bridges are not yet completed, but that when finished, he will pass over his cavalry and whole army, and give protection to the bridges your dispatch refers to.

A. A. HUMPHREYS,
Chief of Staff.

Note from President Lincoln to General Halleck, July 20, 1863:

Seeing General Meade's dispatch of yesterday to yourself, causes me to fear that he supposes the Government here is demanding of him to bring on a general engagement with Lee as soon as possible. I am claiming no such thing of him. In fact, my judgment is against it; which judgment, of course, I will yield if yours and his are contrary. If he could not safely engage Lee at Williamsport, it seems absurd to suppose he can safely engage him now when he has scarcely more than two-thirds the force he had at Williamsport, while it must be that Lee has been reinforced. True, I advised General Meade to pursue Lee across the Potomac, hoping, as has proved true, that he would thereby clear the Baltimore & Ohio Railroad and get some advantages by harassing him on his retreat. Those being past, I am unwilling he should now get into a general engagement on the impression that we here are pressing him, and I would be glad for you to so inform him, unless your own judgment is against it.

A. LINCOLN.

ALEXANDRIA, July 20, 1863.

General Haupt:
Following just received from General King:

FAIRFAX STATION, July 20, 1863.

General Haupt:
Yours just received. My Headquarters are now at Fairfax Court House, and my main force is there. I will furnish any guard you wish if you will let me know when and where they are wanted. How far is the road now in running order? Have you sufficient guards now for your trains and working parties?

RUFUS KING,
Brigadier-General.

So far the guard furnished is sufficient. If more soldiers are needed to-morrow, we will ask for them. The General knows we are pushing ahead, I suppose, and whether we should meet our troops at Manassas. If not, would it not be well to have a force advanced there from Fairfax? The third bridge is completed over Pope's head, and workmen are on the fourth.

J. H. DEVEREUX.

FAIRFAX COURT HOUSE,
July 21, 1863, 11:30 A. M.

General Haupt, Chief of Construction, Washington, D. C.:
Colonel Lowell started at daylight from Centreville, to reconnoiter in the direction of Manassas and also towards Thoroughfare Gap. He took all our spare cavalry with him. You may hear from him on your way. I can furnish you an infantry guard, one or two companies, if you desire it, from the regiment now at Fairfax Station. I will direct the Colonel to follow your instructions in this respect.

RUFUS KING,
Brigadier-General.

July 22, 1863.

General Haupt:
Shall I send construction force towards Warrenton Junction, following General Gregg, or wait at Manassas for the present?

A. ANDERSON.

My answer was that "the construction can follow General Gregg."

WASHINGTON, July 23, 1863.

Brigadier-General Gregg:
Your dispatch is received. I will communicate with General Halleck and arrange to have the railroad bridge guarded by infantry. The protection of the railroad requires that the gaps of the Blue Ridge and

fords of the Occoquan be carefully guarded. If your force is insufficient for this service, it should be performed by others. If you make a reconnoissance to Culpepper, please inform me as early as practicable of the condition of the road and bridges. If any bridges are destroyed, we will at once, on being advised, take measures to reconstruct them.

H. HAUPT,
Brigadier-General.

ALEXANDRIA DEPOT, July 26, 1863.
General Herman Haupt:
  No. 1 train this A. M. found, when a mile and a half east of Burkes, a rail taken out of the track and horseshoes on rail. Engine was reversed and brakes put hard down. Engine jumped the break and, with two cars, passed on. Had it been rail on opposite side, the whole train would have run off the track down a twelve-foot bank. Before train was checked twelve rebels in grey and blue coats and pants, and all with guns, pushed out of bushes, whilst the guard of the Fourth Delaware then took a hand and, after a few shots, jumped off the train and had a foot-race through the woods after the rebels. One fat rebel particularly distinguished himself in getting out of sight. The guard saved the train and its convoy, and Providence saved a smash-up which, for some time, would have prevented the Army of the Potomac from receiving supplies.
  It is pitiful that a handful of rebels can be allowed the chance of so retarding the progress of our army in such measure as an accident like this might cause. I earnestly ask that 200 men be at once stationed from Accotink to Burkes. General Meade has ordered the road repaired at once to the river, and the Rappahannock bridge rebuilt. All stores and material have been forwarded to-day on regular time.

J. H. DEVEREUX.

WASHINGTON, July 27, 1863.
Received 10:20 A. M.
General R. Ingalls, Headquarters Army of the Potomac:
  Another attempt was made to throw off and capture our trains near Burkes yesterday. Rails were taken out and horseshoes placed upon the track. Fortunately the rails were taken up on the inside and not on the outside of the curve, and the train was not thrown off. Twelve rebels in grey and blue costumes, armed with guns, made their appearance and were chased by the train guard, but none were captured.
  These attempts to throw off trains are made daily, and unless the practice can be broken up, there is no security in your communications. To operate the road with reasonable security, we must have the gaps of the Blue Ridge so occupied that Lee's cavalry cannot get through, the fords of the Occoquan guarded, the country patrolled by cavalry, and notice given to the inhabitants that in case of any further attempts to disturb track or telegraph, all able-bodied residents within ten miles will be arrested and placed under guard.
  Please communicate with General Meade and have an order issued, giving notice to the inhabitants, something to this effect:
  "Notice is hereby given that if any attempt shall be made to destroy the track, bridges, or telegraph, or any of the lines of railroad used by the Army of the Potomac, the residents in the vicinity for a distance of ten miles will be held responsible in person and property,

RAFT OF BLANKET BOATS WITHOUT LOAD.

and all the able-bodied citizens arrested. If the offenders can be discovered, their punishment will be death."

I will endeavor to see you to-morrow. Would it be well to search houses and seize arms? This, I know, is an extreme measure, but I am confident that those who appear to be farmers during the day are the parties who injure us at night.

H. HAUPT.

ALEXANDRIA, July 23, 1863, 11:20 A. M.

General Rufus King, Centreville:

Yesterday morning, on returning from a reconnoissance to White Plains, I passed the western-bound train at Burkes' about 5 A. M. Conductor reported that his train had been fired into at Accotink, eight miles from Alexandria. As I had no train guard with me, I returned to Fairfax, procured two companies, and scoured the woods about Accotink, but found no enemy. Fresh horse-tracks, however, were numerous. I learn this morning that before the train passed rails had been taken out and obstructions placed upon the track by these guerrillas, but some of the track men had seen and repaired the damage.

These men are supposed to be part of Mosby's gang. I heard of them the evening on which I was over the Gap road as being at Wolf Run Shoals, and I also heard of the proximity of Mosby's men at Thoroughfare and other points.

To enable us to operate the road with any security, we must have cavalry pickets along the Occoquan and at the Gaps of the Blue Ridge; also patrols through the country. Every citizen of suitable age for draft, who is not in the army, should be regarded with suspicion and closely watched, for I am told that many of them have been exempted from draft on condition of joining Mosby's band, who are guerrillas by night and farmers by day. Our trains will be run as much as possible by daylight and with train guards, but with a heavy business we cannot avoid running at night, and train guards afford but little protection.

Please send copy of this to General Gregg. I wish to examine the line of the Orange & Alexandria Railroad as far as protection can be afforded to our railroad forces. Can you, or can General Gregg ascertain, by a cavalry reconnoissance, the condition of the railroad and bridges between Culpepper and Manassas?

H. HAUPT,
In Charge of Military Railroads.

The following reply was received from General King:

CENTREVILLE, July 23, 1863, 5:30 P. M.

Brigadier-General Herman Haupt, Washington:

Your dispatch is received. I will employ my cavalry as far as possible in scouting along the line of the Orange & Alexandria Railroad as far as Bull Run, and also through the country between this point and the ridge. They will be instructed to watch narrowly all suspected persons, and to look out especially for the guerrillas who make up Mosby's gang. I have not force enough at my command to make the reconnoissance you wish towards Culpepper, but I have sent a copy of your message to General Gregg, who is at Briscoe with a brigade of cavalry, and requested him to do it.

RUFUS KING,
Brigadier-General.

FAIRFAX STATION, July 23, 1863.

General Haupt:

I will go out again to White Plains, if your road there is in working condition. I would like to leave early in the morning from foot of 14th street, end of Long Bridge. Will you please inform me if I can be sent through quickly on a special, and at what hour I must start? It is very probable now that we will wish to begin using the O. & A. R. R. as well as the Manassas Gap. I wish to send grain now to Gainesville.

RUFUS INGALLS,
Brigadier-General,
Chief Quartermaster.

ALEXANDRIA DEPOT, July 27, 1863.

Colonel D. C. McCallum:

To post you I would report: In addition to reconstructing road from Alexandria to Warrenton and from Manassas to White Plains, we have forwarded to the Army of the Potomac in this last opening five hundred and thirty loaded cars, sending to Warrenton Junction, forty miles, yesterday, one hundred and twenty-seven loaded cars, and to-day one hundred and fifty-nine loaded cars. Part of these have been sent from Warrenton Junction to Warrenton, but the branch track is still bad and greasy.

Last night two engines were three hours getting ten cars up the branch. The army reached Warrenton before the road was opened beyond Manassas, short and out of everything. One hundred thousand men and eight thousand animals are to be fed daily, but they desire ten days' rations to be sent at once, at eight tons to the car, and most of them had ten tons. We sent to-day twelve hundred and seventy-two tons with the last train this P. M. We cleared every loaded car from the yard and they have reached Warrenton Junction, but the branch track detains part of them there, and with all other demands, that of pressing the road forward and reconstructing Rappahannock bridge is not the least in importance.

J. H. D.

HEADQUARTERS ARMY OF THE POTOMAC,
July 27, 1863, 1 P. M.

General Haupt:

Your dispatch was read to General Meade, who said he had communicated with General Heintzelman to know at what points his troops would guard the roads; soon as informed, he will cause them to be properly protected within his lines. It would certainly seem to be the province of General Heintzelman to guard them as far as Fairfax. Your suggestion for protection ought to be acted upon. It is too late to act after an accident, and yet that is our usual practice. I think this army will protect the roads without failure this side of Centreville and Manassas. General Meade wishes to have the bridges repaired over the Rappahannock as soon as possible.

RUFUS INGALLS,
Brigadier-General.

HEADQUARTERS ARMY OF THE POTOMAC,
July 27, 1863.

General Haupt:

Arrangements have already been made to take possession of the south bank at the Rappahannock Station as soon as the river is fordable or the pontoons arrive, which have been ordered up by rail. Meantime, the bridge has been secured from any further interference by the enemy. As soon as we are on the south bank, A. Anderson, Chief Engineer of Construction, and yourself will be informed.

By order of General Meade.

WARREN,
Chief Engineer.

July 28, 1863, General Halleck wrote a conciliatory letter to General Meade commending his action in the battle of Gettysburg, and stated that he should not have been surprised or vexed at the President's disappointment at the escape of Lee's army. He thought that Lee's defeat was so certain that he felt no little impatience at his unexpected escape. He assures General Meade that he had lost none of the confidence which he felt when he recommended him for the command.

CHAPTER XVII.

RESTORING WRECKED RAILROADS EXPE-
DITIOUSLY.

THE subsequent operations during my connection with the service were of the usual character, and are not of sufficient interest or importance to be reported in detail. Bridges were destroyed and reconstructed, that over Bull Run for the seventh time; trains troubled by guerrillas; contraband articles smuggled into camps by sutlers and others, etc. The following served to check guerrilla operations:

HEADQUARTERS ARMY OF THE POTOMAC,
July 30, 1863.
PROCLAMATION.

The numerous depredations committed by citizens, or rebel soldiers in disguise, harbored and concealed by citizens, along the Orange & Alexandria Railroad and within our lines, call for prompt and exemplary punishment. Under the instructions of the Government, therefore, every citizen against whom there is sufficient evidence of his having engaged in these practices, will be arrested and confined for punishment, or put beyond the lines.

The people within ten miles of the railroad are notified that they will be held responsible in their persons and property, for any injury done to the road, trains, depots, or stations by citizens, guerrillas, or persons in disguise; and in case of such injury they will be impressed as laborers to repair all damages.

If these measures should not stop such depredations, it will become the unpleasant duty of the undersigned, in the execution of his instructions, to direct that the entire inhabitants of the district of country along the railroad be put across the lines, and their property taken for Government uses.
GEO. G. MEADE,
Major-General Commanding.

I applied for and received authority to arm, drill and make the Military Railroad organization, to some extent, self-protective, and procured action regulating passes, transportation of supplies and newsboys.

GERMANTOWN, August 1, 1863, 3:10 P. M.
Brigadier-General Haupt:

I am instructed by the Major-General Commanding to inform you that we hold both banks of the Rappahannock near the railroad bridge, and that its repair may now be commenced.
Very respectfully, your obedient servant,
A. A. HUMPHREYS,
Major-General,
Chief of Staff.

We had to be masters of construction as well as destruction, so, for the benefit of the army, I submitted a report on experiments I had made to determine the most expeditious mode of straightening rails and destroying communications that had been broken by the enemy, as follows:

WASHINGTON, D. C., August 4, 1863.

To Major-General H. W. Halleck, General-in-Chief United States Army.

GENERAL: In obedience to the instructions contained in Special Order, No. 286, I commenced the reconstruction of the Cumberland Valley and Franklin Railroads, near Chambersburg, Pa., for the purpose of forwarding troops and supplies to Hagerstown, to aid the armies operating in that vicinity.

I found about ten miles of these roads destroyed in the manner usually adopted by the enemy; the cross-ties had been piled, the fence-rails from both sides of the road mixed with them and fired; the rails placed on top of these piles, and when heated, bent at various angles, and left in that condition.

After experimenting for a few hours, I found that about three-fourths of all the damaged rails could be straightened without heating, and in less than one-tenth of the time required to injure them by the means which the enemy had adopted. The remaining fourth part could also be straightened and made fit for use, but not without heating.

As a general rule, I found that all rails that had been bent with a curve of one foot or more radius could be straightened cold in from two to four minutes to each rail; while those which had been heated to a high degree, and bent at a sharp angle, could not be restored without heating and hammering.

As the results of these experiments may be of much value to the public service, and avoid the delay and expense of procuring new iron, as has been the usual practice heretofore in the reconstruction of roads that have been injured by the enemy, I have caused the operations to be repeated and photographed, forming a series illustrative of the operation of *reconstruction,* as a sequel to the series showing the most expeditious and effectual modes of *destruction,* which formed the subject of a former report.

A very rapid, effective and portable contrivance for straightening rails, which I used on the Hagerstown Road, consists of five blocks of wood, each about ten inches square and five feet long. The top block was notched slightly, to receive the base of the rail and cause it to lie with the plane of the base vertical. The pieces of scantling three by four or four by four, were placed across the ends. Twelve or sixteen men at each end would press down or relieve the pressure at the words of command, "down," "up." The rail was moved forward or back at the word of command, or turned. After a very short drill the intelligent contrabands, who furnished the motive power, were able to straighten a rail in an average of from two to three minutes sufficiently near to a straight line to permit it to be laid in the track, and so nearly straight that a continuance of the operation would not generally result in any improvement. The rail, after this operation, could be laid in the track and spiked; it would be so nearly straight that trains could be run over it safely; but a short bend would always remain, which could be removed by the jack-screw apparatus after it was in the track.

After finishing the rails within a convenient distance, the blocks were carried forward to the next pile.

By distributing the gangs, several miles of rails could be straightened in a day.

Sometimes the rails would be bent in the direction of the plane of the vertical rib, and be too stiff to straighten by simple pressure. In this case the rail was raised to the height of the head and allowed to fall on a cross-tie at the words of command, "ready," "drop;" once or twice dropping did not fail to take out the vertical bend. (See illustration on page 181).

Another mode was used very successfully in straightening a large amount of bent iron at the depot in Chambersburg. In this case the power was applied by means of a rope attached to the end of the rail, forming a fulcrum. Two posts firmly planted in the ground, about two and one-half feet apart, would be very convenient for straightening rails on this plan. The rail must be supported beyond the fulcrum, or a bend will be formed at this point.

When the rail is so much bent that it cannot be straightened cold, it should be thrown out, and no time lost in attempting to improve it. When the track is laid, these rails should be carried to a convenient place where a furnace can be prepared for heating them. Two parallel walls of brick, stone or even of clay, with bars laid across to hold the wood or coal, will answer for a furnace. When heated, the rails are laid upon a straightening table and hammered until the bends are removed, after which the rail is cooled before removal by pouring on water.

The straightening table is prepared in a very simple manner, by taking a piece of timber twelve inches square, and as long as a rail, placing two rails base downwards on the top surface of the timber, and another rail base upwards between the first two; the whole being firmly spiked, the base of the top rail forms the plane surface on which the rails are straightened.

The short bends or kinks in the rails, whether in the track or out of it, are readily removed by the apparatus represented in illustration on page 171. The pile of iron shown in the picture is a portion of that destroyed by the rebels on the Loudoun & Hampshire Railroad, and brought into Alexandria, where it now lies. A portion of this iron was heated and bent around trees, from which it could be removed only by cutting the trees down.

This report, with the accompanying photographs,* is very respectfully submitted by

H. HAUPT,
Brigadier-General,
In Charge of United States Military Railroads.

One of the most effective features of my plan of organization was approved as follows:

Washington, August 7, 1863.

Major-General Halleck, General-in-Chief United States Army.

General: The difficulty of procuring guards for the protection of the employes of the Military Railroad Department and for the security

---

* NOTE.—The Photographic Department was under the charge of Captain A. J. Russell, 141st Regiment, N. Y. Volunteers, a photographer and an artist who was specially detailed for the service at my request. After the war Captain Russell was for many years on the staff of artists for Leslie's Magazine.

LARGER RAFT OF BLANKET BOATS FERRYING INFANTRY ACROSS THE POTOMAC RIVER.

of the public property entrusted to their care, induces me to recommend that the organization be made self-protective.

I propose to have the men formed into companies, drilled and armed and will proceed to carry this recommendation into effect if approved by you, so soon as the necessary orders are given for arms and ammunition.

Very respectfully submitted,

H. HAUPT,

In Charge of United States Military Railroads.

Approved. Requisitions for arms, etc., signed by General Haupt will be filled.

August 8, 1863.

H. W. HALLECK,
General-in-Chief.

HEADQUARTERS ARMY OF THE POTOMAC,
August 20, 1863.

GENERAL ORDERS,
  No. 78.

1. Passes from Headquarters to be given by the Provost Marshal General, or by his authority. Said passes will authorize the return of the parties, but will not include the transportation for property beyond necessary personal baggage.

2. All orders for transportation of property must be given by the Quartermaster's Department.

3. Supplies for officers may be procured by sending an agent with a list of the articles to be obtained, signed by a General Officer and approved by the Provost Marshal General, or by his authority.

4. Sutlers and their property to be entirely excluded from transportation by rail for the present.

5. Newsboys will not be permitted to travel on trains, but packages of papers may be sent to local agents, under charge of a baggagemaster, for sale or distribution.

6. No passes to civilians to visit the Army of the Potomac shall be given, except by Adjutant General of the Army, and the General in command of the Army of the Potomac.

7. The principal depot quartermasters at Washington, Alexandria and at other depots upon the line of the road can pass officers and agents of their departments, and also officers and agents of other departments traveling on necessary public business, who can procure orders for transportation from them.

8. All orders for cars must be sent to the Superintendent of the Military Railroad, through the proper officers of the Quartermaster's Department in charge of depots.

9. No officers, other than those herein specified, will be permitted to give passes beyond the limits of their commands.

10. All boxes or packages sent to, or marked with the name of any officer shall be accompanied with an accurate list of contents, and shall be placed in custody of the Provost Marshal at the place of destination, to be delivered to the consignee upon satisfactory evidence that the package contains necessary supplies for his individual use and contains nothing else.

11. All persons seeking transportation on any railroad shall present their passes for examination at the office of the Superintendent in that city.

12. Provost guards at Washington, Alexandria and other stations will see that the foregoing orders are executed.

13. Train guards for the protection of each train and to preserve order and keep off stragglers will be furnished by commander of troops nearest the points of departure, on requisition of Superintendent of Road.

By command of Major-General Meade.

S. WILLIAMS,
Assistant Adjutant General.

Approved as amended.
By order of the Secretary of War.

JAMES A. HARDIE,
Assistant Adjutant General.

Official:

RUFUS INGALLS,
Brigadier-General,
And Chief Quartermaster Army of the Potomac.

GERMANTOWN, August 20, 1863.

GENERAL: The enclosed is a copy of the order as amended by the Secretary of War which, of course, governs us in future.

I am, very respectfully yours, etc.,

RUFUS INGALLS,
Brigadier-General,
And Chief Quartermaster Army of the Potomac.

Brigadier-General Haupt,
Superintendent United States Military Railroads,
Washington, D. C.

CHAPTER XVIII.

RUPTURE OF OFFICIAL RELATIONS CAUSED BY GOVERNOR ANDREW, OF MASSACHUSETTS.

I N the latter part of August Governor John A. Andrew, of Massachusetts, visited Washington and was in daily conference with the Secretary of War. I had many friends in his office, and one of the assistant secretaries informed me that I was a frequent topic of conversation, and that it had been arranged that the Secretary should compel me to accept my commission unconditionally, and then assign me to some position that would prevent me from going to Massachusetts to trouble the Legislature with my claims for compensation for expenditures made in the construction of the Hoosac Tunnel.

The Governor, notwithstanding the unanimous endorsement of investigating committees and in opposition to the advice of his Executive Council, had insisted that the work should be taken out of my hands and placed under the control of commissioners, and not a single dollar had been repaid for the expenditures I had made upon the work. I was willing to accept expenditures with simple interest, and waive all claims for profits or for damages, but the Governor was not willing that I should receive a cent.

My presence in Boston during the session of the Legislature was a great annoyance to him, and to the Chairman of the Board of Commissioners, whose plans I was compelled, in self-defense, to criticise, and his ignorance and extravagance to expose; but as the Governor of Massachusetts was active and powerful in furnishing men and other support to the war, the Secretary of War was compelled to side with Andrew and sacrifice me.

Accordingly, I soon after received the following notice:

WASHINGTON, September 1, 1863.

GENERAL: I do not observe on file any acceptance of your appointment as Brigadier-General. Inasmuch as the Secretary of War has ordered that all appointments the acceptance of which shall not have been filed by September 5, 1863, be taken as vacated, it becomes necessary to file your acceptance at once.

Very respectfully, your obedient servant,
JAMES A. HARDIE,
Assistant Adjutant General.

Brigadier-General H. Haupt,
Washington, D. C.

262   *REMINISCENCES OF*

On the receipt of this notice, I turned to my files and found that my commission as Brigadier-General had been dated September 5, 1862, just one year before the date named, and it seemed evident that this General Order had been made to fit my particular case. I waited until September 5, and then sent the following letter to the Secretary:

WASHINGTON, September 5, 1863.

Hon. E. M. Stanton, Secretary of War.

SIR: I am in receipt of a communication from Colonel Hardie, Acting Assistant Secretary of War, informing me that all commissions that are not formally accepted by this date will be considered as vacated.

I have uniformly declined to accept military rank unconditionally, and have given you my reasons for it. I cannot part with the control of my time and of my freedom of action to so great an extent as I must do if I accept a commission unconditionally.

Interests involving more than a million of dollars; the private fortunes of my associates and myself, my reputation as an engineer and a man, are in jeopardy from the efforts of active and unscrupulous enemies. They can only be saved by my personal exertions.

But not even to save them, not to protect private interests were they tens of millions, should I suffer the country to sustain injury from neglect or omission of anything that I could do, or had engaged to do, to save it. At the same time, when I know that the public interests do not, and my private interests do require my attention for a short time, I must be at liberty to act as my judgment dictates.

I could not, if my presence were required in Boston, resign for a week and be reappointed. I might not obtain a leave if I asked for it. I must, if I accept unconditionally, be placed in the same category as other officers, although not another officer in the service, perhaps, can be found whose acceptance has not been a benefit to him, while with me it would involve the loss of everything. Even while I have been in Washington parties in Massachusetts, to whom I have not been legally or equitably indebted a single dollar, have brought suit on fictitious claims of which I had no notice, and from my non-appearance have obtained judgment, taken execution and seized on personal property.

The conduct of the State authorities, and of some of the people of Massachusetts interested in the Western Railroad, has been infamous, and I must hold myself in a position to settle accounts with my enemies if opportunity offers. It is probable that many times the compensation of a Brigadier-General for the time that I have been in Washington would not compensate me for the losses consequent upon my being here, if I cannot secure legislation to repair the damage.

These losses do not disturb me greatly. I have confidence enough in the good sense and justice of the people of Massachusetts to believe that when I have time and opportunity for explanation, the wrongs done through misrepresentation of facts will be set right; and, if I can be useful to the country in no other way than by accepting a commission, I would put the yoke upon my neck and the fetters upon my wrists and labor to save the Union. But is this necessary? The members of the Cabinet are civilians; the Assistant Secretaries of the War and Navy are civilians; the chiefs of most of the bureaus are civilians; why cannot the Chief of the Bureau of Military Railroads be a civilian also, if you will clothe him with the power necessary to secure efficiency and prevent military interference with his duties?

You refused my acceptance unless untrammeled with conditions, and I declined to accept unconditionally. My name is, I suppose, or will be, dropped from the rolls, where I never asked that it should be entered, although the appointment for meritorious services was a source of much gratification, and I am not ungrateful for your expressions of confidence in me and of obligations for what has been accomplished.

During the whole time that I have been connected with the public service, now a year and a half, I have received no pay except for personal expenses for a portion of the time. After my last interview with you on the subject, I concluded to make no more explanations and to trouble you no further about my account, which you had hesitated to allow, but to raise money from other sources, by loans or otherwise, to pay my way until the war was over, and then if the account was not paid, I would make the Government a present of the amount and retire.

The condition of Military Railroad affairs in the West, as appears from the reports of the Special Agent, is becoming worse and worse. It is almost too late now to apply a remedy. I hope that I will not be called upon at so late an hour to make the attempt. The labor would be excessive and the result problematical; still, I will endeavor to carry out your wishes, and I am willing, if you desire it, to continue my supervision over operations in the East where results have been attained with which I am much gratified. There are no longer difficulties about transportation, deficiencies of supplies, delays of army movements while waiting for stores, accidents and blockades. All these have ceased since my efforts have been sustained by the orders of yourself and General Halleck, and roads and bridges have been reconstructed in less than half the time ever before considered practicable.

I repeat, that so long as I can be useful to your Department, or to the country in this crisis, I am willing to work, cost what it may in labor and sacrifice, but when my usefulness is at an end I wish to leave. No office in the gift of the President would tempt me to accept it as I am now situated, unless consideration of duty should imperatively require it, and when my services are not required, my time and the control of them I desire to use for other purposes.

If you desire that I should continue the ambiguity that exists in regard to my position should be removed. You might appoint me Chief of a Bureau of Military Railroads. I have not had, since Pope's campaign, any official position. My title then was Chief of Construction and Transportation of the Army of Virginia. Since then I have appended to my signature in official communications "In charge of United States Military Railroads."

Please decide whether, in your opinion, the interests of the service will be best promoted by my continuance or withdrawal; and if you wish me to continue, prescribe the position which I am to occupy, the authority to exercise, the powers to remedy defects and correct abuses with which I am to be clothed, and the geographical limits over which these powers are to be exercised.

Respectfully submitted,

H. HAUPT.

A few days after the receipt of this letter the Secretary sent for me. He seemed to be irritated bcause I would not yield, and remarked that the commission had been given to me for meritorious services; that my name had been sent to the Senate by the President and confirmed; that I should consider it a high honor, and that my refusal to accept was an act of disrespect to the President, to himself and to the Government; and further, that I could not be paid lawfully unless the commission was accepted.

I replied that pay was no consideration. I was losing many times the amount of pay by neglect of other interests. He could pay me from the contingent fund, if so inclined. If not, I could do without it; that I *did* appreciate the honor conferred and was grateful for it. If he did not wish to make a record of any conditions as establishing a precedent, I was willing to rely upon his word.

I represented that in the winter there was a long period of suspension of military operations during which my presence was not required. I referred to our first interview when he asked me to undertake the reconstruction of the Fredericksburg Railroad, saying that my services would only be required for a few weeks; that as soon as McDowell could move Richmond would fall and the war be ended; and added that while I was willing to remain so long as my services were needed, when they were no longer needed he had it in his power to relieve me. The Secretary exclaimed, "I will relieve you at once, sir!" and soon after the following order was issued:

WASHINGTON CITY, September 14, 1863.

SIR: You are hereby relieved from further duty in the War Department.

You will turn over your office, books, papers and all other property under your control belonging to the United States, to Colonel D. C. McCallum, Superintendent of Military Railroads.

Very respectfully, your obedient servant,

EDWIN M. STANTON,
Secretary of War.

To Herman Haupt, Esq.,
In Charge of Military Railroads,
Washington, D. C.

The action of the Secretary occasioned much surprise. Hon. John Covode and other members of the Committee on the Conduct of the War went to the Secretary to know what it meant, but without results, and efforts were made to induce the President to insist upon a withdrawal of Stanton's order. The President, although apparently regretting the action, declined to take any steps to reverse it.

My retirement called forth letters of regret from Assistant Secretary Watson, who had always supported me, and also from

RAFT OF BLANKET BOATS FERRYING FIELD ARTILLERY AND MEN OVER POTOMAC RIVER.

officers in high positions, who expressed commendation in strong and gratifying terms. There is a letter before me now, dated September 27, 1863, in which I was informed that if I would use my pen and tell what I knew, there was a party in Congress, both in the Senate and House, that would bring such a pressure as to compel Stanton's resignation; but I had absolutely no inclination to engage in such a contest, even had I believed it could succeed.

CHAPTER XIX.

FINAL REPORT.

THE following report to the Secretary of War was my last official act in connection with the Bureau of United States Military Railroads:

WASHINGTON, D. C., September 9, 1863.

Hon. E. M. Stanton, Secretary of War.

SIR: A brief review of operations in the Bureau of United States Military Railroads since my connection with it is herewith respectfully submitted:

In April, 1862, I was summoned to Washington by a telegram from you, and requested to assist in the reconstruction of the railroad from Acquia Creek to Fredericksburg. The Army of the Potomac was at that time in front of Yorktown; the Army of the Rappahannock rested near the Potomac; neither could move, as was supposed, without the coöperation of the other, and such coöperation was impossible without the railroad as a means of communication with the depots on the base of the Potomac.

The injury of the railroad consisted of the wharves and buildings at Acquia Creek, which had been burned; three miles of track torn up, the ties consumed, and rails carried south of Fredericksburg. The bridges across Potomac and Ackakeek Creek and the Rappahannock River destroyed; and two miles of strap rail in a very unsafe condition, which required to be relaid.

Although engaged at the time in a professional enterprise which was entirely dependent on my personal efforts for success, and although the protection of property and reputation, which were jeopardized by the hostile and unjust action of the State administration in Massachusetts, required ceaseless vigilance and effort, I did not feel at liberty to allow personal interests to stand in the way of the success of the military operations of the army, and believing that I could be useful, and that my services would not be required for a longer time than three or four weeks, I consented to undertake the work of reconstructing the road to Fredericksburg.

The only laborers to be procured consisted of soldiers detailed from the ranks, many of them entirely unaccustomed to labor, others unwilling; and what was worst of all, the details would be changed daily, so that after spending a great part of the day in organizing the forces, the next day new details would be sent out and the process would have to be repeated.

My remonstrances led to a change in this organization; a permanent detail was made, forming the members of a Construction Corps, but the men were without experience or skill, and much effort was required to infuse into them a proper emulation and induce efforts to hasten the completion of the work. The difficulties were much increased by the state of the weather; the rain fell almost daily, and the track was laid in a lake of mud; but with all these disadvantages, the work was carried on day and night, light being furnished at night by means of lanterns, and the supply very limited at that.

One day was lost in waiting for iron, which was supplied from Alexandria, but in three working days the three miles of track were relaid, during which time most of the ties were manufactured in the woods. In forwarding this work, as also on various occasions subsequently, very important aid was rendered by Major Barstow, of General McDowell's staff, now Assistant Adjutant General of the Army of the Potomac.

Ackakeek bridge was commenced on Saturday, at 2 p. m., and on the next day, at about the same hour, a train passed over it. This bridge, 120 feet long and about 30 feet high, was erected in fifteen hours.

In reference to the Potomac Creek bridge, General McDowell, in his remarks before the Court of Inquiry, uses the following language:

"The Potomac Run bridge is a most remarkable structure. When it is considered that in the campaigns of Napoleon the trestle-bridges of more than one story, even of moderate height, were regarded as impracticable, and that, too, for common military roads, it is not difficult to understand why distinguished Europeans should express surprise at so bold a specimen of American military engineering. It is a structure which ignores all the rules and precedents of military science as laid down in books. It is constructed chiefly of round sticks cut from the woods, and not even divested of its bark; the legs of the trestles are braced with round poles. It is in four stories, three of trestles and one of crib-work. The total height from the deepest part of the stream to the rails is nearly 80 feet. It carries daily from ten to twenty heavy trains in both directions, and has withstood several severe freshets and storms without injury.

"The bridge was built in May, 1862, in nine working days, during which time the greater part of the material was cut and hauled. It contains more than two million feet of lumber. The original structure which it replaced required as many months as this did days."

The bridge across the Rappahannock was under the immediate supervision of Daniel Stone, Esq., the experienced bridge architect of Philadelphia. It was longer than the Potomac Creek bridge, but not so high.

These structures were all completed and the road opened for use in about three weeks, when I expected to return to Massachusetts to protect my interests in that State, but General McDowell remonstrated so earnestly against this course, and represented that my continuance with the army was essential to the success of his movements, that I felt it my duty to remain until after the opening of the Manassas Gap Road to Front Royal, to which place the Army of the Rappahannock had been ordered for the purpose of intercepting the retreat of General Jackson.

By this time the efficiency of the Construction Corps was so much increased that in June, 1862, they reconstructed five bridges of from 60 to 120 feet span in one day, and in three days opened the Manassas Gap Railroad to Front Royal, reaching that place with a continuous track and reinforcements of 5,000 men only one day after the advance of the army had arrived there by forced marches.

Soon after General McDowell was relieved, and General Pope placed in command. This officer did not seem to place so high a value on my labors as his predecessor. He gave me no instructions, and having declined to accept a commission, I returned to Massachusetts, after leaving my address at the War Department, with the information that if my services were again required for any temporary duty I could be sent for, but that the condition of my affairs would not permit me to connect myself permanently with the army, or be absent for long periods of time from Massachusetts.

I was not long permitted to be absent. General Pope tried the experiment of operating a Military Railroad, and the results were unsatisfactory. In about ten days from my departure I received a telegram from the War Department requesting my immediate return, with a declaration that without my aid to organize and manage the operations of the Military Railroads it was impossible to keep the army supplied.

I again dropped all professional and business engagements, reported at the War Department, and proceeded to the Headquarters of General Pope, near Cedar Mountain. The road was in a state of blockade, very few trains moving, everything in great confusion; the primary cause being military interference. General Pope issued a stringent order, in terms which I suggested, forbidding officers of any rank to interfere with the management of the roads. Rules were made and enforced, punctuality insisted upon, and in two or three days regularity was again restored. Since this time, with a single exception, when an officer of high rank undertook to place me in arrest for respectfully declining to obey orders which he had no right to give, the operations of the Military Railroads in Virginia have been conducted with extraordinary regularity and exemption from accidents; and no army movements have ever been delayed a single hour for want of any supplies or transportation which it was the province of the railroads to furnish.

While the Army of Virginia was in position behind the Rappahannock the enemy, in superior numbers, succeeded in turning its right flank. The first information of this movement was conveyed by an attack of Stuart's cavalry at Catlett's, August 22, 1862, followed soon after by an attempt to capture several of our trains at Bristow. Unfortunately, General Pope had ordered a large portion of the rolling stock to the front, from which exposed position it could not be withdrawn after the break in the communications in the rear, and as a consequence seven first-class locomotives fell into the hands of the enemy and 277 freight cars were destroyed.

During the battle which followed great exertions were made to preserve and maintain intact the communications with the army. Troops were sent by rail to hold bridges across Bull Run, supplies were forwarded, and General Pope notified at what station his wagons could receive them; telegraph operators and scouts were sent out to make and report observations, which were promptly communicated to Headquarters at Washington. Services of great value were rendered by the officers and employes of the Military Railway Bureau, both in transportation and construction. They remained at stations loading cars and carrying away stores long after the retreat of our forces and the departure of the guards had left them without any military protection whatever, and when the enemy on the common roads was in advance of the positions so occupied. They volunteered for the service and succeeded in reconstructing a bridge and bringing off General Taylor and the wounded men of his command at Bull Run after the General in command, with whom I was directed to consult, had declined to send a military force for this purpose in consequence of the risk. Night and day, during this period of intense excitement, the railway employes remained at their posts, performing uncomplainingly the most dangerous duties without rest or regular food. From the Superintendent to the lowest grade of operatives, they are all entitled to much credit for the important services rendered on that occasion.

The retreat of General Pope was followed by the invasion of Maryland and raids into Pennsylvania; operations on the railroads of Virginia were suspended, but some employment was found for the Construction Corps in assisting in rebuilding the bridge across the Potomac at Harper's Ferry, for which we were fortunately in a condition to aid the Baltimore & Ohio Railroad Company by furnishing material.

The battles of South Mountain and Antietam were followed by the retreat of the enemy and the reoccupation of the country north of the Rappahannock by our forces. The Orange & Alexandria Railroad was soon repaired and put in running order. Great doubts existed as to the ability of this road to supply the army, which then consisted of the two Armies of Virginia and the Potomac united; but with the efficient and cordial coöperation of the Chief Quartermaster, General Ingalls, so large an amount of stores was forwarded that during the brief sojourn at Warrenton nearly four thousand tons were accumulated in excess of requirements, which were afterwards brought back and sent to Acquia Creek. About two thousand tons were forwarded daily while the army remained in the vicinity of Warrenton, and this business was accommodated without accident or delay. This result is most extraordinary, when the difficulties of operating a Military Railroad are considered, but it is due chiefly to the fact that the stringent orders of General Halleck prevented any military interference with the running of the trains, and the excellent arrangements of General Ingalls secured the prompt return of cars.

Anticipating the necessity of a change in the line of operations to the Fredericksburg Railroad, I had, with the approval of General Halleck, ordered a million feet of lumber, which very opportunely commenced to arrive on the very day when work was resumed at Acquia Creek. The reconstruction and opening of the railriad between Acquia Creek and Falmouth was accomplished in a very brief period of time, under the direction of William W. Wright, Esq., as engineer and superintendent, and the road was operated with great regularity and success during the whole period that the Army of the Potomac remained at Falmouth.

After the occupation of Falmouth by the forces under General Burnside, in the fall of 1862, the high bridge across Potomac Creek was repaired. The damage done by the enemy consisted in the destruction of parts of two spans, which were promptly restored. No opportunity was offered of attempting the reconstruction of the railroad bridge across the Rappahannock until the day of the first battle of Fredericksburg, when our forces having possession of the city, I commenced work on the bridge.

At this time the construction party consisted of only thirty carpenters under the supervision of E. C. Smeed. The Construction Corps which I had organized under General McDowell had been disbanded by General Pope and, owing to the diversity of opinion which existed as to the propriety of employing soldiers or civilians, no reorganization on a scale sufficient for efficiency had been made. General

Burnside had, at my solicitation, given peremptory orders that 200 soldiers should report for duty to me at daylight, and I went personally to the commanding officer to see that the detail was made and the men notified. The soldiers made their appearance next morning, but as soon as the battle became exciting, it was found impossible to keep them at work; they scattered over the hills and behind trees, leaving only the bridge carpenters. These men worked for several hours under a warm fire, until the pulley block of the hoisting apparatus was broken, the timber on which the men were at work struck several times by shells and the ropes cut. As they were too few in number to accomplish any important results, and as the bridge could be finished after the battle as soon as it would be required for use, I permitted the men to seek shelter and wait until the next day before resuming operations.

Next day operations were resumed, and a span on each side well advanced towards completion; but the following night Fredericksburg was evacuated, and no opportunity has ever been offered since that time of reconstructing the bridge.

General Burnside was succeeded by General Hooker in command of the Army of the Potomac, who, if successful in his movement against the enemy on the Rappahannock, expected to advance towards Richmond with great rapidity. General Hooker sent for me before the battle of Chancellorsville, informed me of his plans and requested me to have everything in readiness for very active operations. I was prepared to reconstruct the road and bridges with a rapidity exceeding anything that the Construction Corps had previously accomplished. About 1,600 lineal feet of bridging had been prepared, 1,000 feet of which was in spans of 60 feet, the trusses comprising which were to be transported on cars to the end of the track, then hauled by oxen to the sites of the bridges and hoisted into place as a whole by means of apparatus prepared for this purpose. About seventy car-loads of material were in readiness for the "On to Richmond" movement at the time of the battle of Chancellorsville, but the enemy was so unaccommodating as not to give us an opportunity of using them.

While waiting for the onward movement, the opportunity was improved for replacing the trestle-bridge across Potomac Creek by a substantial truss-bridge. The new bridge was erected and the old one removed without delaying a single one of the numerous trains running on the road for a single minute, a performance which the officers at Headquarters supposed to be impossible. Objections had been made to the reconstruction of the bridge, under the impression that it must necessarily, for some days at least, interfere with army transportation. The new bridge was a very beautiful and substantial structure. It was built on a new plan designed as a general one for military truss-bridges. Its peculiarities were that it was adapted to any span or location; could be used either for deck or through bridges; could be constructed to any extent in advance, and kept on hand ready for an emergency. It required no skilled labor to frame and raise it, the auger and the saw being almost the only tools required to put it together. All the parts were alike and interchangeable; any timber could be turned or reversed end for end, and it would fit equally well. It was not necessary to put any part of the bridge together until it was erected on the spot which it was intended to occupy, and it could be raised in one-half or one-third the time of any other bridge. The trusses of the Potomac Creek bridge, four hundred feet long in three spans, were raised in about a day and a half, and this was the first bridge of the

Arks Made of Frames Covered With Canvas for Transferring Military Stores and Cars by Water.

kind ever constructed. I have but little doubt that with a proper drill and more perfect organization 600 lineal feet of this military truss-bridge might be set up in a single day.

After the reconstruction of the Potomac Creek bridge nothing of special interest occurred until after the battle of Chancellorsville. Regularity, order and absence of all complaints distinguished the operations of the railroads in Virginia so far as they were under our charge. This continued until the movement of the enemy towards Maryland and Pennsylvania compelled the abandonment of the Fredericksburg line, and Acquia Creek, with its expensive wharves and warehouses, was again evacuated and subsequently destroyed by the enemy.

The evacuation was effected without any loss of movable property; everything was carried away, even to the sashes of the buildings. The cars, loaded with stores at Falmouth, were put on barges at Acquia Creek, towed to Alexandria, landed without break of bulk, and sent to the front over the Orange & Alexandria Railroad.

The success of this movement convinced all who had previously been skeptical in regard to the advantages of sending loaded cars on barges, and if it should ever again become necessary to reoccupy the Fredericksburg line, I am most decided in the opinion that the wharves, warehouses and buildings at Acquia Creek should never again be reconstructed on a scale approaching to its former magnitude, but that the distribution should be made from cars loaded at Alexandria and Washington, and sent without break of bulk to Falmouth, Fredericksburg, or other more advanced stations on this line, as fast as they came into our possession.

The duties which the Railway Bureau was called upon to perform subsequent to the successful evacuation of Acquia Creek were connected with the second invasion of Maryland and Pennsylvania in June of the present year. A few days sufficed to replenish the supplies of the Army of the Potomac by way of the Orange & Alexandria Railroad, so that the pursuit of the enemy in the direction of Frederick was resumed. While at and near Frederick, the Baltimore & Ohio Railroad formed the line of supply, but some embarrassment was caused by that prolific source of Military Railway troubles—the detention or appropriation of trains by military authority, exercised independently of the Superintendent of the line. Having relieved the blockade which the interference had occasioned, I proceeded to take military possession of the Western Maryland Railroad, extending from the Relay House, on the Northern Central Railroad, to Westminster. The operation of this road under the circumstances was a remarkable success, and showed how much could be accomplished by expedients. The road was crooked, the grades unfavorable, there were neither water-stations, sidings, turn-tables, nor other conveniences for more than two or three trains per day, and no fuel. The supply of the army required about thirty trains per day in both directions.

To meet these difficulties, cars, engines, and full sets of train hands, also coal and split wood were brought from Alexandria; water was dipped from a dam by buckets, an old turn-table was put in order to turn the engines, sidings were dispensed with by the prompt unloading of the cars on the main track under the efficient supervision of Major Painter, of the Quartermaster's Department, and, with the presence and personal exertions of Adna Anderson, Esq., Chief Engineer of Construction on the Military Railroads, the extraordinary service so suddenly required of the road was satisfactorily performed.

After organizing the transportation on the Western Maryland Railroad, and placing it in competent hands, my attention was next directed to the reopening of the communication with Harrisburg by means of the Northern Central Railroad. On this road nineteen bridges, some of them of considerable magnitude, had been completely destroyed. I divided the Construction Corps into two divisions, and each of them into subdivisions. One division, under E. C. Smeed, as superintendent, I sent to Harrisburg via Philadelphia, with a train of tools and materials, with instructions to commence at Harrisburg and work south. The second division, under George W. Nagle, as superintendent, was instructed to work north until it met the first. One of the subdivisions of the second party I took with me, and personally attended to the reopening of the communication with Littlestown and Gettysburg. Littlestown was reached on Saturday, July 4, the very day of Lee's retreat, where I found General Sickles, and made immediate arrangements for his removal. The next morning I reported to General Meade at Headquarters near Gettysburg that in a few hours he would be again in communication with the capital, and with his depots, both by rail and telegraph.

While engaged in this work, earnest solicitations were made for the reconstruction of the railroad between Harrisburg and Chambersburg, but as the Construction Corps had more on hand than could possibly be managed, I requested Colonel Thomas A. Scott, Vice-President of the Pennsylvania Railroad Company, to assist in the reconstruction of the Cumberland Valley Railroad, and take men from the shops under his control, until I could relieve a portion of my own forces from other duties. Colonel Scott promptly responded to this request and, for several days, superintended the work in person.

As soon as the road to Gettysburg was opened, I marched 200 men over the mountain to Chambersburg under charge of J. B. Clough, Principal Assistant Engineer of Construction, carrying tools and rations in wagons, which it was necessary to impress for that purpose, and set them to work to reconstruct the Chambersburg and Franklin Railroads. The remainder of the Construction Corps, after completing the bridges on the Northern Central Railroad, were directed to proceed with their trains via Harrisburg and report at Chambersburg. While the Corps was on the way, and had nearly reached Chambersburg, a telegram was received from Washington informing me of the escape of Lee. I immediately turned back the trains and directed them to be forwarded with all possible dispatch to Alexandria, stopped work on the Franklin Road, and with the remainder of the men returned with all haste to Alexandria to resume operations on the Orange & Alexandria line.

Telegrams were sent to Superintendents of other roads requesting the prompt return of all cars and engines belonging to the Government, and a sufficient number were collected to forward all necessary supplies before the Army of the Potomac had reached the line of the Manassas Gap Railroad.

It affords much gratification to be able to state that the Armies of the Rappahannock, of Virginia and of the Potomac, while dependent for supplies on the railroads in my charge, have never suffered inconvenience or been delayed in their movements from any deficiency; in fact, it is a question whether rapid movement was not retarded by the very superabundance of supplies. No movement ever took place without involving the necessity of reloading and transporting by rail hundreds, and sometimes thousands of tons which had been sent forward in excess of the consumption and of the ability of the wagons to remove. These results are due chiefly to two causes: the great efficiency of the Superintendents, J. H. Devereux and William W. Wright, and their subordinates, and the stringent orders of Major-General Halleck, which prevented that interference by officers with train movements which, previous to my connection with Military Railroad operations, had been the cause of constant and vexatious blockades.

I have now presented a brief report, in the form of a personal narrative, of such operations of the Military Railroads Bureau as came under my personal observation. This has properly been made in very general terms, as I preferred to refer for details to the reports of the officers to whom they were more particularly entrusted, which reports are appended hereto.

Information in regard to disbursements and accounts has been furnished by Colonel D. C. McCallum, Military Director and General Superintendent of United States Railroads.

The report of Adna Anderson, Chief Engineer of Construction, will exhibit the operations of the Construction Corps.

The report of J. H. Devereux, Esq., Superintendent of Orange & Alexandria, Loudoun & Hampshire, Manassas Gap & Washington and Alexandria Railroads, will exhibit the doings on those roads.

The report of W. W. Wright, Superintendent and Engineer of the Richmond, Fredericksburg & Potomac Railroad, and for a time also Military Superintendent of the Cumberland Valley and Franklin Railroads, will exhibit the operations on those lines.

The Petersburg & Suffolk and Seaboard & Roanoke Railroads have been under the charge of E. L. Wentz, Esq., as Superintendent and Engineer, who will also report the doings in construction and transportation on those lines.

These are all the Military Railroads that have been directly under my charge; for the management of others I have not been in any way responsible. Although directed by the Secretary of War to cause an inspection to be made of the various Military Railroads in the West, and to report such suggestions and recommendations as would promote their efficiency and economy, I never received authority to correct abuses or remedy defects, and my recommendations have not been acted upon.

The report of F. H. Forbes, Esq., Special Agent, is submitted, and the attention of the Department particularly directed thereto.

While the report of Mr. Forbes gives evidence of a commendable fidelity and attention to duty on the part of some of the officers connected with the railway organization in the West, the general impression produced by the report is that of inefficiency, want of system and order, inexperience and, too often, utter disregard of economy and great waste of public property. Sometimes, too, there are strong reasons to suspect collusion between Government officers and contractors. The most prolific source of irregularity in operations, resulting in detention of trains, embarrassment of operations and waste of property has been caused in the West, as it formerly was in the East, by interference of officers with the duties of the Superintendent. It might be supposed that military men, recognizing the importance of subordination, would be the last to interfere with the orders of a Superintendent or require a violation of them on the part of his employes; but, unfortunately, there has existed a thorough contempt for civilians, particularly on the part of officers of low grade, and very few are willing to look beyond their own personal gratification or convenience, or care for the embarrass-ments to other Departments that a determination to accommodate them-selves may cause. The only remedy for this evil is that which was applied by General Halleck to the railroads under my charge, when it was ordered that any officer who interfered with the movements of the trains should be dismissed, and my authority over the railroad was declared to be supreme. It is too evident to require argument or illus-tration, that a railroad is a complicated machine, requiring for its successful operation a Superintendent possessed of qualifications not often found; it must have one head, and only one, and through that head alone should orders be given affecting the movement of trains. Self-evident as appears the propriety of these positions, they have not been generally recognized or acted upon, but have been continually violated.

What is needed is a uniform code of rules, regulations and signals for the operation of all Military Railroads of the United States; a central bureau at Washington; a system of regular periodical reports, giving the names, location, condition, amount of rolling stock, miles in operation, characteristics, persons in charge, doings in construction and transportation, salaries of employes, and other particulars on all the Military Railroads; but even with this, no efforts for improvement or reform can be successful without the approval and cordial coöpera-tion of the officer in command of the Department, who must have a real-izing sense of the necessity of order and system, and who will not permit his own temporary convenience, or that of his officers, to violate the established rules of operation, and throw the trains into confusion.

Claims by railroad corporations will, no doubt, be presented for damages caused by the raids of the enemy, or for suspension of ordinary business during the occupancy of such roads for military purposes.

In all such cases I am of the opinion that no payment should be made by the Government except for actual damages that can be proved to have been sustained, none for the loss of prospective profits antici-pated by corporations from taxing Government transportation. The business and receipts of a road during its ordinary condition can be readily ascertained by taking the average of several years before the war, and adding the indicated annual percentage of income; or, if the occupation has been only for a short time, then by comparing corre-sponding periods before the war at the same seasons. The deficiency of receipts during the period of military occupancy should be made good, as also any damages caused by such occupancy. If allowances be made for damages caused by raids, the labor and material expended by Government in reconstruction should be deducted or considered in the award.

The exposed position of the depot grounds at Alexandria, which invited raids; the large amount of rolling stock and other valuable property accumulated there, and the fact that attempts had been made to fire the buildings, induced me to ask permission of General Halleck to construct some artificial protection. The permission was granted without hesitation, and after a careful examination of the ground, I concluded to enclose an area occupying several squares with a substan-tial stockade. The stockade will not only exclude persons who have no right to enter the enclosure, but it will be capable of a very efficient defense in case of attack. The straight lines which form the sides have been broken by intermediate bastions, so that every part is well flanked; the bastions are formed by heavier logs than the rest of the stockade, and have two tiers of loop-holes. In case of attack they will be defended by practiced riflemen armed with magazine rifles. Two positions which command the exterior approaches have been prepared for artillery. The work was done by the Construction Corps at a time when they had no other employment, and is very creditable to them.

The Construction Corps and a portion of the employes in the Transportation Department have been drilled daily under the direction of Lieutenant-Colonel John Clark.

The Construction Corps consists of about 200 bridge carpenters and 300 "contrabands." They are not often suffered to remain idle, but when not actually employed in advance movements, are required to cut wood, piles and cross-ties, repair track, straighten rails, build block-houses and stockades, frame bridges in advance of requirements in construction, and perform various other services, in which they have attained great efficiency.

Owing to the frequent exposure of these men in positions where they are liable to capture, I obtained permission from General Halleck to organize, arm, and drill all the employes of the Military Railroads Bureau, in number about one thousand men, with a view to self-defense. They have entered into the plan with much zeal and spirit. In case of attack, I have no doubt they will give a good account of themselves.

In the operations of the Military Railroads which have been under my charge, various new modes of facilitating transportation, of reconstructing roads and bridges, of destroying and repairing communications, and of rapidly throwing troops across streams, have presented themselves as the results of observation and experience, the introduction of which would increase the efficiency and economy of the service.

For the purpose of giving an intelligible explanation of these plans, the operations were photographed and reports made to General Halleck, accompanied with the illustrations. These reports were printed, and with the accompanying photographs sent to officers in command of departments, posts and expeditions, where the introduction might lead to valuable results. To these officers the information should be confined during the continuance of the war; any publication of details previous to its termination would be improper.

The artist was detailed from one of the regiments and receives no compensation except his ordinary pay. The expense of the photographs is inconsiderable.

Some of the operations which have been thus illustrated consist of plans of transporting loaded cars on floats so as to connect the water termini of different railroads, and transfer cars from one road to another without break of bulk or lapse of time.

Plans for constructing floating docks, wharves, warehouses and bridges, so as to avoid delay in establishing landings and river depots, or loss of stores or improvements. if an evacuation becomes necessary.

Plans for destroying bridges with apparatus so portable that it can be carried in the pocket, and in a period of time not exceeding five minutes.

Plans for destroying track at the rate of five miles in an hour, with apparatus that can be carried in saddle-bags, and which twists and bends rails so effectually that they cannot be again used.

Plans for straightening rails and reconstructing roads that have been destroyed by the enemy.

Plans for various new kinds of trusses, trestle and suspension bridges, designed to permit the use of rough sticks and other material that will not require transportation.

Plans and expedients for crossing streams with boats that two men can construct of rough sticks in four hours, requiring transportation of only about eight pounds of ropes, cords, and material to each man. By means of these boats, rafts, ferries and bridges can be formed capable of crossing infantry at the rate of from 10,000 to 20,000 men per hour; also artillery and wagon-trains. They will render possible operations which have been considered impossible by the best military engineers.

All these operations have been tested experimentally and illustrated by photographs exhibiting actual results. The Construction Corps has rendered valuable service in making these experiments at times when they would have been otherwise unemployed. Instead of allowing the men to remain idle in camp, they have been constantly exercised and employed in some way by which they could be made to pay expenses.

This report, with a complete set of photographs illustrative of operations in construction and transportation, is herewith respectfully submitted.

H. HAUPT,
In Charge of United States Military Railroads.

PLATFORM FOR CONSTRUCTING ARKS, AND ARK READY FOR LAUNCHING.

CHAPTER XX.

DESCRIPTION OF PHOTOGRAPHIC ILLUS-
TRATIONS.

ONLY a portion of the photographs of the achievements and experiments of the Military Railroads Construction Corps can be presented herein; but a description of certain of those not reproduced may be quite as instructive and interesting, especially to military men and engineers, as the pictures themselves.

The title-page of the quarto volume containing the entire series stated:

Photographic Illustrations of Operations in Construction and Transportation, as used to facilitate the movements of the Armies of the Rappahannock, of Virginia, and of the Potomac, including experiments to determine the most expeditious and practical modes to be resorted to in the construction, destruction, and reconstruction of roads and bridges. This series of photographs is sent to officers of departments, posts, and expeditions, with a view to increase the efficiency and economy of the public service, and especially to suggest expedients whereby our own communications can be most readily preserved or restored, and those of the enemy most rapidly and effectually destroyed.

No. 1. Illustrates a mode of transportation which was adopted with great advantage on the Potomac (see page 291) in establishing a communication between Alexandria and Aquia Creek. It can be used to connect the various roads which have their termini on navigable rivers, and would prove of great advantage on the Western waters.

The floats used on the Potomac consisted of two large-sized Schuylkill barges, across which long timbers were placed supporting eight tracks. On these tracks loaded cars were run at Alexandria, towed to Aquia Creek, landed without break of bulk, and sent to advanced stations, where their contents were distributed. This is the first known attempt to transport cars by water with their cargoes unbroken.

At the time of the abandonment of the Fredericksburg Railroad, in June, 1863, supplies from Falmouth and other stations in the front were loaded in cars, the cars run on floats at Aquia Creek, sent to Alexandria, landed without break of bulk, and sent forward to meet the army which had marched overland to the line of the Orange & Alexandria Railroad. All the cars and engines were safely removed, and none of the stores lost or destroyed. Without the floats this would have been impossible.

With suitable arrangements trains can be loaded on or unloaded from the barges in a very few minutes, and by this means the multiplication of depots, the break of bulk, with the handling, waste and expense which it involves, the steamers and transports, and the risk of capture from the establishment of depots in exposed positions, would, to a great extent, be avoided. It was estimated that the general introduction of this system on the Potomac for the supply of the Army at Fredericksburg would have saved at the rate of a million and a half of dollars per annum. On the Ohio and Mississippi Rivers there may also be opportunities of using the plan with great advantage.

No. 4. Represents arks 60 feet long, 20 feet wide, and from 6 to 8 feet high. The sides are formed of round sticks, flatted where they come together, and about 6 inches in diameter. The sticks are connected by spikes and treenails. Two-inch planks are spiked vertically in the cribwork, covered with two thicknesses of canvas, coated on both sides with pitch, and the canvas then covered with boards. (See page 273.)

These arks may be used for a great variety of purposes connected with army transportation, some of which are as follows:

a. Transports for carrying lumber, commissary or quartermaster's stores.

b. Lashed together in lots of four, forming a float 120 feet by 40 feet, they will carry 16 cars, which constitute a full train on the Virginia railroads, and all the cars can be loaded and unloaded without changing the position of the float.

c. Five arks, placed side by side and covered by a canvas roof, will form a warehouse 100 feet by 60 feet, from which supplies may be issued; and when empty, the warehouse itself may be towed to the depot to be refilled.

d. Placed together, end to end, they form a wharf sufficiently wide for two railway tracks, upon which, when anchored by piles, trains can be safely run; and the capacity for loading or unloading vessels may be increased to any desired extent by increasing the number of floats at the end of the wharf. In case of evacuation, the wharves and floating warehouses may be towed to a place of safety, rendering the destruction of buildings and stores unnecessary.

e. Built about 8 feet high, with a roof of logs, they may be used as floating block-houses, for the transportation of troops on rivers, where ordinary transports would be exposed to fire from the banks; or for the protection of warehouses and other property at river landings.

f. Filled with bunks, they may form floating hospitals, or may be used for the accommodation of mechanics and laborers employed on work near streams.

g. The weight of a locomotive engine will depress an ark but 8 inches; they may, therefore, be used to support railway bridges capable of carrying trains across wide and deep streams. The spans may be built in advance on the arks, one at each end, towed into position, fastened together, anchored in any suitable way, and a railway communication opened in a very short time. A draw in such a bridge can be formed by making a span movable.

Provision should be made for bailing or pumping any water that may run or leak into the arks.

No. 5. Represents the platform on which the bottoms of the arks are constructed. It is elevated 10 feet above the launching ways, supported by stout hinges in the middle so as to afford facilities for turning over the bottom of the ark when it has been finished ready to receive the sides. The inclined braces which support the projecting part of the platform are removed when the bottom is to be turned, and the maneuver is effected by ropes passing round the windlasses shown on the back part of the platform. (See page 281.)

Near the water is seen an ark on the ways, nearly finished.

No. 14. EXPERIMENTAL SUSPENSION TRUSSES OF BOARDS.—The experiments on this truss gave very important results, and indicate the possibility of applying the principles even to railway bridges. The supports of the bridge consisted of two catenaries, each of six 1-inch boards, 12 inches wide; the span was 100 feet, versed sine 10 feet. The boards were nailed together at intervals of 4 inches, with tenpenny nails; and after the catenary was formed, cut spikes were driven through. The anchorage, which was not very secure, gave way with 84,000 pounds, but the boards were not pulled apart. The experiment will be repeated by coating the surfaces of the boards with pitch, compressing them with half-inch bolts one foot apart, and driving spikes at intervals of four inches. It is believed that this arrangement will possess extraordinary powers of resistance, and the combination being impervious to water, will also possess great durability.

In constructing a suspension bridge upon this principle, to replace a bridge of one or more spans that has been destroyed, three of the layers of boards which form the catenaries are nailed together on the bank at one end of the bridge, supported, if necessary, by rollers, and drawn into place across the opening by a cable and capstan on the opposite side. When the catenary of three boards is placed, it will form a runway across the opening; other boards are then added, taking care to break joints at equal distances. Holes are then bored, bolts inserted and tightly screwed, and lastly the spikes are driven. The anchorage is secured by spreading the boards at the ends by means of wedges, in the shape of a fan, to prevent it from pulling through the timbers which embrace it; or in several other ways secure anchorage may be obtained.

As boards can be carried by men for several miles, this mode of construction for military bridges may sometimes possess great advantages. A very important application of this principle may be made to the construction of a board suspension bridge for ordinary military purposes. The board catenaries drawn across the stream, anchored to posts, and floating on the water, may be raised, at intervals of 30 or 40 feet, by means of a scow, and trestles placed under, giving as many points of support as may be considered necessary. Such a bridge could be constructed with great rapidity.

No. 17. EXPEDIENTS FOR CROSSING STREAMS.—Promises to be of very great value in military operations. It consists of a frame (see page 217) covered with an India-rubber blanket, or with painted canvas, or any other material impervious to water.

The frames are made of round or split sticks, not much larger than chair sticks, put together by means of the pocket auger represented on page 191.

To afford sufficient capacity, the best size for the blanket is 8 feet long by 5 feet wide. This will allow two men to sit in each boat, facing each other, with their legs extended. The frames are 16 inches high, 28 inches wide and 64 inches long, outside dimensions. The blanket is surrounded by eyelets and tied to the top rail of the frame by strings.

Although these boats may be used singly, for scouting and for other purposes, yet their most important use promises to be in throwing large bodies of troops suddenly across a stream, even in the face of an enemy of equal strength, and enabling them, by the rapidity of the maneuver, to occupy and hold their ground before the enemy can concentrate to oppose them. To accomplish this movement, which books on military science declare to be impracticable, a point should be selected where artillery can command the opposite bank, and where troops can be massed unobserved. When all is ready, two regiments of engineer troops, each man carrying his boat, advance rapidly to the stream, throw in the boats, lash them together in rafts of 25, send over ropes to tie to trees on both sides, and in a few minutes a ferry is extemporized, capable with two ropes, of throwing troops across at the rate of 10,000 men per hour; one of the ropes being used for the loaded rafts, and the other to return the empty ones (see page 257). Each raft will carry 50 to 65 men; and to avoid confusion and delay, the men who manage the rafts should be drilled. Cavalry may be passed over by holding the bridles of the horses; artillery (see page 265), by flooring the rafts with poles. In No. 17 (see page 233) two boats of smaller dimensions than those prescribed carry four men, but the men should sit flat on the bottom, not on boards across the top.

No. 18. EXPEDIENTS FOR CROSSING STREAMS.—Blanket boats on the Potomac (see page 241) some distance from shore. A pair of boats carries four men, and a single small boat, made of an ordinary blanket, one man, who is sitting on the bottom. Boats of blankets of the ordinary size are too small. They have buoyancy enough to carry a man, but he must be very expert in the use of a canoe or he will upset.

No. 19. EXPEDIENTS FOR CROSSING STREAMS.—Frame of a blanket boat (see page 217) of proper size. The outside dimensions are: height 16 inches, breadth 28 inches, length 64 inches. The rails of the frame are one inch and a half, round or square; the connecting pieces one inch, round or square. The material may be obtained from fence rails, poles or split timber. It is not absolutely necessary that an India-rubber blanket should be used for covering the frames; any kind of tight canvas will answer as well. Pieces of sail cloth or condemned tents may be used for this purpose to great advantage. A coat of thick paint will render them impervious to water.

No. 20. EXPEDIENTS FOR CROSSING STREAMS.—Pocket auger (see page 191) used to construct the frames of the blanket boats. It consists of a hollow case about 6 inches long, which contains a $\frac{3}{4}$-inch auger for boring holes in the rails, and in the end is a hollow auger for cutting round tenons $\frac{3}{4}$-inch diameter and $1\frac{1}{2}$ inches long. The auger can be carried with little more inconvenience than a jack-knife.

No. 21. EXPEDIENTS FOR CROSSING STREAMS.—A pair of small pontoons (see page 225), designed to facilitate scouting operations. They should be about 10 inches diameter and 7 or 8 feet long. They can be carried by a strap around the waist and concealed by an overcoat. A boat can be made of these by running poles through the loops, and then placing sticks across. They were originally designed by General Haupt for the use of surveying parties, but for scouting expeditions they may be of great value.

No. 24. EXPERIMENTAL BRIDGE TRUSSES.—Truss for military bridges (see pages 61, 71, 81, 91), which is composed of boards nailed and spiked together. The span is 60 feet; the height of truss six feet. The form is that of a fish or two arches curved in opposite directions.

The lower arch is composed of six boards, the upper arch of five. The braces are of two-inch plank, and through the trusses, vertically, inch bolts are passed. These trusses were tested by forming a bridge of two of them, which was loaded with railroad iron until it broke. The weight was applied by first piling a number of bars on the bridge, then pulling over a car loaded with twenty tons by means of a rope, so as to avoid risk to the men. The bridge broke (see page 91) with 108,000 pounds.

This was a highly satisfactory experiment, and although the trusses were designed simply for ordinary military bridges, they would safely have carried a locomotive. When they broke, the weight stood on the bridge five minutes before it came down. Much stronger trusses than those experimented upon, can be made by pitching the surface of the boards, bolting them with half-inch bolts at intervals of a foot, and driving spikes through at intervals of four inches. Two such trusses would carry a train, but three or four could be used if preferred.

Instead of the two arches turned in opposite directions, one of them may be replaced by a straight chord.

No. 27. Second Experiment with Board Trusses.—This truss was 60 feet long, the clear span 56 feet, height of truss six feet. The top and bottom arches were each composed of six boards, one inch thick and twelve inches wide; the surfaces of the boards were covered with pitch; the boards, as they were successively placed, were nailed with tenpenny nails, four inches apart; at intervals of one foot were placed two half-inch bolts, compressing the boards tightly, and spikes, six inches long, were driven through the boards at intervals of four inches. Boards were also nailed vertically on the sides.

The bridge was loaded until it broke. The breaking weight was 95 tons, 30 tons of which were on the car; the equivalent was about 105 tons, uniformly distributed.

When the truss broke, it appeared that the built-chord had acted as a solid piece; there was no slipping of the boards upon each other. The fractures of the six boards, on each lower chord, were nearly at the same point. Assuming five of the boards to have resisted the tensile strain, the breaking strain was 2,900 pounds per square inch. The top chords did not break.

No. 36. Experiment with Board Trusses.—Experiments having proved that trusses could be made of boards of sufficient strength to carry railway trains, it was concluded to construct 1,000 lineal feet of bridging of this description (see page 61) preparatory to the forward movement of the Army of the Potomac.

The construction of these bridges furnished employment to the Construction Corps when they had no other work. It was intended that the trusses should be carried whole and placed in position, without the use of false works, resting the ends on wooden piers when the trusses were shorter than the spans which they replaced.

Each pair of trusses was to form a span of 60 feet of bridging. The trusses were to be placed about 10 feet apart, braced by planks, and the ties placed directly on the top chords, as shown in plate.

These trusses were composed of nine boards in each chord. The surfaces were not pitched. The half-inch bolts were in pairs one foot apart, as in the trusses previously constructed. Cut spikes, six inches long, were driven from both sides at intervals of four inches. Boards were also nailed vertically on the sides of the trusses covering the edges of the other boards.

A pair of these trusses were experimented upon and tested by first loading them uniformly with one ton per lineal foot, in addition to the weight of the bridge, and then running on a car loaded with 30 tons of rails. The strain thus produced was supposed to be twice as great as that caused by the passage of any ordinary railroad train.

The bridge stood the test without any yielding or slipping of the boards in the middle of the span. Only one board appeared to have slipped about the sixteenth part of an inch, but even this was doubtful.

There were about one hundred of these valuable photographs illustrating the peculiar inventions of General Haupt to promote the operations of war, but the remainder, where not reproduced in this volume, require no description.

CHAPTER XXI.

SUBSEQUENT ACHIEVEMENTS OF THE MILITARY RAILROAD CORPS.

AFTER the repulse of General W. S. Rosecrans in September, 1863, East Tennessee was considered in great jeopardy, and Secretary Stanton decided to send a portion of the Army of the Potomac to reinforce the armies in the West. An article in the *Century* of March, 1887, states that General Halleck considered the movement impracticable, as it would be impossible to get the transfer effected in time. After much discussion, the President was inclined to side with General Halleck. Stanton requested an adjournment until evening, and in the meantime sent for my successor, Colonel McCallum, and presented the question:

Assuming that you have entire control of rail and telegraph, what is the shortest time in which you can transfer the required number of troops, with artillery, ammunition and supplies, to the objective point?

McCallum made his figures and reported a date earlier than that which the Secretary considered necessary. At the adjourned meeting Colonel McCallum was sent for and gave his figures, and was ordered at once to commence the movement, which was successfully accomplished, 22,000 men, artillery, ammunition and supplies being moved from near Catlett's Station, on the Orange & Alexandria Railroad, to a point 1,166 miles distant in eight days. McCallum was rewarded by a commission as Brigadier-General.

But it was in Sherman's great campaign, in his world-renowned march to the sea, that the wonderful efficiency of the Construction Corps was most strikingly exhibited. The marvelous celerity with which bridges were reconstructed and broken communications restored inspired so much confidence in General Sherman that he would risk advances when dependent upon extended rail lines of hundreds of miles in his rear for supplies, and that, too, when these lines were subject to constant breaks from guerrilla bands and hostile citizens.

In this famous march, the transportation was under the direction of W. W. Wright, the repairs of roads under Adna Anderson, and the bridges under E. C. Smeed. Wright, being much of his time at Headquarters and receiving instructions from General

Sherman and from his Chief Quartermaster, appears to have been the only officer of the Corps recognized by General Sherman in his Memoirs, and to him all the credit has been given; but Wright managed the transportation only; the reconstruction of the roads was in the hands of General Anderson, who held a more difficult position.

There could have been no transportation without a continuous track, and there could have been no continuous track without bridges.

The bridges were the key of the situation, and they were under the charge of E. C. Smeed, and to this diffident, unassuming man, whose name was not even mentioned, more than to any other, I give the credit of the success of Sherman's great campaign.

Sherman could not have moved without supplies; he could not have had supplies without the railroads, and the railroads could not have been used without the bridges, and I firmly believe that no other man living could have been found capable of reconstructing the bridges with equal celerity.

During this campaign I received a letter from Smeed informing me that he had built a bridge across the Chattahoochee, which contained twice the amount of timber of the Potomac Creek bridge, and was built in just half the time, or four and a half days, the timber being taken from the stump.

The records of the whole world cannot find the equal of such a performance, but it must be remembered that Smeed had a corps of men thoroughly organized and drilled, veterans in military bridge construction, while at Potomac Creek I had details of common soldiers, changed every day, unskilled, untrained and many of them useless for any purpose.

I was very anxious to get an account from Smeed himself of the reconstruction of this Chattahoochee bridge to include in these Memoirs, and wrote to him two or three times without reply. I finally concluded that his well-known and extreme diffidence rendered him indisposed to place himself in any position that would render him conspicuous; but after his death, in 1892, his daughter, Mrs. Kate Smeed Cress, of Emporia, Kansas, wrote to me that she had found amongst her father's papers an unfinished letter addressed to me, which she would forward if desired. Of course it was desired, and the following is a copy of the letter:

OMAHA, NEB., May, 1899.

DEAR GENERAL: Replying to yours, asking to be furnished with a brief account of my operations while connected with the Construction Department of the Military Railways of the Military Division of the Mississippi, I will say:

In the fall of 1863, while at Alexandria, Virginia, I received an order to report for duty to General D. C. McCallum at Bridgeport,

Float of Two Canal Boats Transferring Eight Loaded Cars from Alexandria to Acquia Creek.

Alabama. I started the same day I got the order and went direct to Stevenson. While there I learned by telegraph from Colonel W. W. Wright that General McCallum and himself were in New York waiting for men to be recruited for railway service in the Southwest, and that they would not come on South for some time. I also learned, while in Stevenson, that the base of supplies for the army then in Chattanooga was at Bridgeport, Alabama.

Being unable to render any service where I was, I went on to Bridgeport, the terminus of the railway. Finding nothing I could do there towards opening the railway further South, I went on about twenty-five miles further to a point where a long and high bridge that carries the railway over a deep, wide valley, had been burned. There I found a party of workmen engaged in rebuilding it. The person in charge of the work said they were working under orders of Colonel Anderson—you, no doubt, know him; he was formerly an engineer on the Pennsylvania Railroad. These men had been at work here for considerable time and the construction of the bridge was well under way. The methods employed in the construction were not the best; they were orthodox, but to a member of the Construction Corps of Virginia they did seem a little old-fashioned and unsuited to the occasion. Steps were immediately taken to change the mode of operation, and introduce better and more expeditious methods of construction, which, I think, succeeded fairly well, as the bridge was finished in a few days that would have taken, under the old regime, as many weeks.

On my return to camp, I found General McCallum and Colonel Wright; they had come on by rail and, being unable to cross the bridge, waited there for me to return, which I did that evening, and after being assured by me that the railway would be ready for trains the next day, they concluded to remain over night in my camp.

The next morning the bridge was finished and several trains loaded with supplies crossed over it and ran into Chattanooga.

General McCallum and Colonel Wright rode into Chattanooga on the first train, and that was the only part either of them took in opening up the railway communications with Chattanooga, although I have often heard each of them speak of their great achievement in opening up the railway to carry food to the starving army in Chattanooga.

After the railway was opened to Chattanooga, Colonel Wright was placed in charge of railway construction in the Southwest, with headquarters in Chattanooga.

As soon as the railway was in good running order I was ordered by Colonel Wright to open up communications between Chattanooga and Knoxville. For this service I had two companies of the Construction Corps that had just come on from Virginia, they being a part of the old force employed there by me before I went South.

The track force went by rail, taking their tools and supplies with them, and repaired the railway as they advanced.

The bridgemen took their tools and supplies in army wagons, and marched about forty miles to Charleston, the place where the bridge over the Hiwassee River had been burned. The bridge, although quite long and high, was finished before the trackmen arrived there. As soon as the track force came up the work of repairing the road was pushed on as far as London, about twenty-five miles from Knoxville.

While at London I received an order to turn the forces over to Colonel E. L. Wentz, and to report for duty to Colonel John Clark, at Nashville, Tennessee, to complete an unfinished railway between Nashville and Johnsonville. When I arrived on the work, I found the road in running order for about twenty-five miles out from Nashville; the remaining forty-five miles that had been built to reach Johnsonville was in work. The grading was being done by colored troops, the track and bridges by Engineer troops—a brigade of the former and two regiments of the latter having been detailed for that service. The work was being done under the old established rules generally followed in such cases, viz., the earth being wheeled out of the cuts to make the fills. The timber for the bridges were squared and framed together according to old established customs. The cross-ties were being bedded to a straight edge, and the rails were being laid and spiked down in the usual manner. In order to open the line as soon as possible, the track was laid before the grading was finished and the cuts taken out and the fills brought to grade afterwards. Our new methods were introduced in bridge-building and track-laying, and by these means the road was opened to Johnsonville in about thirty days.

All these operations were preliminary to the Atlanta campaign.

When the Atlanta movement began I was in Nashville, Tennessee, and did not expect to go with the Construction Corps on that campaign, as another engineer, Colonel Eicholtz, had been selected for that service. But some time after the movement south from Chattanooga began, I received a telegram to proceed to Chattanooga and join the Construction Corps in the field as soon as possible. I started immediately on receipt of the order and joined the Corps near Big Shanty, Georgia. After I joined the Corps, Colonel Wright and Colonel Eicholtz remained with it until the railway was repaired to Marietta. Soon after I joined the Corps Colonel Wright and Colonel Eicholtz returned to Chattanooga, and I saw very little of Colonel Wright and nothing of Colonel Eicholtz until the railway was opened to Atlanta. Colonel Wright occasionally made short visits to the front, but never remained with us very long.

Our operations here in the Southwest were conducted quite similar to the Front Royal campaign in Virginia; you, of course, remember how we did the work there. Our forces here were better organized and equipped, and consequently more efficient than the raw details employed there. Our tools for bridge-building consisted chiefly of axes, cross-cut saws, spiking mauls, augers, ropes, blocks and tackle, timber-rollers, scaffolding plank, when we could get them, and two good sets of balance beams, and a few carpenters' tools, the latter seldom used. We always carried a full supply of wrought bridge spikes, that were liberally used in our temporary works. For track service we had a regular set of track tools for laying track, and in addition we always carried hooks for taking up track and bending rails.* You remember the first of these hooks were made in Alexandria, Virginia. I see General Howard, in his *Century* article, gives Colonel Poe the credit for inventing it. You know who invented it.

Our transportation by rail consisted of locomotives, box cars for supplies, flat cars for materials and stock cars for animals. Our land transportation was all done with ox teams, which were drawn from the Commissary and returned to the Commissary when we were out of beef and a new provision return made out for more meat rations. Our camp equipment consisted of a sufficient supply of tents and the regular camp equipage for men. The men were organized in squads of about twenty

---

* NOTE.—Invented by E. C. Smeed during Hooker's campaign, and previously described herein.

each, with a foreman in charge of each squad. Each squad had its own cook, camp equipage, tools, etc. The squads were independent of each other; in other words, any one of the squads could be detached for special duty without interfering with the organization of another squad.

The successive steps taken to build a bridge over a large stream would be as follows: A sufficient number of axmen, teamsters and teams would be left in the rear, where good timber for our purposes was plenty, to cut and hew (we usually flatted the timber on two sides) and deliver on the cars a sufficient quantity of timber to build the bridge. As fast as the timber could be loaded on the cars it would be forwarded to the bridge site. The framers and raisers would proceed to the bridge site and begin the work of clearing away the rubbish, unloading tools, pitching camp, etc. By the time this had been finished the first lot of timber would have arrived and been unloaded on the ground.

As soon as this was done the squads would be assigned to their special duties and begin their work at once. The raisers would begin operations by rigging and running out their balance beams at both ends of the bridge. The framers would frame and put a bent together on the ground ready to be launched into the stream or raised from the ground into place, according to circumstances. By the time a bent was put together, the leveler would be ready to give the exact length for cutting off the feet of the posts; in the meantime, the raisers would have their balance beams rigged and the falls lowered ready to raise the bent into position. As soon as the bent was stayed, the balance beams would be run out for the next bent. This operation would be repeated in this way from both ends of the bridge until all the bents were in place. While the shore bents were being put up, another squad would build a temporary ferry for crossing the stream, which consisted of a raft rigged similar to a rope ferry. The ferry would always be located just above the bridge site, so that the bents of the bridge that came in the stream could be fastened to the raft and floated into position under the bridge, ready to be raised into place. If the water was deep and the current swift, several bars of railway iron would be spiked to the feet of the posts to assist in sinking them. When a bridge was two, three or four sections high, very little attention was paid to the height of the first sections, but the leveler would take the elevation of the top of the first section as soon as it was raised and determine the exact height of all the upper sections, and they would be framed to the proper height. As the work progressed, another squad would spike on, where needed, additional braces. These braces were made of round poles about six inches in diameter, flatted where they came in contact with the main timbers and well spiked to them as fast as the bents were raised and braced. Another squad of men would put on the track stringers, which were made of round logs hewn flat on the top sides and where they rested on the bents. The track stringers were never spliced nor butted together on a cap, but were always lapped by each other; the bays were generally about sixteen feet long. We used two, four or six stringers in each bay, depending entirely on the size and quality of the timbers in them. The next and last operation was laying the track. Common hewn cross-ties were used; they were spiked to the track stringers with long bent spikes, and the rails spiked down to them in the usual way.

Generally the track was repaired up to the bridge site before the bridges were begun. Exceptions were sometimes made where long stretches of track had been destroyed and where timbers for rebuilding a bridge could be obtained near at hand. In such cases the bridgemen would build the bridges in advance of the track work. The bridges built in this way were rough and strong; they would sometimes settle out of line and surface under the weight of the first trains, but they were easily relieved and surfaced again. Considering the circumstances and materials we had to work with, the bridges were built in a very short time. As for an example of military bridge-building, the bridge over the Chattahoochee River, near Atlanta, Georgia, although being a large one, about 800 feet long and nearly 100 feet high, was built in four and a half days.

The water service required special attention, and was done by men detailed for that service.

The advance engines were supplied with water carried from wells, small streams, or water courses, to the tender in buckets or camp kettles by men formed in line passing the buckets from one to another. The water tanks were built in advance of the regular supply trains. No fixed rules were followed in building them; they generally consisted of a tub about twelve feet in diameter and eight feet deep, set upon a framed stand. Water would be supplied to them from the nearest spring or water course.

The above is a general outline of the way the railway building was carried on during the Atlanta campaign. We had to encounter many difficulties not enumerated here, but they were all matters of detail in railway building in an enemy's country that were met and overcome.

The foregoing letter is unsigned and ends abruptly. The system of operations was precisely the same as that first introduced by me in the campaign of the Army of the Rappahannock under General McDowell in 1862, in which operations E. C. Smeed was my most efficient assistant.

The brief mention of the Chattahoochee bridge is worthy of note and characteristic of the modesty of the writer. This bridge I regard as the most extraordinary feat in military bridge construction that the world has ever seen.

A bridge 780 feet long and more than 90 feet high, constructed in four and a half days, the timber being cut from the stump, is certainly without parallel.

It is not surprising that the accounts of building these bridges, published during the war, were considered fabulous by the military engineers of Europe, and that I was requested in 1868, by a unanimous vote of the British Association for the Advancement of Science at the Dundee meeting, to explain how such structures had been erected. The explanation was followed by a vote of thanks and the tender of a banquet by the Royal Engineers.

CHAPTER XXII.

MY ASSOCIATES AND SUPERIORS.

THESE notes, covering an important period of the war, contain many papers which are not found in the records of the Rebellion, and statements of facts known only to myself, which throw strong sidelights upon the main facts of history.

I have purposely omitted the reports of the Special Agent sent to examine into the condition of affairs in the West and Southwest. They exhibited gross mismanagement, wanton waste, and wholesale destruction of public property, and also contain statements affecting the integrity of individuals which should at the time have been made the subject of investigation by a Congressional Committee. These reports were all submitted to the Secretary of War, but as no public action was taken by him, and no investigation made by Congress, it would be ungenerous, after so great a lapse of time, to throw a cloud upon the reputation of those who might have made a good defense, or, at least, have made explanations that would have removed in part, at least, the odium which appeared to attach to them.

My intimate association with heads of departments and with the commanders of armies in the field, renders it expedient for me to give some expressions of opinion derived from personal contact, and thus help to remove some popular errors.

PRESIDENT LINCOLN.—My first interview with President Lincoln was in 1861, before my connection with the service. On the occasion of a visit to Washington, Hon. John Covode, of Pennsylvania, asked me to go with him to see the President.

Covode was not a man who paid any attention to the rules of etiquette. He took me to the White House, and without sending a card, walked up stairs, then along the hall to a room, opened the door without knocking, and ushered me into the august presence of Abraham Lincoln. The President was alone, seated in a chair, tilted back, with his heels upon the sill of an open window, clad in a linen duster, for the weather was warm.

Covode was greeted very cordially, and then I was introduced with some rather extravagant words of commendation, when Covode remarked: "Mr. President, I always thought it strange that the first time we met we seemed to know each other, and I think I have discovered the reason. You are called 'Honest Abe' and I 'Honest John,' and honest men are so mighty scarce in Washington that, of course, we knew each other at sight."

The President laughed, and then said: "That reminds me of a little story." It was about two little newsboys, and was appropriate, but I have forgotten the point.

I met the President occasionally afterwards during my connection with the service, but never intruded upon him unless I had something of importance to communicate. I was always received with cordiality.

On one occasion I had returned from a visit to the army with Covode, who was a prominent and useful member of the Committee on the Conduct of the War. He asked me to go with him to see the President. It was a period of gloom. We found the President much depressed. Covode reported the dissatisfaction in the army and the criticisms on his policy, and had proceeded for some time, when the President suddenly turned, placed his hand upon his knee and said:

"Covode, stop! Stop right there! Not another word! I am full, brim full up to here"—drawing his hand across his neck.

The President was tired of hearing criticisms upon his policy; he knew that he was doing his duty as best he could, and the verdict of posterity has been entered up in his favor.

The President respected the sanctity of the Sabbath and disapproved of unnecessary work upon that day. I accompanied him on his visit to McDowell at Falmouth, when the General told him that he would not be ready to start before Sunday on the march to Richmond, but knowing his objections to initiating movements that day, he would leave it to his judgment. The reply was: "Take a good ready and start Monday morning."

It was on his return from this visit that he told members of the War Committee that I had built the Potomac Creek bridge out of nothing but beanpoles and cornstalks.

In Pope's second battle of Manassas I have reason to believe that the President passed many days without sleep, for at all hours of the night I received telegrams from him asking if I had no further intelligence to communicate.

He was sorely tried by McClellan's inactivity, and his letters and dispatches were often pathetic: "If you don't intend to use that army, won't you lend it to me?" "What has your cavalry been doing since the battle of Antietam that would fatigue anything?"

It is useless to indulge in any eulogies of President Lincoln. His heart was tender and full of sympathy, with no room for

GENERAL HAUPT'S STOCKADE AT ALEXANDRIA, VA.

enmity. His intellect was penetrating and intuitive, his judgment almost infallible. In him the South lost their best friend, and the Nation, with the possible exception of Washington, their greatest President.

SECRETARY EDWIN M. STANTON.—I had some acquaintance with Mr. Stanton when he was practicing law in Pittsburg, but was not intimate. He was a man of marked ability and of strong characteristics. He was, I believe, honest, patriotic and fearless, but at times impulsive and headstrong. He made enemies and was denounced by those who unsuccessfully opposed him or felt the force of his power, as unjust and tyrannical.

Although I incurred his displeasure by interesting myself in behalf of parties who had been charged with and punished for disloyalty, when I believed there was no ground for it, I was treated in general with much consideration by the Secretary, and furnished with a card, "Admit the bearer at any hour day or night." At times he was lavish in compliments; at other times he charged me with disrespect for not obeying orders that I believed to be impracticable and unreasonable.

On the whole, our relations were satisfactory until he was compelled to choose between Governor Andrew and myself, and, of course, chose the former.

PETER H. WATSON.—Mr. Watson was Assistant Secretary of War. He had been associated with Mr. Stanton as a lawyer, and was his most intimate friend. He was a man of bright intellect and sound sense; discreet, prudent and eminently practical, and acted as a balance-wheel in the Department.

Between Watson and myself there never was a ripple of antagonism. When I was recalled to resume charge of the railroads in 1863, no one welcomed my return more cordially. He gave me authority to arrest and imprison parties guilty of treasonable practices; placed at my disposal part of the contingent fund to employ detectives to ferret out abuses and frauds, and no one regretted my retirement more sincerely.

He held important positions after the war, and was at one time President of the Erie Railroad.

GENERAL HENRY W. HALLECK.—In July, 1862, General Halleck was summoned to Washington as General in chief command of all the armies of the United States, and military adviser of the President. Previous to that time he had been in command of the Department of the Missouri, Headquarters at St. Louis.

He had been a counsellor-at-law at San Francisco, author of numerous works on Military Science, an LL. D., a man of superior attainments and eminently fitted for the responsible position to which he had been called. Secretary Stanton had known him professionally in California and may have been the cause of his promotion.

Before this time there had been no military head to the armies, each commander acting independently with such instructions as he received from the War Department or the President.

My office was on G street, near the War Department, and Halleck's office was a few doors east. I was with him frequently and, after his appointment, consulted him instead of the Secretary in regard to the operations of my Department. General George W. Cullom was his Chief of Staff, and Colonel J. C. Kelton his Adjutant General.

I formed a very high opinion of General Halleck's sound judgment, prudence and discretion, and was encouraged by him to express opinions and make suggestions freely in all matters pertaining to the operations under my charge.

There is, and has been, a widespread misapprehension in regard to the interference of General Halleck with the Generals in command of armies in the field, and he has been censured by the press for giving orders which trammelled their liberty of action, and resulted in disaster. This, I think, is an error, and does him great injustice.

I have already narrated the interview between the President and General Halleck after the battle of Fredericksburg, when he positively refused to issue orders for the retirement of the army to the north side of the river. He told the President decidedly that if such orders were issued, he must give them on his own responsibility. He said if he were personally present he might take such responsibility, and then enunciated his position in these words—a position from which I never knew him to depart: "I hold that a General in command of an army in the field is, or ought to be, the best judge of the situation. He should be allowed full liberty to exercise his own discretion and not be trammelled with orders from those who are not in a situation to know all the conditions which influence a decision."

In his dispatches to Hooker he refused to give him detailed instructions, and stated that it was proper for those at Washington merely to indicate the objects to be accomplished; it was the duty of the Generals in the field to use their own discretion as to the best means of accomplishing those objects. The general directions were: Do not manœuvre in such a manner as to leave the capital exposed; keep as near the enemy as you can; use your cavalry to obtain information as to his position and movements; if he spreads out, strike as opportunity offers; it is more important to defeat and destroy the army of the enemy than to take Richmond.

General Halleck has been severely censured for the orders given to Meade after the battle of Gettysburg. I am, perhaps, responsible for these orders more than any one else.

At my interview with General Meade on the next morning after Lee's retreat, I felt sure that if the rest of several days which he proposed to take were really taken, the enemy would escape, and I urged General Halleck to give orders to commence the pursuit immediately and prevent Lee from effecting a crossing of the Potomac back into Virginia.

When Lee did escape it was natural that great dissatisfaction should be felt, and it was to have been expected that such dissatisfaction should also be expressed when the fruits of the splendid victory at Gettysburg had been lost by inaction.

MAJOR-GENERAL IRVIN MCDOWELL.—Of all the commanders of the Armies of the East during my connection with them, I considered General McDowell the most able, but at the same time the most unfortunate and the most unpopular.

My relations with McDowell were more intimate personally than with any other General in command. I was a member of his staff, enjoyed his confidence and was authorized by him to attach his name to any orders I might find it necessary to issue. He wished me to be with him as much as possible, to make his camp my Headquarters, and assured me that a camp bed and plate were always at my service; but this could not be, as my duties required a constant change of location.

McDowell never forgot what he was pleased to consider my kindness to him when he came to West Point as a new cadet and was received by me as a tent-mate, assisted and protected from hazing. I claim, therefore, that I should know McDowell thoroughly, and whether the public opinions in regard to him were correct.

He was a man of fine education, with superior conversational powers, but a very strict disciplinarian. He sought to increase the mobility of his army by cutting off unnecessary transportation. He had no use for regimental bands, and objected to the barrels of lager and the cases of wines and liquors which increased the wagon trains and delayed movements.

He himself used no stimulants, and could not regard them as a necessity for others, which made him obnoxious, especially to the German regiments.

16

He regarded newspaper reporters as a nuisance. They retaliated by writing him down, and their papers, circulating amongst the camps, manufactured a public opinion amongst the rank and file, much to the injury of the commander.

On one occasion a band came to serenade him, but he was so much occupied in studying maps and papers that he probably did not hear them, and they went off with uncomplimentary epithets.

He was thoroughly systematic, and when sending an order always sent a duplicate and required an indorsement, as evidence of receipt. This practice proved of value before the Court of Inquiry, when a German General, having repeatedly denied receiving a certain order, McDowell took a paper from a package and asked him if he recognized his own signature. The only answer was, "Well! I forgot it."

There is no question that McDowell felt hampered by instructions from Washington, and was not always permitted to exercise his own judgment to the full; but it was not the same with subsequent commanders to an equal extent.

After the unsuccessful movement to Front Royal, against which McDowell had so earnestly protested, and truly predicted the result, the public clamor demanded his removal, which was made by the President with great reluctance, as I believe he enjoyed his entire confidence.

One of his staff related an instance of his coolness under fire. They were riding along an open valley, when a rebel battery on a hill opened fire upon them. On the opposite side of the valley were a large number of artillery horses. He sent an officer of his staff to have them removed to a place of safety, seeming, as my informant said, more concerned about the safety of the horses than the safety of his staff.

Had Halleck come into command sooner, or had McDowell remained in command later, I think favorable results would have come to fruit earlier.

MAJOR-GENERAL JOHN POPE.—With General Pope I was not so well acquainted. I never had more than three or four personal interviews with him.

He did not recognize my position when he came into command, although McDowell told him he was making a great mistake. He seemed to think it a simple matter to run a railroad, and that his Quartermasters could manage it. I, therefore, returned to Massachusetts, but was soon recalled by Assistant Secretary Watson with the information that there was not a wheel moving on any of the roads.

In the interview on the battlefield of Cedar Mountain he was quite courteous, and directed his Chief of Staff, Colonel Ruggles, to issue any order I might dictate. This was the first interview; the second was on the banks of the Rappahannock when, from the reports made in my presence, I suspected a flank movement, of which Pope thought there was no danger, but which was then actually taking place, and from which I narrowly escaped capture at Catlett's.

The next interview was after the battle, when Pope and McDowell gave me a full account, in their camp, from which I formed and maintained for years very unfavorable impressions of the conduct of Fitz John Porter, which were not removed until Porter's counsel, John C. Bullit, of Philadelphia, put in my hands the testimony before the court. This modified my opinion so far as this particular officer is concerned, but I still think that if there had been proper coöperation on the part of the Army of the Potomac under General McClellan, a complete victory would have been gained.

As to Pope's generalship, I do not feel competent to express an opinion, but McDowell, on whose judgment I relied, considered him an officer of more than ordinary ability.

MAJOR-GENERAL GEORGE B. McCLELLAN.—General McClellan was the idol of the army and the favorite of the public. He was the very antipode of McDowell in his characteristics. He possessed personal magnetism, was affable and courteous, treated newspaper reporters with the greatest consideration, and they in return wrote him up as a hero, as they falsely wrote down McDowell as a brute. The newspapers, much more than military capacity or achievement, made the public sentiment of the army and of the people.

I was not a participant in McClellan's operations on the Peninsula, but I had much to do with him after his return. His first interview with me, which continued some hours, impressed me with the idea that his caution was excessive, and that he was not a man to incur risks or assume responsibilities, which opinion was not changed upon further acquaintance. He did not seem anxious to get his army into the fight at Manassas, but rather to make the capital secure by placing his men in the forts surrounding it, and telegraphed that he did not despair of saving the capital, when perhaps no one else supposed the capital could be in any danger.

He gained a splendid victory at Antietam, where good generalship seems to have been exhibited, but he suffered his beaten enemy to escape. I am not disposed, however, to criticise this fact too severely. It may not have been possible to prevent it.

Lee had bridges there, which he did not possess after his retreat from Gettysburg.

The battle of Antietam was on the 17th, and on the 19th Lee was across. It would have required a knowledge of Lee's intentions and far greater celerity of movement than was exhibited by the Army of the Potomac, or any other of the Armies of the East, to have prevented this movement. Stonewall Jackson might have done it. I know of no one else who could. Jackson could follow up an advantage and not lose the fruits of victory by stopping to rest. I may be in error, but such is my opinion.

After Antietam there was a long delay before starting in pursuit. The General was always wanting something, and when that something was supplied he would think of something more, until at last the long-tried patience of the President was exhausted and, in reply to a statement that the horses were fatigued, he begged to be informed what the horses had been doing since the battle of Antietam that would fatigue anything.

My observations of McClellan would lead me to characterize him as The Unready.

John Covode, a Congressman from Pennsylvania, in his homely phraseology, used to say that "McClellan has been raised to so high a pinnacle that he is afraid to move in any direction for fear that he will fall and break his neck."

MAJOR-GENERAL AMBROSE E. BURNSIDE.—Whatever may have been the failings of General Burnside, it cannot be charged that he was characterized by any large amount of self-conceit. I accompanied General Halleck, at his request, on the occasion of the visit to camp when Burnside was appointed to succeed McClellan. He was very reluctant to accept it; declared emphatically that he was not fit for it; that there were many better men in the service, but that if the President and General Halleck insisted upon it, he would do the best he could, and could promise no more.

Burnside had not the system and order which distinguished McDowell, and his ideas of practical operations were sometimes very crude. On one occasion he wanted a new wharf built below Acquia Creek, and asked me how much time would be required.

I answered, "About three weeks." He exclaimed, "three weeks! I want it in three days. I will detail twenty thousand men for the service."

I explained that more than a limited number of men could not work; they would only be in the way, and that some time would be required to collect tools and material. His idea seemed to be that if 50,000 days' work were required to complete a structure, he could detail 50,000 men and do it in one day.

Burnside had promised to give no orders about rail transportation, except through me, but he sometimes forgot and gave orders to subordinates which invariably led to trouble.

His movement to Falmouth was not upon the lines indicated by the President and General Halleck as the best, and was probably a mistake, but he was allowed to use his own judgment.

A greater mistake was made in his assault on the heights at Fredericksburg, which were too strong to be taken in front. If there had been more prompt movement of his forces on the left flank, the position might have been taken; but this is simply my opinion. I was with Burnside during the battle. This battle was the only event of importance during General Burnside's career, which was brief, and General Hooker became his successor.

MAJOR-GENERAL JOSEPH HOOKER.—In conferring the command upon General Hooker, the President wrote one of his characteristic letters, in which he told him that he had placed him in command, not for the things that he had done, but in spite of them.

I well remember Hooker when he came to West Point as a cadet, a remarkably handsome youth with a florid complexion, which he always retained.

Hooker's accession to the command was followed by a long period of cessation of military operations, during which my Corps was occupied in the shops and yards of Alexandria in preparing for the "On to Richmond" movement in the spring.

My relations with Hooker were entirely satisfactory. He never interfered with transportation movements, and communicated his plans to me confidentially, so that I should be fully prepared when a movement was commenced.

Of the personal habits of General Hooker I am unable to speak. He was charged with fondness for stimulants, but I never saw him when I thought he was under their influence.

When the movement commenced in the spring of 1863, a heavy rainfall embarrassed his movements by rendering roads almost impassable, causing delays which betrayed his movements to the enemy, and compelled him to modify his original plans.

The retreat after Chancellorsville was not approved by some of his best Corps Commanders, especially by Reynolds and Meade, and was probably a serious error, as his forces at the time were said to have been superior to those of the enemy.

My report to General Halleck of the interview with General Hooker at Fairfax had probably much influence upon the promptitude with which his request to be relieved was acted upon; but he would no doubt have been retired if the request had not been made.

MAJOR-GENERAL GEORGE GORDON MEADE.—General Meade graduated from West Point in 1835, in the same class with myself. His class rank was 19 in a class of fifty-six members. He was not distinguished at the Military Academy by any prominent characteristics, was dignified, courteous and gentlemanly, but rather reserved and without personal magnetism. I was not particularly intimate with him while at the Academy.

General Meade married a daughter of the distinguished lawyer, John Sargent, of Philadelphia, and upon making a call upon him after his marriage, I was introduced to Henry A. Wise, of Virginia, who had married another daughter.

After this, our next meeting was in the Army of the Potomac.

His appointment to the command of the army was wholly unexpected and, under the circumstances, a crushing weight of responsibility was imposed upon him. He had no knowledge of where the enemy was, or where his own forces were scattered, and it is difficult to conceive of a more embarrassing position.

Good fortune directed my steps to Harrisburg on the night of June 30. After hearing the reports of the movement of the enemy I was able to interpret them correctly, and advised Meade the same night by telegraph and courier that Lee was concentrating his forces at Gettysburg to fall upon and crush his Army Corps in detail, before they could be concentrated.

The battle commenced by an attack upon the First Corps. Its able commander, John F. Reynolds, was killed and his men were driven back, fighting through the town to the Cemetery Ridge, which was a very strong position, and where a stand was made until reinforcements could arrive and the whole army was concentrated at that point.

General Meade arrived on the second day. He had no intention of fighting a battle at Gettysburg. His intention, as he told me in the interview on Sunday after the battle, was to fall back towards Baltimore and occupy a defensive position along Pipe Creek, but circumstances beyond his control changed his plans.

That Meade allowed the fruits of his brilliant victory to be lost by tardy movement is as undeniable as it was unfortunate. Lee retreated July 4, and did not get across the Potomac until July 14—double the time that would have been necessary, under skillful engineers, to build bridges and make his escape.

I have no wish to detract from the high reputation won by General Meade at Gettysburg, but, while I was not sure that McClellan could have prevented the escape of Lee at Antietam, I was just as sure that Meade could have succeeded after Gettysburg. I was well acquainted with all the country to the Potomac and knew all the roads and the topography. I had gone to Gettysburg in 1836 to locate the Gettysburg Railroad across the South

Mountain to Hagerstown, had married in Gettysburg and lived there ten years, part of the time as Professor of Mathematics and Civil Engineering in Pennsylvania College.

The residence which I built on the Seminary Ridge was in the battlefield, and one of Longstreet's batteries was in front of this house, and from what I know of the country along the Potomac, it would be difficult to convince me that prompt movement would not have insured the capture of Lee's army and ended the war then and there.

I had myself, when locating the railroad, walked from a more distant point on the Potomac to Gettysburg in one day, and could not believe that it was impossible for troops to march a shorter distance in two days.

GENERAL U. S. GRANT.—I never met General Grant in the army and had formed an unfavorable opinion of him as a man who was not naturally gifted, of not more than ordinary intelligence, taciturn because he had nothing to say, and whose elevation was due more to favorable circumstances than to genius; his successes to the weakness and exhaustion of his adversary and his own unlimited resources.

But I was mistaken. At the celebration of the opening of the Northern Pacific Railroad, General Grant and also Generals Cass and Newton and Secretary Evarts had been assigned to the sections of the train under my special charge, and to my private car. I was with him daily for a week, during which time I had a good opportunity of becoming well acquainted with my special guests.

I found General Grant really very well informed, his conversational powers much above the average, his affability and condescension to inferiors great, no affectation or conceit about the man, but perfect simplicity and disregard of self. At the various stations the assembled crowd cheered for Grant. They seemed to care for no one else. When they called for a speech, he said that speech-making was not his forte; that he had brought Secretary Evarts with him who was an accomplished orator, and, as he had communicated his ideas to him, Secretary Evarts' speeches might be regarded as an expression of his own opinions.

Women crowded around the platforms, holding up their infants to be kissed. To see Grant was the great event of their lives, something to talk over at their humble firesides and transmit the narrative to children's children.

General Grant shook hands with all who offered, although frequent ablutions were rendered necessary as a consequence. During the whole trip he touched no stimulants; in fact, the occupants of my car formed a very dry party.

CHAPTER XXIII.

PERSONNEL OF THE BUREAU OF MILITARY RAILROADS.

THE operations of the Construction Corps during the campaigns of 1862 and 1863, under my leadership, had raised it to a condition of marvelous efficiency. Colonel D. C. McCallum, who had been my predecessor and who became my successor, was a thorough master of transportation, when he could be relieved from military interference and have a telegraphic line under his entire control—conditions that did not exist previous to my charge.

New cadets, or "plebes," as they are called at West Point, regard cadets in the higher classes with great veneration, and, after leaving the Academy, junior graduates retain respect for their seniors. This was, no doubt, of advantage to me in assuming charge of the Military Railroads. With the exception of General Heintzelman, there was no Corps or Army Commander that I can recall whose first commission in the army antedated my own.

This fact, in connection with the order making my authority supreme, effectually put a stop to that scourge of Military Railroads, interference and conflicting orders by the different commanders along the lines.

McCallum was a civilian, and civilians were considered as entitled to no respect when the convenience of officers was involved. I do not, therefore, claim that the improved condition of affairs, after I took charge, was due to superior ability.

D. C. McCallum.—D. C. McCallum had been for many years the General Superintendent of the Erie Railroad, and was one of the most experienced managers in the country. He could sit in his New York office and move his trains by telegraph with the utmost precision, but the conditions were widely different on the Military Railroads. When the wires were not down they were in use by the military authorities, who would not allow them to be interrupted.

McCallum was a splendid office man, thoroughly familiar with every detail of requisitions, accounts and red-tape, which I was not. Moreover, I did not care to learn, so it did not take long to come to a perfect understanding and division of duties which suited us both. McCallum took the office and I took the field, and did not trouble myself with accounts, except when matters of claims were referred to me, as they frequently were by the Secretary of War, for investigation and report.

WILLIAM H. WHITON.—William H. Whiton was Chief Clerk. He was a gentleman of education, intelligence, independent circumstances and high social position. He had married a daughter of Mr. Lord, the first President of the Erie Railroad, and owned a fine estate on the Hudson River near Piermont. His reasons for accepting the position of Chief Clerk were patriotism and personal friendship for McCallum. He was a thorough accountant, and the right man in the right place.

JOHN H. DEVEREUX.—I had no acquaintance with J. H. Devereux before I took charge of the Military Railroads, and my first impressions were not favorable. He was a warm friend of McCallum, whom I superseded, and there was naturally some dissatisfaction in consequence of this change, which was shared by many others; but further acquaintance broke the ice, and when we knew each other our relations became fraternal. Our friendship continued until his death.

Devereux was a man of superior and cultivated intellect, an accomplished gentleman, a zealous and active churchman, a conscientious Christian, a master of all transportation details, and a man of great powers of endurance. He could remain at his post for nights in succession without sleep; his discipline was kind but inflexible, and his judgment almost infallible.

After retiring from the service he became General Superintendent of the Cleveland & Pittsburg Railroad, and was one day surprised by the visit of a committee who tendered him the Presidency of an important line of railroad centering in Cleveland, with a salary of $25,000 per annum and a bonus, in addition, of $100,000. This position he accepted and retained until his death, recognized as one of the leading railroad men of the country.

While connected with the Military Railroads, he managed the transportation on the roads centering in Alexandria, and a more efficient Superintendent could not have been found.

As a churchman he was usually one of the lay delegates in Episcopal conventions and took a prominent part in their discussions.

ADNA ANDERSON.—General Anderson was another individual with whom I had no acquaintance until after my connection with the Military Railroads. He was quiet and taciturn, and although

I saw him frequently as I passed through the office, we seldom spoke to each other, and I took but little notice of him.

One day Devereux said to me: "Do not be offended at the liberty I propose to take, but I have observed that you have little or nothing to say to Anderson. You do not know him. If you would cultivate him, you would find him to be a very superior man."

I did cultivate him from that time and did find him to be very superior. He was not only an able, intelligent and scientific civil engineer, but also thoroughly familiar with all details of transportation and accounts.

I gave him charge of the Construction Corps as Chief Engineer, and whenever there was any duty to perform requiring prompt action, energy and sound judgment, Anderson was the man above all others that I called upon to assume the charge. He it was who managed the transportation so successfully over the Western Maryland Railroad during the battle of Gettysburg, and he had charge of the Construction Corps during Sherman's celebrated campaign, although Sherman probably did not know him and did not give him credit for the results to which his own success and reputation were largely due.

After the war I saw but little of Anderson until 1881, when we were again brought into contact on the Northern Pacific Railroad. He was Chief Engineer of Construction, and I the General Manager of Transportation.

WILLIAM W WRIGHT.—William W. Wright had been my pupil at Gettysburg in mathematics and engineering, and my Assistant Engineer on the Pennsylvania Railroad, where his intelligence, activity and efficiency gave me great satisfaction. Knowing him to be the man for the place, I gave him charge of the transportation on the Acquia Creek & Fredericksburg Railroad, which was well managed.

He accompanied General Sherman in his march to the sea, and managed the transportation on the whole system of Military Railroads used in that memorable campaign, securing results which, considering the difficulties encountered, were truly marvelous.

General Sherman has referred to Wright in his Memoirs in terms of the highest commendation, but I regret that he overlooked Anderson and Smeed, without whose efficient service in construction no transportation could have been effected; but these gentlemen were in the field, and at a distance, and did not come under the eye of the General in command, while Wright spent much of his time at Headquarters, and an opportunity was offered for better acquaintance.

E. C. SMEED.—I may be considered extravagant in the strong expressions of commendation I have used in regard to members of my staff in the Construction and Transportation Corps of the Military Railroads, but amongst them all Smeed is the man whom I most delight to honor, and especially so as Generals Sherman and McCallum, while making favorable mention of others, have omitted entirely the man whom I consider most worthy of especial notice.

Before the war Smeed held a subordinate position on the Catawissa Railroad in Pennsylvania as a Road Supervisor, in charge of bridges and trestles. He came to Virginia in the employ of Daniel Stone as a foreman of carpenters, and was with a number of others assigned to me when I commenced work on the Fredericksburg Railroad.

He attracted my attention by the manner in which he handled his men, and at the Potomac Creek bridge I placed him in general charge of all the gangs. He was the best organizer of work I ever saw, possessed unlimited resources in adopting expedients to secure rapid progress.

If he could not get the material he wanted, he would use what he could get. If trees or buildings were near, he would never delay work to wait for transportation.

A spirit of emulation was encouraged in his gangs, and they would rival each other to secure the greatest daily progress. Without Smeed I never would have been able to build the Potomac Creek bridge in the space of time which General McDowell thought so wonderful a performance.

Smeed was a man without education, reserved, diffident and slow to make the acquaintance of strangers, but he was a close student and in time became an expert mathematician, and able to make the most intricate calculations on the strains of bridges and trusses.

Smeed's inventive genius produced the simple, portable and efficient apparatus which destroyed track and twisted rails so they could not be again used, and it was chiefly through Smeed's efforts, working night and day, through rain or sunshine, that the numerous bridges on the Northern Central and Gettysburg Railroads were reconstructed in about five days, and General Meade placed in communication with Washington, both by rail and telegraph, on the very next day after Lee's retreat—a result which, Meade told me, he had not believed possible for two weeks.

Smeed accompanied General Sherman's army in his march to the sea, and had charge of bridge construction. The Trumpet of Fame has never published his exploits of that period. I never saw them noticed in bulletins, or by the press, but his Chattahoochee bridge is the greatest feat of the kind that the world has ever seen.

Without Smeed, Sherman's military railroads could not have been reconstructed with the celerity with which the work was accomplished. Without the roads, there could have been no transportation of supplies; without supplies the army could not have moved in the enemy's country and the campaign would have been a failure. Let Smeed have the credit that is due to him.

After the war, by force of merit, Smeed raised himself to a high position; became Chief Engineer of the Kansas Pacific Railroad, where Jay Gould discovered his value. I tried to get him with me on the Northern Pacific, but Gould bid $4,000 per year higher than I could bid and I had to let him stay.

Such were the men who formed my staff on the Military Railroads, and to whom the merit of results was largely due. If I can claim credit for myself, it is chiefly in discovering their qualifications, and in placing them in positions to render them available.

There were others, and many others, worthy of mention, but I cannot refer to them individually. There was G. W. Nagle and his three brothers, George Speer and other bridge foremen, each with his own permanent gang; men who could run on planks on tops of high trestles with the agility of squirrels. There was Tinglepaugh, who managed the drove of oxen—"Haupt's horned cavalry" as they were called—whose services were invaluable.

Many of the conductors had been brought by Thomas A. Scott, when Assistant Secretary of War, from the Pennsylvania Railroad. Some of them had been appointed by me when I was General Superintendent of the road, and a more efficient set of men could not have been found.

The train dispatchers and operators were also entitled to much credit. They occupied advanced positions near the enemy to report his movements and held positions after the military had retired until nearly surrounded, then escaped through the bushes. One of the most efficient (McCrickett) was killed by guerrillas. The engine on which he was riding was switched off the track on a high embankment by means of a telegraph wire attached to a rail and pulled by men concealed in a thicket. Several others were killed at the same time.

Engineers and firemen were so often fired upon that it became necessary to use boiler plate cabs for their protection, but they never hesitated to perform a duty, and volunteers could always be found for extra-hazardous risks, of which there were many.

Most of these men have gone to their rest unhonored and unknown, but their fidelity and sacrifices entitle them to as much consideration as those, who, occupying higher positions, were more conspicuous marks for public favor. There is one at least, who can appreciate their services and who takes pride in doing justice to their memory.

They wrought night and day without intermission when a necessity for such service existed; they knew just what to do and how to do it; they laid track and built bridges at night by the light of lanterns, uttering no complaint, and defying storms and dangers.

With the exception of the superior officers and the foremen, the Construction Corps consisted almost entirely of so-called "contrabands." Thousands of these refugees had flocked into Washington, and from them were selected several hundred healthy, able-bodied men familiar with the use of the ax. These Africans worked with enthusiasm, and each gang with a laudable emulation to excel others in the progress made in a given time.

In rebuilding to restore communications, permanency was not considered. It was not a question of months, or of weeks, as in erecting permanent structures, but one of hours.

The Potomac Creek bridge was reconstructed, as General McDowell declared, in as many days as the former structure, which it replaced, had required months, and yet for all the purposes of the campaign it was just as useful. The nineteen bridges destroyed by the enemy on the Northern Central Railroad were rebuilt in a few days, and all the bridges on the branches leading to Gettysburg were reconstructed during the battle, communication with Washington being re-established by noon of the day after Lee's retreat!

While Generals who fought the battles have been eulogized and costly statues erected to their memories, the humble Corps, through whose fidelity and efficiency victories were rendered possible, have found no historian to do them honor.

If there ever should be recognition of their great services, the faithful contrabands will be justly entitled to their share; no other class of men would have exhibited so much patience and endurance under days and nights of continued and sleepless labor.

APPENDIX.

WAR DEPARTMENT,
WASHINGTON, July 26, 1861.

To the Officers U. S. A.:
Please furnish, upon requisitions from A. Carnejie,* Superintendent in charge of railways, such facilities, rations, etc., as he may desire for the forces under his charge.

THOMAS A. SCOTT,
General Manager Government Railways and Telegraphs.

AN ACT to authorize the President of the United States in certain cases to take possession of railroad and telegraph lines, and for other purposes.

Be it enacted by the Senate and House of Representatives of the United States of America in Congress assembled, That the President of the United States, when in his judgment the public safety may require it, be, and he is hereby, authorized to take possession of any or all the telegraph lines in the United States, their offices and appurtenances; to take possession of any or all the railroad lines in the United States, their rolling stock, their offices, shops, buildings, and all their appendages and appurtenances; to prescribe rules and regulations for the holding, using, and maintaining of the aforesaid telegraph and railroad lines, and to extend, repair, and complete the same, in the manner most conducive to the safety and interest of the Government; to place under military control all the officers, agents, and employes belonging to the telegraph and railroad lines thus taken possession of by the President, so that they shall be considered as a post road and a part of the military establishment of the United States, subject to all the restrictions imposed by the Rules and Articles of War.

SEC. 2. *And be it further enacted,* That any attempt by any party or parties whomsoever, in any State or District in which the laws of the United States are opposed, or the execution thereof obstructed by insurgents and rebels against the United States, too powerful to be suppressed by the ordinary course of judicial proceedings, to resist or interfere with the unrestrained use by Government of the property described in the preceding section, or any attempt to injure or destroy the property aforesaid, shall be punished as a military offense, by death, or such other penalty as a court martial may impose.

SEC. 3. *And be it further enacted,* That three commissioners shall be appointed by the President of the United States, by and with the advice and consent of the Senate, to assess and determine the damages suffered, or the compensation to which any railroad or telegraph

---

* Andrew Carnegie, the great ironmaster and philanthropist.

320

company may be entitled by reason of the railroad or telegraph line being seized and used under the authority conferred by this act, and their award shall be submitted to Congress for their action.

SEC. 4. *And be it further enacted,* That the transportation of troops, munitions of war, equipments, military property and stores, throughout the United States, shall be under the immediate control and supervision of the Secretary of War and such agents as he may appoint; and all rules, regulations, articles, usages, and laws in conflict with this provision are hereby annulled.

SEC. 5. *And be it further enacted,* That the compensation of each of the commissioners aforesaid, shall be eight dollars per day while in actual service; and that the provisions of this act, so far as it relates to the operating and using said railroads and telegraphs, shall not be in force any longer than is necessary for the suppression of this rebellion.

Approved January 31, 1862.

[EXTRACT FROM GENERAL D. C. MCCALLUM'S FINAL REPORT.]

With few exceptions, the operations of the Military Railroads have been conducted under orders issued by the Secretary of War, or by army commanders in the field.

During February, 1862, I received the following important verbal order from the Secretary of War: "I shall expect you to have on hand at all times the necessary men and materials to enable you to comply promptly with any order given, *nor must there be any failure."*

It was made the duty of the Director and General Manager to arrange the Military Railroad oganization upon a basis sufficiently comprehensive to permit the extension of the system indefinitely; to perfect the *modus operandi* for working the various lines; to determine as to the number of men to be employed in the several departments, and the compensation to be paid therefor; the amount and kind of machinery to be purchased, and the direction as to the distribution of the same.

Having had a somewhat extensive railroad experience, both before and since the Rebellion, I consider this order of the Secretary of War to have been the very foundation of success; without it the whole railroad system, which has proved an importnot element in conducting military movements, would have been not only a costly but ludicrous failure. The fact should be understood that the management of railroads is just as much a distinct profession as is that of the art of war, and should be so regarded.

The difficulty of procuring a sufficient force of competent railroad men, both in the construction and transportation departments, was almost insurmountable. Owing to the peculiar nature of the service and the rapid expansion of the railroad system, the supply of railroad operatives in the country has always been limited; many had entered the army in various positions, thus diminishing the actual number in civil life, while the stimulus imparted by the war to the business of Northern railroads had greatly enhanced the value of the services of those who remained at their posts, thus rendering the home demand for skillful labor far in advance of the supply. When the large number of men necessary to equip these military lines were sought for, it was extremely difficult to induce those who were really valuable to leave secure positions and enter upon a new and untried field of action.

The difference between civil and military railroad service is marked and decided. Not only were the men continually exposed to great danger from the regular forces of the enemy, guerrillas, scouting parties, etc., but, owing to the circumstances under which military railroads must be constructed and operated, what are considered the ordinary risks upon civil railroads are vastly increased on military lines.

The hardships, exposure, and perils to which trainmen especially were subjected during the movements incident to an active campaign were much greater than that endured by any other class of civil employes of the Government—equalled only by that of the soldier while engaged in a raid into the enemy's country. It was by no means unusual for men to be out with their trains from five to ten days, without sleep, except what could be snatched upon their engines and cars while the same were standing to be loaded or unloaded, with but scanty food, or perhaps no food at all, for days together, while continually occupied in a manner to keep every faculty strained to its utmost. Many incidents during the war, but more especially during the Atlanta campaign, exhibited a fortitude, endurance, and self-devotion on the part of these men not exceeded in any branch of the service. All were thoroughly imbued with the fact that upon the success of railroad operations, in forwarding supplies to the front, depended, in great part, the success of our armies; that although defeat might be the result, even if supplies were abundantly furnished, it was evident there could be no advance without; and I hazard nothing in saying, that should failure have taken place either in keeping the lines in repair or in operating them, General Sherman's campaign, instead of proving, as it did, a great success, would have resulted in disaster and defeat; and the greater the army to supply the more precarious its position. Since the end of the rebellion I have been informed by railroad officers who were in the service of the enemy during the war, "that they were less surprised at the success of General Sherman, in a military point of view, than they were at the rapidity with which railroad breaks were repaired and the regularity with which trains were moved to the front;" and it was only when the method of operating was fully explained that it could be comprehended.

The attempt to furnish an army of one hundred thousand (100,000) men and sixty thousand (60,000) animals with supplies from a base three hundred and sixty (360) miles distant, by one line of single-track railroad, located almost the entire distance through the country of an active and most vindictive enemy, is without precedent in the history of warfare, and to make it successful required an enormous outlay for labor and a vast consumption of material, together with all the forethought, energy, patience, and watchfulness of which men are capable.

This line, from the fact of its great length, was imperfectly guarded, as troops could not be spared from the front for that purpose. This rendered the railroad service one of great risk and hazard, and at times it was only by the force of military authority that men could be held to service. As an item showing the real danger attending military railroad operations, it may be stated that during the last six months of the fiscal year ending June 30, 1865, the wrecking train picked up and carried to Nashville sixteen (16) wrecked locomotives and two hundred and ninety-four (294) car-loads of car wheels, bridge iron, etc. These wrecks were caused by guerrillas and rebel raids.

The Chattanooga & Atlanta, or Western & Atlantic Railroad extends from Chattanooga to Atlanta, 136 miles, with a branch from Kingston to Rome seventeen miles long.

The reconstruction and maintenance of this line was, in many respects, the most difficult of any military railroad operations during the war. By it the Confederate army under General Johnston made its retreat from Buzzard Roost to Atlanta; and in falling back from one strong position to another it did such damage to the road as was supposed would delay or prevent Sherman's pursuit, but in this it was unsuccessful. However great the damage done, it was so speedily repaired that General Sherman soon ceased to fear any delay from this cause, and made his advance movements with perfect confidence that the railroad in his rear would be "all right."

Being, from the nature of the case, entirely ignorant of the obstacles to be encountered at each advance, the construction force was at all times prepared for any emergency—either to build bridges of formidable dimensions, or lay miles of track, or, perhaps, push back to some point on the line and repair damages done by guerrillas or raiding parties. These attacks on the line to the rear were of such frequent occurrence, and often of so serious a character, that to insure speedy repairs it became necessary to station detachments of the Construction Corps at various points along the road, and also to collect supplies of construction materials, such as iron, rails, chairs, spikes, cross-ties, and bridge timber, at points where they would be comparatively safe and easily obtained when required. These precautionary measures proved to be of the utmost importance in keeping the road open.

The detachments stationed along the line were composed of bridge-builders and track-layers, with an ample supply of tools for all kinds of work. Each detachment was under the command of a competent engineer or supervisor, who had orders to move in either direction, within certain limits, as soon as a break occurred, and make the necessary repairs without delay, working day and night when necessary. Under this arrangement small breaks were repaired at once, at any point on the line, even when the telegraph wires were cut and special orders could not be communicated to the working parties. When "big breaks" occurred, one or more divisions of the Construction Corps were moved as rapidly as possible thereto, either from Chattanooga or the front. Construction trains, loaded with the requisite tools and materials, were kept ready at each end of the road to move at a moment's notice.

Guerrillas and raiding parties were more or less successful in destroying portions of track during the whole time we held this line; but the crowning effort was made by the enemy in October, 1864, when Hood, getting to Sherman's rear, threw his whole army on the road—first at Big Shanty, and afterward north of Resaca—and destroyed in the aggregate thirty-five and one-half miles of track and 455 lineal feet of bridges, killing and capturing a large number of our men. Fortunately, however, the detachments of the Construction Corps which escaped were so distributed that even before Hood had left the road two strong working parties were at work, one on each end of the break at Big Shanty, and this gap of ten miles was closed and the force ready to move to the great break of twenty-five miles in length north of Resaca as soon as the enemy had left it. The destruction by Hood's army of our depots of supplies compelled us to cut nearly all the cross-ties required to re-lay this track, and to send a distance for rails.

The cross-ties were cut near the line of the road, and many of them carried by hand to the track, as the teams to be furnished for hauling them did not get to the work until it was nearly completed. The rails used on the southern end of the break had to be taken up and brought from the railroads south of Atlanta, and those for the northern end were mostly brought from Nashville, nearly two hundred miles distant.

Notwithstanding all the disadvantages under which the labor was performed, this twenty-five miles of track was laid and the trains were running over it in seven and a half days from the time the work was commenced.

The economy so commendable and essential upon civil railroads was compelled to give way to the lavish expenditure of war; and the question to be answered was not, "How much will it cost?" but rather, "Can it be done at any cost?"

The greatest number of men employed at the same date during the war was:

In Virginia	4,542
In North Carolina	3,387
In military division of the Mississippi	17,035
Total number of men	24,964

The total number of miles operated.

In Virginia	611
In North Carolina	293
In military division of the Mississippi	1,201
Total	2,105

The number of engines.

In Virginia	72
In North Carolina	38
In military division of the Mississippi	260
In Georgia	14
Provided but not used	35
Total	419

The number of cars.

In Virginia	1,733
In North Carolina	422
In military division of the Mississippi	3,383
In Georgia	213
Provided but not used	579
Total	6,330

Lineal feet of bridges built or rebuilt.

In Virginia	34,931
In North Carolina	3,263
In Missouri	1,680
In military division of the Mississippi	97,544
Total number of feet	137,418

Or twenty-six miles and one hundred and thirty-eight feet.

The length of track laid or relaid.

	Miles.	Feet.
In Virginia	177	2,961
In North Carolina	30	4,632
In military division of the Mississippi	433	2,323
Total	641	4,636

The following statement exhibits the amount expended during the war in constructing and operating the United States Military Railroads, said sum having been furnished from the appropriation made for the expenditures of the Quartermaster's Department:

Virginia.

For labor	$5,227,145 24	
For materials	4,920,317 27	
		$10,147,462 51

North Carolina.

For labor	1,086,224 60	
For materials	1,510,435 45	
		2,596,660 05

Military Division of the Mississippi.

For labor	16,792,193 05	
For materials	12,870,588 06	
		29,662,781 11

Department of the Gulf.

For materials		55,238 88

Total		42,462,142 55
Property sold under Executive Order of August 8, 1865	7,428,204 96	
Property sold for cash	3,466,739 33	
Receipts from passengers and freight	1,525,493 04	
Receipts from hire of rolling stock	103,528 50	
Property on hand (estimated)	100,000 00	
		12,623,965 83
Net expenditures		$29,838,176 72

It was impossible for this Department to keep an accurate account of the persons and material transported, as whole corps and even armies, with all their artillery and equipments, were moved upon verbal orders from commanders sometimes hundreds of miles, and frequently in face of the enemy. As an illustration, one of the largest movements of this character was that of the Fourth Army Corps in 1865, from Carter's Station, in East Tennessee, to Nashville, three hundred and seventy-three (373) miles, and which employed one thousand four hundred and ninety-eight (1,498) cars.

In conclusion permit me to say that the Government was peculiarly fortunate in securing the services of civilian officers of great nerve, honesty, and capability, to whom the whole country owes a debt of gratitude.

Among them I take the liberty of naming, as principal assistants: A. Anderson, Chief Superintendent and Engineer; Colonel W. W. Wright, Chief Engineer in the Military Division of the Mississippi, and Chief Engineer and General Superintendent in the Department of North Carolina; J. J. Moore, General Superintendent and Chief Engineer of Railroads in Virginia; E . L. Wentz, General Superintendent and Chief Engineer of Railroads in Virginia, and afterward for a time General Superintendent of Railroads in the Division of the Mississippi; W. J. Stevens, General Superintendent of United States Military Railroads, Division of the Mississippi; L. H. Eicholtz, Acting Chief Engineer, Military Division of the Mississippi, during the absence of Colonel W. W. Wright in North Carolina; A. F. Goodhue, Engineer and Superintendent Military Railroads, West Tennessee and Arkansas. Also the following commissioned officers: Brevet Brigadier-General H.

L. Robinson, Acting Quartermaster, Washington, D. C.; Brevet Major F. J. Crilly, Acting Quartermaster, Nashville, Tennessee; and Captain G. S. Roper, Commissary of Subsistence, Nashville, Tennessee.

I have the honor to be, very respectfully,

Your obedient servant,

D. C. McCALLUM,

Brevet Brigadier-General, Director and General Manager
Military Railroads United States.

Hon. Edwin M. Stanton,

Secretary of War.

INDEX.

327

* Nearly all letters in war time are sent by telegraph.

THE RAILROADS

An Arno Press Collection

Adams, Charles Francis, Jr. **Railroads: Their Origin and Problems.** 1878

Boyd, William Harland. **The Shasta Route, 1863-1887** (Doctoral Dissertation, University of California, Berkeley, 1943). 1981

Brooks, John Graham. **An American Citizen.** 1910

Bruchey, Stuart, editor. **Memoirs of Three Railroad Pioneers.** 1981

Carr, Hobart C. **Early History of Iowa Railroads** (Masters Thesis, State University of Iowa, 1938). 1981

Cary, John W. **The Organization and History of the Chicago, Milwaukee & St. Paul Railway Company.** 1893

Chandler, Alfred D., Jr. **Henry Varnum Poor.** 1956

Chandler, Alfred D., Jr., editor. **The Railroads: The Nation's First Big Business.** 1965

Cherington, Charles R. **The Regulation of Railroad Abandonments.** 1948

Cleveland, Frederick A. and Fred Wilbur Powell. **Railroad Promotion and Capitalization in the United States.** 1909

Crippen, Waldo. **The Kansas Pacific Railroad** (Masters Thesis, University of Chicago, 1932). 1981

Daggett, Stuart. **Railroad Consolidation West of the Mississippi River.** 1933

Dixon, Frank H[aigh]. **State Railroad Control with a History of Its Development in Iowa.** 1896

Dufwa, Thamar Emelia. **Transcontinental Railroad Legislation, 1835-1862** (Masters Thesis, University of North Dakota, 1933). 1981

Eckenrode, H[amilton] J. and Pocahontas Wight Edmunds. **E.H. Harriman.** 1933.

Epstein, Ralph C. **GATX: A History of the General American Transportation Corporation, 1898-1948.** 1948

Fisher, John S. **A Builder of the West.** 1939

Fournier, Leslie T. **Railway Nationalization in Canada.** 1950

Galloway, John Debo. **The First Transcontinental Railroad.** 1950

George, Peter James. **Government Subsidies and the Construction of the Canadian Pacific Railway** (Doctoral Dissertation, University of Toronto, 1967). 1981

Granger, J.T. **A Brief Biographical Sketch of the Life of Major-General Grenville M. Dodge.** 1893

Grodinsky, Julius. **The Iowa Pool.** 1950

Grodinsky, Julius. **Jay Gould.** 1957

Hamburg, James Fredric. **The Influence of Railroads Upon the Processes and Patterns of Settlement in South Dakota** (Doctoral Dissertation, University of North Carolina, Chapel Hill, 1969). 1981

Harnsberger, John L. **Jay Cooke and Minnesota** (Doctoral Dissertation, University of Minnesota, 1956). 1981

Haupt, Herman. **Reminiscences of General Herman Haupt.** 1901

Heap, Gwinn Harris. **Central Route to the Pacific.** 1853

Herring, James M. **The Problem of Weak Railroads.** 1929

Holbrook, Stewart H. **The Age of the Moguls.** 1953

Hughes, Sarah Forbes, editor. **Letters and Recollections of John Murray Forbes.** 1900. 2 vols.

Kennan, George. **The Chicago & Alton Case.** 1916

Kennan, George. **E.H. Harriman.** 1922. 2 vols.

Kennan, George. **Misrepresentation in Railroad Affairs.** 1916

Lewis, Oscar. **The Big Four.** 1938

Longley, Ronald Stewart. **Sir Francis Hincks.** 1943

Lopata, Edwin L. **Local Aid to Railroads in Missouri.** 1937

Lovett, H[enry] A[lmon]. **Canada and the Grand Trunk, 1829-1924.** 1924

McAlpine, R.W. **The Life and Times of Col. James Fisk, Jr.** 1872

MacVeagh, Rogers. **The Transportation Act 1920.** 1923

Million, John W. **State Aid to Railways in Missouri.** 1896

Morris, Keith. **The Story of the Canadian Pacific Railway.** 1916

Mosk, Sanford A. **Land Tenure Problems in the Santa Fe Railroad Grant Area.** 1944

Newcomb, H.T. **The Work of the Interstate Commerce Commission.** 1905

Ogilvie, John Stuart. **Life and Death of Jay Gould and How He Made His Millions.** 1892

Perkins, J.R. **Trails, Rails and War.** 1929

Petrowski, William Robinson. **The Kansas Pacific** (Doctoral Dissertation, University of Wisconsin, 1966). 1981

Reed, S.G. **A History of The Texas Railroads and of Transportation Conditions Under Spain and Mexico and the Republic and the State.** 1941

Reeder, Clarence A., Jr. **The History of Utah's Railroads, 1869-1883** (Doctoral Dissertation, University of Utah, 1970). 1981

Ripley, William Z[ebina]. **Railroads: Finance and Organization.** 1915

Robinson, John R. **The Octopus.** 1894

Russel, Robert R[oyal]. **Improvement of Communication With the Pacific Coast as an Issue in American Politics, 1783-1864.** 1948

Sanborn, John Bell. **Congressional Grants of Land in Aid of Railways.** 1899

Secretan, J.H.E. **Canada's Great Highway.** 1924

Smith, Philip R. **Improved Surface Transportation and Nebraska's Population Distribution, 1860-1960** (Doctoral Dissertation, University of Nebraska, 1971). 1981

Stafford, Marshall P. **The Life of James Fisk, Jr.** 1871

Starr, John W[illiam], Jr. **Lincoln and the Railroads.** 1927

Sutton, Robert Mize. **The Illinois Central Railroad in Peace and War. 1858-1868** (Doctoral Dissertation, University of Illinois at Urbana-Champaign, 1948). 1981

Talbot, Frederick A. **The Making of a Great Canadian Railway.** 1912

Taylor, George Rogers and Irene D. Neu. **The American Railroad Network, 1861-1890.** 1956

Trent, Logan Douglas. **The Credit Mobilier** (Masters Thesis, University of North Dakota, 1935). 1981

Villard, Henry. **The Early History of Transportation in Oregon.** 1944

Wendt, Lloyd and Herman Kogan. **Bet a Million!** 1949

Wheelwright, William Bond. **Life and Times of Alvah Crocker.** 1923.